Hunger Movements in Early Victorian Literature

T0270813

In *Hunger Movements in Early Victorian Literature*, Lesa Scholl explores the ways in which the language of starvation interacts with narratives of emotional and intellectual want to create a dynamic, evolving notion of hunger. Scholl's interdisciplinary study emphasises literary analysis, sensory history, and political economy to interrogate the progression of hunger in Britain from the early 1830s to the late 1860s. Examining works by Charles Dickens, Harriet Martineau, George Eliot, Elizabeth Gaskell, Henry Mayhew, and Charlotte Brontë, Scholl argues for the centrality of hunger in social development and understanding. She shows how the rhetoric of hunger moves beyond critiques of physical starvation to a paradigm in which the dominant narrative of civilisation is predicated on the continual progress and evolution of literal and metaphorical taste. Her study makes a persuasive case for how hunger, as a signifier of both individual and corporate ambition, is a necessarily self-interested and increasingly violent agent of progress within the discourse of political economy that emerged in the eighteenth century and subsequently shaped nineteenth-century social and political life.

Lesa Scholl is the Dean of Emmanuel College within the University of Queensland, Australia, and an Honorary Research Fellow with the University of Exeter, UK.

Hunger Movements in Early Victorian Literature

Want, riots, migration

Lesa Scholl

Routledge
Taylor & Francis Group

LONDON AND NEW YORK

First published 2016 by Routledge

2 Park Square, Milton Park, Abingdon, Oxfordshire OX14 4RN
52 Vanderbilt Avenue, New York, NY 10017

Routledge is an imprint of the Taylor & Francis Group, an informa business

First issued in paperback 2019

British Library Cataloguing in Publication Data
A catalogue record for this book is available from the British Library

Library of Congress Cataloging in Publication Data
A catalog record for this book has been requested

ISBN: 978-1-4724-5715-8 (hbk)
ISBN: 978-0-367-03063-6 (pbk)

Typeset in Times New Roman
by Swales & Willis Ltd, Exeter, Devon, UK

For my parents,
who never let me go hungry
and
enabled me to develop my own tastes.

Contents

Acknowledgements

While producing this book, I have been privileged in regard to the number of people and institutions that have supported its progress. The project began through many conversations with Helen Groth, whose generosity astounded me, and also with significant input from Julian Murphet. Regenia Gagnier has been particularly supportive and encouraging of my work, through many discussions as well as hours of reading. Grace Moore and Tricia Zakreski have also gone beyond the call of duty in reading draft chapters and giving me perceptive feedback. My work has also benefited through many conversations with scholars and colleagues from around the globe. Special mention must be made of Mark Smith, Ayesha Mukherjee, Hilary Fraser, Sarina Gruver Moore, Emily Morris, Kate Hext, Kate Newey, Corinna Wagner, Jude Piesse, Christopher Stokes, Kelly Wade-Johnson, Jennifer Greenwood, Charlotte Chambers, Myles Lawrence, Michael D'Arcy, Prue Ahrens, Michelle Smith, Rohan McWilliam, Katherine Inglis, Dino Felluga, Mike Sanders, Julia Kuehn, and Brecht de Groote.

Institutionally, I am firstly grateful to Emmanuel College, especially Stewart Gill, who has encouraged the pursuit of my research, Emmanuel's Senior Common Room Research Group, and my colleagues at the University of Queensland. I was able to spend several months at the University of Exeter, where I enjoyed the extraordinary hospitality of the Centre for Victorian Studies at the Streatham campus, and the Centre for Environmental Arts and Humanities in Penryn. I would also like to acknowledge my colleagues in various organisations, and in particular the Australasian Victorian Studies Association, the Midwest Victorian Studies Association, the British Association of Victorian Studies, the North American Victorian Studies Association.

On a more personal level, I have received support from friends, many of whom give me free accommodation during conferences and research trips, and know me only in a state of jetlag. Thank you to Susan and Ben Harris, Katie Pennycuick, and Katie and Neil Booth for their years of hospitality and for understanding when I'm not on holiday. It's comforting to know I can have a sense of home wherever I am in the world.

Finally, I want to thank Ann Donahue, for whose editorship of this book I am extremely grateful. Apart from her efficiency, professionalism, kindness, and good humour, I have been so inspired by the wonderful conversations we've had, as well as her insight and faith in my work.

Introduction

Hunger, taste, mobility

> Hunger is one of the beneficent and terrible instincts. It is, indeed, the very fire of life, underlying all impulses to labour, and moving man to noble activities by its imperious demands. Look where we may, we see it as the motive power which sets the vast array of human machinery in action . . . [b]ut when its progress is unchecked, it becomes a devouring flame, destroying all that is noble in man.
>
> (George Henry Lewes, *The Physiology of Common Life* (1859), 1–2)

> However much we might like to think of hunger as happening elsewhere, to strangers in far-off lands ravaged by famine, it is always just around the corner. . . . It connects us in elemental ways to others, because we believe that in the modern world no one deserves to live with hunger, let alone die of it.
>
> (James Vernon, *Hunger: A Modern History* (2007), 1)

The word *hunger*, when associated with nineteenth-century Britain, conjures an array of images, from the criminal deported to the colonies for stealing bread to feed his or her family, to the iconic 1849 depiction of the starving Irishwoman Bridget O'Donnell with her waiflike children,[1] to workhouses, settlement laws, and the general exploitation of the poor. These images exist alongside representations of the spoils of empire, celebrations of human progress and industry, and the seemingly necessary extremes of excess and greed that are inherent in the continuing path toward civilisation and modernity. The chasm between rich and poor, between the starving and those living in luxurious excess, remains central to contemporary British economic narratives, most recently, perhaps, in the heated debates regarding food banks. Within a social context built upon neo-classical economic theory, the progressive world of modernity continues, like its Victorian past, to seek to justify the existence of hunger in a world of statistical plenty. The narratives of deflection that emerge are hauntingly reminiscent of the Victorian age, from the displacement of hunger onto the other, as James Vernon notes, to a perverted moral

---

1 In 'The Condition of Ireland,' *Illustrated London News* (22 December 1849), 404.

economy that distinguishes between the deserving and undeserving poor, as well as perhaps the most insidious form: where hunger is rewritten as something positive, a metaphorical hunger aligned with ambition—a powerful force that drives humanity toward progress, thereby justifying the excesses of wealth as if it were necessary to national and global economic health. Yet, as George Henry Lewes noted in 1859, *excesses* of hunger, regardless of the *type* of hunger, lead not to progress, but to devastation.

The sentiment of Charles Dickens's Sissy Jupe in *Hard Times* (1854) embodies a powerful resistance to the obsessive adherence to economic statistics as evidence of progress. She is deemed 'wrong' by Mr M'Choakumchild for remarking, in response to the hypothetical occurrence of only twenty-five people starving to death on the streets of a town of one million inhabitants, that she 'thought it must be hard upon those who were starved, whether the others were a million, or a million million.'[2] Dickens's critique of political economy, the forerunner of neo-classical economic theory, emerges within a body of work in which public intellectuals of the nineteenth century used the mechanisms of literary narrative to expose the fundamental flaws of a reified view and social application of economic theory. The key authors I address in this study—Charles Dickens, Elizabeth Gaskell, George Eliot, Charlotte Brontë, Harriet Martineau, and Henry Mayhew—were each concerned with economic narratives and social justice, and each, most importantly, sought to give voice to characters in fiction who, in 'real' life, would not have that level of political space. Their constructions of multiple narrative possibilities reveal the complex nature of hunger and want, and the difficulties in trying to solve social problems that seem to be beyond the reach of human intervention. Vernon suggests that the eighteenth-century economists Adam Smith and Thomas Malthus 'were the first to establish the modern political economy of hunger,' and that while they departed from each other in terms of whether hunger was 'man-made or a divinely ordained phenomenon, as well as whether the market economy would eradicate hunger or depended upon it as a spur to industry, the two agreed that the market should be left to produce plenty or want freely, without intervention from the state.'[3] The reification of the self-regulating market, epitomised in Smith's infamous 'invisible hand,' was the focus of critique of many literary figures, who, through their fictional narratives, were able to give faces, names, and, most crucially, voices, to the hypothetical twenty-five starving figures. The reality, however, of mid-nineteenth-century Britain, was that the starving were many more than M'Choakumchild's hypothesis; and the cries for social reform emerged from the desperate hunger of those dismissed by economic statistics. Riots and protests emerge through the period as a marker of those wanting to be counted—metaphorically and literally—within a political arena that wanted to deny their existence.

2 Charles Dickens, *Hard Times* (1854; Oxford: Oxford University Press, 1989), 75.
3 Vernon, *Hunger*, 3–4.

Hunger Movements is loosely positioned between the 1832 and 1867 Reform Acts in order to emphasise the central thesis that the need to have a political voice and a sense of belonging is intrinsically connected to seasons of food scarcity, and individual and communal hunger. Within the Whiggish vision of continual progress, this kind of hunger becomes essential to the progress of the nation, refining political constructions and compelling reform. Indeed, in *The Hunger Artists* (1993), Maud Ellmann positions corporate or communal hunger as a catalyst for social progress. Ellmann argues that while the individual experience of hunger is subjective, relative, and socially impotent,

> [i]t is only in the unified collective, like a regiment of soldiers, or the workers in a factory, or a social class which has matured into a 'class unto itself,' that the experience of hunger sheds its intonations of submission and clarifies itself as solidarity or insurrection.[4]

Ellmann's observation of the power of corporate hunger is crucial to my understanding of the connection between physical and social hunger; yet I would add that the unified collective in this sense is necessarily made up of hungry individuals, among whom the drive of hunger is not necessarily the same. The spectrum of hungers, physical and social, can be vast; yet within a seemingly common momentum—even if just by virtue of timing—they can hold powerful sway. I am also concerned, though, with the paradoxes of hunger, especially in that they can simultaneously create and break down communities. The dual nature of hunger in this regard is why I define hunger as a catalyst, not so much for human progress or human destruction, but for human mobility. Hunger compels people—individuals and groups—to move: either to protest against their position of hunger; to migrate geographically; or to seek advancement up the social strata. From this perspective, the connection between physical and social hunger is predicated on social inequalities, as expressed by Adam Smith in *The Theory of Moral Sentiments* (1759): it is through 'look[ing] around and admir[ing] the condition of the rich' that man is compelled to change his situation, leading to labour and productivity. For the broader society, then, the individual human nature 'rouses and keeps in continual motion the industry of mankind' out of his self-interested 'ambition' to acquire property.[5] It seems extraordinary that the so-called progress made by liberal capitalism in the one hundred years between Smith and Lewes leads Lewes to claim that if 'food be abundant and easy of access ... civilisation becomes impossible.'[6] Lewes is not uncritical of hunger, yet it still remains problematic that he buys into its myth of progress.

---

4 Maud Ellmann, *The Hunger Artists: Starving, Writing & Imprisonment* (London: Virago Press, 1993), 6.

5 Adam Smith, *The Theory of Moral Sentiments* (1759; London: George Bell, 1907), 263.

6 Lewes, *Physiology of Common Life* (Edinburgh and London: William Blackwood and Sons, 1859), 2.

Self-regulation: the market and the individual

Some form of hunger seems an inevitable part of the human condition, from the gentle prod of a healthy appetite to dire starvation, or, at the other end of the spectrum, the uncontrollable impulses of addiction. Hunger is necessarily chaotic. It is the individual's capacity to control their hunger that determines their level of social agency. If hunger cannot be eradicated, the quest, then, must be for equilibrium between hunger and satiety. I refer to this equilibrium throughout this study as the 'luxury of moderation'—an ironic term, but pointed: I argue that the ability to moderate (or regulate) one's own appetite is a luxury that few can afford, due to the overarching unequal distribution of wealth. In the narratives I address, individuals are driven to extreme behaviours in regard to food and social power out of the fear of scarcity as much as actual starvation. These behaviours extend from excessive hoarding to food destruction, as well as rioting and self-starvation. Memories of seasons of scarcity as well as narratives of potential future want create a scarcity mentality that is as much a driving force of social unrest as the reality of hunger. In the midst of these figures are those who have the capacity to choose when, how much, and what they eat, and are therefore not psychologically fraught with the fear that what they currently have will not be renewed. They are in control of their appetites. This control is, I argue, at the core of social agency: these individuals are self-regulating. Taste, to which I will return, operates as a mechanism of this control—the ability to choose what to eat, which can then be extended into metaphorical, aesthetic taste. Taste becomes a form of cultural capital that can be acquired separately from economic capital; in this way, there is provision for social advancement, with taste being positioned as a radical element that disrupts the stability of economic discourse.

The self-regulating, self-moderating individual is as much of an ideal as the self-regulating market, not the least because they intercept each other. E.P. Thompson observes that for the early political economists, 'the market was never better regulated than when it was left to regulate itself,' but the crucial variable remains that 'the only way in which this self-adjusting economy might break down was through the meddlesome interference of the State and of popular prejudice.'[7] 'Popular prejudice' in this sense could, in fact, arise from a taste for ethics. Regenia Gagnier describes political economy as an ideal dependent on continual progress, 'in which scarcity was perceived to be a relation of productive forces to Nature,' but the rub is in the belief that '[o]nce society had *developed* its progressive forces, humanity could *progress* ethically and politically.'[8] Gagnier's observation reveals the power of political economy's narrative to dismiss moral and ethical causes on the basis that they are secondary to the abstract concept of progress; and most importantly, in a context of *continual* development, progress will never end—therefore,

7 E.P. Thompson, 'The Moral Economy of the English Crowd in the Eighteenth Century,' *Past and Present*, 50 (1971): 76–136, 90.

8 Regenia Gagnier, *The Insatiability of Human Wants: Economics and Aesthetics in Market Society* (Chicago and London: Chicago University Press, 2000), 2. Gagnier's emphasis.

the imperatives of ethics will never be at the fore. Within the nineteenth century, working against this bleak amoral ideal, interference at various social and political levels would persist, negating the self-adjusting model. However, in combining the utilitarian ideals of political economy with its de-moralising claim, this economic vision in times of scarcity narrates a discourse of a starving few being sacrificed for the sake of the many in society—as enunciated by Dickens's M'Choakumchild. As the narratives I address show, though, in *practice* the many are sacrificed for the luxury of a few.

The development of taste

In examining the representation of food and hunger in British narratives from the 1830s through to the 1860s, there appears to be a transition from food being the object of desire, from the devastated harvests of the early part of the century through to the Hungry Forties, to food being a signifier of desire in the later texts. In this way, I would suggest, taste begins to supersede hunger in the historical trajectory. Taste is always present, though, as is hunger, and so it is more helpful to view this transition in terms of a change in ratio. As Richard Menke discusses convincingly in his reading of Christina Rossetti's *Goblin Market*,[9] there were still bad harvests in the late 1850s, as there will continue to be. But the preoccupation in the middle of the century is more about access to specific *tastes* than access to food generally. Menke refers, for example, to the weekly accounts in the *Economist* of fruit scarcity in the British market, and the journal's preoccupation with the specific scarcity of lemons and oranges:

> On April 23 it reports a '[m]arket bare of oranges,' a week later one emptied not only of oranges but now also of lemons. By May 7, the 'backward season for fruit of home growth' seemed 'likely to clear the market of foreign produce' as well, as Britons substituted imported for homegrown fruit. Anyone in England who sought a sweet orange to eat or wanted a lemon for punch would likely have had to do without. Given the destruction of the new fruit crop and the subsequent scarcity of imported fruit, England in late April 1859 must have been a particularly fruit-less place.[10]

The move toward taste could be accounted for in a number of ways or narratives. The general increased prosperity of the nation and British Empire, including its access to colonial resources, would be a significant factor, as would a seeming decrease in the level of fear of abject poverty and starvation. There were better educational prospects for the working classes, and the consequent capacity to acquire social and economic capital, primarily due to the work of the Chartists.

---

9 Richard Menke, 'The Political Economy of Fruit,' in *The Culture of Christina Rossetti: Female Poetics and Victorian Contexts*, ed. Mary Arseneau, Antony H. Harrison, and Lorraine Janzen Kooistra (Athens: Ohio University Press, 1999), 105–36.
10 Ibid., 109.

Nor was there the same level of fear in the 1860s of Continental Terror. Britain and the Empire seemed more stable, but at the same time, any idea of class distinction became less unmoveable. Within this context, the refinement of taste became the distinguishing factor in the breakdown of feudalism that began with the industrialisation that had caused such a significant amount of hunger and fear. This particular narrative seems to buy into the idea of hunger leading to progress; but what I want to focus on is the function of taste in counteracting abject hunger in order to promote social dynamism.

Influential Enlightenment discussions on taste have been read most commonly in the figurative sense, but the ideas become even more provocative when physical taste and hunger are related to notions of civilisation. Edmund Burke argues for the universality of taste, connecting it closely to reason: 'it is probable that the standard both of reason and Taste is the same in all human creatures.'[11] Similarly, Immanuel Kant would go on to state in his *Critique of Judgment* (1790) that 'the judgment of taste cannot rest on any subjective end as its ground.'[12] Thus, while Burke acknowledges that it is 'commonly supposed that this delicate and aerial faculty, which seems too volatile to endure even the chains of definition, cannot be properly tried by any test, nor regulated by any standard,' he contends that this is only due to the neglect of philosophers.[13] In 'Of the Standard of Taste' (1757), however, David Hume directly challenges Burke's assertions from a more democratic perspective, referring to the 'great variety of Tastes, as well as of opinions, which prevail in the world,' and pointing out that '[w]e are apt to call *barbarous* whatever departs widely from our own taste and apprehension: But soon find the epithet of reproach retorted on us.'[14] In spite of their disagreement on the relationship between taste and reason, both Hume's and Burke's observations build on Aristotelian ideas of reason that are connected with literal or sensory taste. In *Sense and Sensibilia*, Aristotle wrote that '[i]t is by taste that one distinguishes in food the pleasant from the unpleasant, so as to flee from the latter and pursue the former,'[15] connecting human reason—the ability to savour and think about food[16]—to the ability to distinguish tastes.

The political economy of taste

In *Accounting for Tastes* (1996), Gary Becker suggests that the 'excessive attention' given to mathematical models and formulas in economic theory has led to neglect of social interactions and the role of taste in economic and social

11 Edmund Burke, 'On Taste,' in *A Philosophical Enquiry into the Origin of the Sublime and the Beautiful* (1757; 5th edn, London: J. Dodsley, 1767), 1–40, 1.
12 Immanuel Kant, from the 'Analytic of Aesthetic Judgment,' in *The European Philosophers from Descartes to Nietzsche*, ed. Monroe C. Beardsley (New York: Random House, 1960), 485.
13 Burke, 'On Taste,' 2.
14 David Hume, 'Of the Standard of Taste,' in *Four Dissertations* (London: A. Millar, 1757), 201–40, 203.
15 Aristotle, 'Sense and Sensibilia,' in *The Complete Works of Aristotle*, trans. J.I. Beare, rev. Oxford translation, ed. Jonathan Barnes (2 vols, Princeton: Princeton University Press, 1984), vol. 1, 693–713, 694.
16 Mark M. Smith, *Sensory History* (Oxford and New York: Berg, 2007), 76.

progress.[17] Gagnier similarly suggests that economists need to address the ways in which 'people come to "choose" what they do, by showing how tastes and choices develop and, just as important, are constrained.'[18] Both Becker and Gagnier address taste more broadly than the sensory, but their emphasis on taste, particularly in terms of Gagnier's development and, conversely, the *constraint* of taste, is pertinent to my approach to social identity and agency, and physical hunger. The idea of constraining taste evokes Amartya Sen's groundbreaking work on the relationship between entitlement, endowment, and exchange opportunities in terms of access to food. In this sense, taste, rather than standing against the chaos of hunger, becomes a type of hunger: social identity is determined by the access individuals and communities have to particular tastes. While he does not talk specifically about taste, Sen does refer to 'consumption habits,' and points out that while it may be essentially 'very low-cost' to provide the minimum calorie requirements, the food provided would be 'monumentally boring, and people's food habits are not, in fact, determined by such a cost minimization exercise.'[19] Indeed, building on Sen's crucial argument that '[s]tarvation is the characteristic of some people not *having* enough food to eat' rather than there not *being* enough,[20] it therefore follows that in regard to taste, similar to the injustice of Adam Smith's man envying the prosperity of the wealthy, particular tastes become something to desire—something for which to hunger. To desire particular food, then, becomes a signifier of desiring to belong to a particular cultural or community space, one in which that taste is considered a staple of the diet.

In *The Taste Culture Reader* (2005), Carolyn Korsmeyer observes that '[a]mong the paradoxes that surround taste, few loom larger than the fact that taste is supposed to be little more than a bodily sensation, yet at the same time it provides the metaphor for the finest cultivation of perceptual experience.'[21] Yet it is evident that the Victorians saw a crucial connection between sensory and aesthetic taste. An article on 'The Five Senses' in the journal *The Leisure Hour* in 1866 positions sensory taste in terms of national significance and identity:

> Inasmuch as the Germans stuff their geese with apples and chestnuts, how comes it, if the theory of harmonies in cookery be adopted, that we Britons stuff our geese with sage and onions? If there really be a canon of taste in this matter, then who—the Germans or ourselves—interpret the canon most faithfully? On the harmonic basis Germany might fairly be assumed to hold

17 Gary S. Becker, *Accounting for Tastes* (Cambridge, Mass.: Harvard University Press, 1996), 194.
18 Gagnier, *Insatiability of Human Wants*, 10.
19 Amartya Sen, *Poverty and Famines: An Essay on Entitlement and Deprivation* (1983; Oxford: Oxford Scholarship Online, 2003), 12.
20 Ibid., 1. Sen's emphasis.
21 Carolyn Korsmeyer, 'Introduction: Perspectives on Taste,' in *The Taste Culture Reader: Experiencing Food and Drink*, ed. Carolyn Korsmeyer (2005; Oxford and New York: Berg, 2007), 1–9, 6.

the palm, considering the deep and successful study they have given to musical harmony.[22]

It is noteworthy that the article focuses on difference, rather than the fact that both nations actually stuff geese for cooking. This act, as the commonality, is not questioned: an unstuffed goose is unconscionable. But what is evident through this preoccupation with taste choices is the way in which by the middle of the nineteenth century so much of one's identity, as an individual, as a member of the community, or even as a citizen of the nation, was defined by the tastes considered appropriate to take into one's body. As Ellmann notes, 'it is by ingesting the external world that the subject establishes his body as his own, distinguishing its inside from its outside'; but this identity remains fraught in the acknowledgement that this 'need to incorporate the outside world exposes his fundamental incompleteness.'[23] This incompleteness potently represents an overarching human hunger that is both physical and social. One is defined by one's need to eat as well as *what* one eats, but also by the incapacity to be fully satisfied, either physically or socially. As Keats wrote to Richard Woodhouse in 1819, '[p]erhaps I eat to persuade myself I am somebody.'[24]

The mobility of hunger

Hunger is both transient and constant, a necessary element of human society, yet inherently subjective in its experience and rhetoric. Hunger is both physical and social, and moves through degrees of literal and metaphorical manifestations. In this way, hunger itself is always moving. Ultimately I see physical and social hunger in a dynamic dialogue, one that mirrors the dialogue between scarcity and excess. Sara Millman and Robert W. Kates succinctly observe that the 'history of hunger is interwoven with the history of plenty,'[25] and I would suggest that taste, alongside a Smithian desire for the greener pastures of others, is what binds together these interwoven narratives. There is a narrative necessity to reconcile the unequal distribution of wealth. Vernon's juxtaposition, though, of the Great Exhibition with the Great Irish Famine highlights, through reference to alternative theories of political economy, the cruel reality of inequality: '[w]hile the benefits of free trade predicted by Smith were on display at the Crystal Palace, Ireland appeared to furnish Britons with a grim fulfillment of Malthus's laws of population.'[26] The mobile quality of hunger, then, is perhaps also necessary in a

22 'The Five Senses,' *The Leisure Hour: A Family Journal of Instruction and Recreation* (7 April 1866): 213–16, 215.
23 Ellmann, *Hunger Artists*, 30.
24 Qtd in Ellmann, *Hunger Artists*, 30.
25 Sara Millman and Robert W. Kates, 'Toward Understanding Hunger,' in *Hunger in History: Food Shortage, Poverty, and Deprivation*, ed. Lucile F. Newman (1990; Oxford and Cambridge: Blackwell, 1995), 3–24, 9.
26 Vernon, *Hunger*, 41.

narrative sense as a means to distance oneself, or one's community or nation, from the responsibility of recognising and contending with the force of hunger.

My study seeks to follow, to a degree, the progression of hunger through the first few decades of Victoria's reign, from the perspective that physical want led to riots and protests, and then to migration, both geographically and socially. While my reading of the texts begin with a greater focus on actual starvation and gradually moves to focus more on taste, both hunger and taste-choice are inherent throughout. Chapter 1, 'Rewriting riots past,' joins physical hunger and fear of hunger with the hunger for a nostalgic past, with the mid-century British preoccupation with the French Revolution playing a central role in the fear of social unrest. Beginning with Dickens's and Martineau's provocative historical fictions of the 1789 French Revolution, in which they expose Britain's very real social and economic investment with the Continental turmoil the nation sought to distance itself from, I then go on to address the ways in which Dickens and Eliot use historical fiction to reinsert Britain's own violent heritage of hunger and riots into the mid-century consciousness. Dickens's reinvention of the 1780 Gordon Riots and Eliot's riotous crowds at the time of the first national election after the 1832 Reform Act are written for their mid-century contemporaries, causing the social hunger for an imagined past to emerge. Dickens, Martineau, and Eliot manipulate the past to bolster their own campaigns regarding poverty, wealth distribution, and social agency.

Chapter 2, 'Humanising the mob,' examines the tensions between self-interest and the needs of the community through British-based social unrest, and the ways in which Brontë, Martineau, and Gaskell use the fictional narrative to critique liberal capitalism and to explore community-based alternatives to the master–worker dichotomy. Yet it also looks at the way community is defined, with a restrictive scarcity mentality arising within community feeling alongside the scarcity of food. 'Foreignness' begins to mean more than just one from another country, extending to those from other parts of Britain, and even England. This attitude seems undergirded by the Poor Laws, in which parishes could literally abdicate responsibility for the poor within their community who did not originate there— although there were many cases of parishes hiding people, charitably keeping them until they could claim legitimate asylum in the community. The greatest aversion was kept for the 'foreigner' who came to the community to make their fortune off the backs of the locals; and the unstable truces that form between these figures are indicative of the instability of a nation in flux, in which identity became less connected to cultural and local heritage.

The physical mobility of people throughout Britain was complicated by migration from the Continent due to the European revolutions, and from famine-devastated Ireland. Chapter 3, 'Disenfranchised communities,' addresses more closely the difficulties in constructing identity within a transient population, and the dangers of othering those who do not belong in terms of criminality and foreignness. By contrasting the reception of the Continental Europeans with that of the Irish, the liminal position of the Irish as both British and not-British is brought into focus, most clearly through Henry Mayhew's presentation of the

Irish migrants in London. These migrants are again contrasted with the itinerant workers, always at risk of being charged with vagrancy, who desperately seek the capacity to fill their bellies and those of their families, at the sacrifice of community. For the transient figure, the need to have a sense of home becomes inherent to their sense of identity; and from this perspective, I examine the role of foods from home—that is, from the place of origin—and of portable property in a context in which a stable, recognisable community is a myth.

Chapter 4, 'Educating transgressive tastes,' takes a more marked transition into the role of tastes, developing from a consciousness of particular cultural capital being associated with economic and social security. This chapter examines the implications of both formal and informal education, and the way in which food and the restrictions on food undergird the social lessons being taught. The role of the boarding school in Dickens, Brontë, and Eliot takes on particular significance, in that the provision of food comes through the institution, rather than the family home, and often the escape to school promotes the capacity for the individual to find a new social path through the cultural education they receive. Chapter 4 and Chapter 5, 'Social communion,' both focus more on the progress of individuals as they seek to navigate and manipulate their social and institutional confines. Yet institutions and ideologies loom over these individuals, revealing the tensions between intellectual and physical hunger, the luxury of moderation, and the insatiable desire for more. 'Social communion' focalises ideas of hunger, taste, and community through the ways in which social inclusion and exclusion are written through eating, as well as the way appetites are moderated from without. The conflict between the desire for self-moderation and individuals or institutions seeking to regulate the appetites of others is complicated through the regulator often also providing individuals with alternative tastes, which, in turn, gives them greater space for choosing tastes. The engagement and investment of individuals in regard to food, especially when it is scarce, becomes a signifier for their mobility within the broader social context, especially in terms of their capacity to adapt.

By concluding with a reading of Rossetti's *Goblin Market*, I seek to reflect upon the insatiable momentum of hunger within modernity, as well as the compulsion to *understand* hunger if it cannot be eradicated. '"Taste them and try"—the risks of tasting in an insatiable market' returns to the hunger for equilibrium—the luxury of moderation—in a social context that requires insatiability. The simultaneous desires for satiety, progress, and agency cannot be sufficiently reconciled within a capitalist mechanism that asserts self-interest over the human need to belong to a community. Taste, once a means of control, becomes merely another hunger not to be filled. The American periodical *Harper's New Monthly Magazine* published a series on the senses in 1855. The article on taste observed:

> As long as the food is in our mouth, we feel it, we taste it, we handle it just as we choose. Jaws, and teeth, and tongue are all subject to our will. . . . But the instant the pellet touches those mysterious curtains, it is beyond our control,

and, under ordinary circumstances, becomes even lost to our consciousness. A faint impression of taste is all that lingers behind.[27]

As this passage suggests, while we are in the process of tasting, we are in control; yet if we want to swallow the food—to feed our empty stomachs—that control must be relinquished. Indeed, the lingering taste is a reminder of hunger being perpetually renewed, denying agency because human nature—and the human body—cannot be free of that driving force of hunger. Our negotiations between different kinds of hunger, and our willingness to sacrifice some hungers for others, is the social and cultural space we are allowed. In an economic sense, the capacity to move between these hungers is what extends the individual's capacity for progress within the unending corporate quest for civilisation.

27 'The Senses. I.—Taste,' *Harper's New Monthly Magazine*, 12 (1855): 73–81, 78.

1   Rewriting riots past

> 'What!' exclaimed the Ghost, 'would you so soon put out, with worldly hands, the light I give? Is it not enough that you are one whose passions made this cap, and force me through whole trains of years to wear it low upon my brow!'
>
> (Charles Dickens, *A Christmas Carol* (1843), 27)

> In relation to the violence of the past, we seem helpless, impotent to set right the injustice that has so forcefully shaped the very times that we inhabit.
>
> (David Lloyd, 'The Indigent Sublime' (2005), 152)

When the Ghost of Christmas Past manifests before Ebenezer Scrooge, Dickens's masochistic, self-starving protagonist responds with a near-visceral need to extinguish the ghost's light. His lack of desire to revisit his past is inherently linked to his self-starvation: he is deliberately disconnected from his community, and there is a sense of fear in acknowledging the existence of a past that includes family relationships, love, and friendship. His hunger for those relationships works in tense opposition to his self-denial, as his 'melancholy dinner in his usual melancholy tavern' is juxtaposed with 'having read all the newspapers' before going home to bed.[1] Scrooge eats alone. He wants to be aware of what is happening in the world, but resolutely determines to have no part in it. Yet much as David Lloyd powerfully suggests our investment in the history of the 'times that we inhabit,' the Ghost's claim that Scrooge's 'passions made this cap' forbids such determination. The desire to stifle the past speaks to the repression of trauma, and a 'retreat to omnipotent fantasy' in which 'one possesses . . . powers over the limitations of the real world.'[2] Scrooge's masochism exemplifies the 'preoedipal origins of masochism in narcissistic trauma' that John Kucich attributes to Edmund Bergler's mid-twentieth-century work on psychoanalysis and megalomania; his 'feelings of abandonment, deprivation, and injustice'[3] are the

---

1 Charles Dickens, *A Christmas Carol* (1843; London: Bradbury and Evans, 1858), 11.
2 John Kucich, *Imperial Masochism: British Fiction, Fantasy, and Social Class* (Princeton and Oxford: Princeton University Press, 2007), 22.
3 Ibid.

miser's self-inflicted means to rationalise his placelessness and powerlessness within the present.

Scrooge provides a provocative illustration for early Victorian Britain's approach of repressing and disconnecting the past in order to rationalise the present. In *The Burdens of Perfection* (2008), Andrew H. Miller identifies the need in nineteenth-century moral perfectionism to remove oneself 'from reality to seek company outside this time and space.'[4] Historical fiction played a crucial role in creating this distance, for, as John Bowen observes in his introduction to Dickens's historical novel *Barnaby Rudge* (1841), '[m]odern history rests on our sense that the past is safely over and can become the subject of disinterested knowledge.'[5] Yet this disinterestedness, for the Victorians as much as it was for Scrooge, was a myth of separation. Miller emphasises that the act of distancing in this way actually creates an 'uneasy sensitivity to exposure,' as the consciousness of an audience, and the awareness of other possible narratives outside the constructed ones, evokes self-reflection.[6] Such self-reflection is further complicated, not just by the transient quality of memory, but by hindsight. Simon Dentith reveals the 'threat that hindsight poses to the authenticity or adequacy of the knowledge or feelings that were available to the original actors,' for 'the benefit of hindsight is precisely that more is known now, at the moment of recall, than could possibly have been known *at the time*.'[7] Indeed, the past can be retold from the safe distance of moral judgement; and within this context, historical fiction, with its self-consciously flexible relationship between 'fact' and 'fiction,' focalises and critiques the rationalising, stabilising effects of hindsight. For imperial Britain, the nostalgia of looking back is disrupted by the very distance it seeks to create through 'optative reflections' upon what could have been: '[t]o the extent that realism proposes to give us stories about how things really were, a space naturally opens up within that mode to tell us how things might have been, but were not.'[8] In this way, Victorian Britain is haunted by the past, and the past's investment in the present and future.

Strategies of denial and repression arose in the wake of food riots, machine breaking, Reform Acts, and Chartism, elements of social unrest that seeped from the past into the present, challenging the stability and civility of the British imperial vision. Jeff Nunokawa speaks of the fear of loss in the Victorian consciousness, referring to 'the inevitable loss of property in the nineteenth-century imagination,' written through the literature with the conviction that 'nothing gold can stay.'[9] In this construction, the fear of loss also speaks to the fear of a return

---

4 Andrew H. Miller, *The Burdens of Perfection: On Ethics and Reading in Nineteenth-Century British Literature* (Ithaca and London: Cornell University Press, 2008), 8.

5 John Bowen, Introduction to *Barnaby Rudge; A Tale of the Riots of 'Eighty* (London: Penguin, 2003), xvi.

6 Miller, *Burdens of Perfection*, 8.

7 Simon Dentith, *Nineteenth-Century British Literature Then and Now: Reading with Hindsight* (Farnham: Ashgate, 2014), vii. Dentith's emphasis.

8 Andrew H. Miller, 'Lives Unled in Realist Fiction,' *Representations*, 98.1 (2007): 118–34, 120; 122.

9 Jeff Nunokawa, *The Afterlife of Property: Domestic Security and the Victorian Novel* (Princeton: Princeton University Press, 1994), 7; 122.

to the past, a past of scarcity and violence. However, this fear is problematic in two key ways: first, it denies the present-day existence of scarcity and violence; and second, more crucially, it unwittingly acknowledges the cultural heritage of violence within the civilised British imagination. Therefore, scarcity and violence must be displaced, repressed, or at least rationalised, in order for the empire to maintain its vision of moral and civil superiority. Yet just as Scrooge is haunted by his past, present, and future, so too was Victorian Britain haunted by its heritage of hungry violence, not just relegated to the past, but speaking into the present and defining the nation's future. The nation is defined as much by what it was *not* as what it was. Speaking of the construction of Dickens's realism, Miller writes: 'there are counterfactual lives each character is pointedly not living, defining mirror existences that have branched off along other lines than that down which he or she is, in fact, traveling.'[10] Scrooge's ghostly visitations are the epitome of this kind of optative exploration. As Avery Gordon suggests, 'the ghost is primarily what is missing. . . . What it represents is usually a loss, sometimes of life, sometimes of a path not taken.'[11] In the case of Scrooge, the ghost is also the figure of that which is denied. It is necessarily from an Other time, a time that should be safely distant, but invades and shapes 'the very times that we inhabit'; and, as David Lloyd posits, 'that other time is not necessarily the past, but may intimate an only fitfully imaginable possible future.'[12]

Dickens makes it very clear that the ghostly manifestations are not events that merely happen to Scrooge, but are constructed in varying degrees of consciousness by his self-imposed physical and social hungers. As much as he denies himself the nourishment of food, he denies himself the nourishment of human sympathy. This miserly attitude extends into the comfort of home. He does not care for light, for '[d]arkness is cheap, and Scrooge liked it' (13), but his fire reveals a desire for warmth: 'It was a very low fire indeed; nothing on such a bitter night. He was obliged to sit close to it, and brood over it, before he could extract the least sensation of warmth from such a handful of fuel' (14). While his meanness triumphs in that he refuses to build a larger fire, the fact that Scrooge leans in and broods over his fire suggests that there is a hunger there, one that he will not let himself sate. It therefore follows that *A Christmas Carol*'s cheerful ending is written in terms of Scrooge accepting his own hunger, both physical and social, and being willing to sate it. His transformation is marked in three key ways: by his purchase of a Christmas turkey for Bob Cratchit's family that is too large to be carried by any means other than a cab; by being willing to donate money to the poor; and by unexpectedly taking up his nephew's invitation to Christmas dinner.

Tara Moore observes that 'much of the nineteenth-century literature containing narratives of Christmas speaks directly to national fears of famine,' focusing

---

10 Miller, 'Lives Unled,' 119.
11 Avery Gordon, *Ghostly Matters: Haunting and the Sociological Imagination* (Minneapolis: University of Minnesota Press, 1997), 63–64.
12 David Lloyd, 'The Indigent Sublime: Specters of Irish Hunger,' *Representations*, 92.1 (2005): 152–85, 155.

on the 'developing rhetoric of benevolence' toward the hungry poor.[13] However, presenting Scrooge's transformation in terms of sating his own social and physical hunger highlights the tensions between liberalism, capitalism, masochistic self-sacrifice, and altruism that inevitably contribute to dialogues between the needs of the individual and the broader needs of the community, which figure throughout this study, and were at the heart of early political economy. In this chapter, hunger and haunting provide a unifying factor in the wake of riots and social unrest. Nostalgia for an imagined past can become a form of hunger, but denying the past also creates a counter-hunger, a type of haunting in which the denied past seeks to reassert itself through the collective memory. The disruptive presence of the Gordon Riots in the late eighteenth century, amongst other uprisings, belied the stability of mid-nineteenth-century Britain, as well as the purity and legitimacy of Britain's global dominance. Through Parliament and the legal system, as well as through the media, the nation sought to redefine its heritage by displacing the threat of current instability onto foreign shores (France being the most common scapegoat), by repressing historical national conflicts, and, where this repression was not possible, by creating rationalising narratives to explain away internal unrest in a way that made it belong to another time and place.

There is a powerful reason, then, for the success and popularity of historical fiction throughout the nineteenth century. While Bowen suggests that mid-century novelists tried their hands at historical fiction in order to acquire the gravitas of history,[14] the genre of historical fiction has an agility of purpose that historical writing is often denied. Its affective nature gives individual voice and interiority to historical events, encouraging empathy rather than the safety of objective distance. Historical fiction rewrites the past to address the present, the narrative voices overtly looking back from a space that is contemporary to the reader. Deliberate references and parallels to the present are drawn, reminding the reader of their unbreakable connection to the narrated past, so that the narratives themselves become an act of haunting. The historical narratives of hunger and social chaos I explore in this chapter, by Dickens, Harriet Martineau, and George Eliot, were each written with an explicit purpose to address the social conditions and injustices that were contemporary to the writer, and specifically challenge wilful acts of displacement, repression, and rationalisation. They reassert the past into the present in ways that counter both a nostalgic historical imagination, and a determined blindness to the traumas and hungers of the present. Furthermore, in looking back to address the present, these texts take on a kind of prophetic role, challenging the progress of Britain's future. In these narratives, it is possible for Britain to see, as Scrooge does, that the 'air was filled with phantoms, wandering hither and thither in restless haste, and moaning as they went. . . . The misery with them all was, clearly, that they sought

---

13 Tara Moore, 'Starvation in Victorian Christmas Fiction,' *Victorian Literature and Culture*, 36.2 (2008): 489–505, 489; 491.
14 Bowen, Introduction to *Barnaby Rudge*, xv.

to interfere, for good, in human matters, and had lost the power for ever.'[15] Thus the resurrection of the chaotic past offers the possibility for the nation to reconnect to its cultural heritage, and allow that acknowledgement to inform its approach to the community, in a way that is not possible while that past is being denied. A present disconnected from the past is ineffectual and always under threat, for the past is hungry to be heard.

The dangers of France

> 'Sir, At this late hour, in this exhausted state of the House, and exhausted state of the debate. . . . I pass by the exciting topics of the French revolution—I say not a word on the details of the Bill—they have been treated already with consummate ability. . . . '
>
> (Sir Robert Peel (22 September 1831))[16]

On 30 January 2014, Conservative Home Secretary Theresa May proposed a new clause to the Immigration Bill first presented to the House of Commons on 10 October 2013. This amendment, 'NC18: Deprivation of Citizenship,' would 'enable the deprivation of citizenship in cases where a person's conduct had been determined by the Home Secretary to have been seriously prejudicial to the vital interests of the UK, even if doing so would make the person stateless.'[17] The dispossession and demonisation of the foreign immigrant has a long history, and I will return to these narratives in later chapters. What I want to focus on here is the continuing narrative, evident in this recent amendment, that circumvents the possibility of the 'homegrown terrorist.' Because it is contained within an Immigration Bill, terror arising from those who are British by birth does not have to be considered.[18] This kind of avoidance and denial of domestic terror resonates strongly with the early Victorian governments that saw the threats to Britain as originating in the foreign place, as if denying that violence and unrest could be born organically out of Britain's own socio-political environment.

The most-referenced locus of terror for the mid-century Victorians was France. In *Writing Against Revolution* (2007), Kevin Gilmartin refers to fellow historian Ronald Paulson, who terms the presence of revolutionary experience in British Romantic literature as 'a secondary French reality—history at second hand in

---

15 Dickens, *A Christmas Carol*, 22.

16 *Speech of Sir Robert Peel, Bart. in the House of Commons, 22 September 1831; On the Question 'Whether the Reform Bill Do Now Pass?'* (London: Roake and Varty, 1831), 3.

17 Charley Coleman and Dorothy Hughes, House of Lords Library Note: Immigration Bill (HL Bill 84 of 2013–14), 6 February 2014, LLN 2014/004, at http://www.parliament.uk/briefing-papers/LLN-2014-004.pdf.

18 While there are (increasingly) other laws to counter homegrown terrorism, it remains significant that the dominant political and social narratives regarding homegrown terrorism involve terrorists becoming radicalised through spending time fighting abroad, thus denying that such radicalism could arise independently on home soil.

written reports.'[19] Yet even this idea of secondary history tends to displace and diminish Britain's own revolutionary history. Gilmartin's assessment becomes more acute when he acknowledges that literary references to French revolutions are a part of an 'ideological defence mechanism': 'the threat of subversion was consistently displaced from England to republican France, to North America, and to Ireland, with the trauma of political change getting related and reported as news, rumor, and correspondence.'[20] From another perspective, in *Popular Radicalism* (1988), D.G. Wright suggests that the French Revolution provided inspiration for the tradition of working-class radicalism in Britain. Indeed, the starving French peasant was prominent in the British imagination, with good reason: Linda Colley observes that in the eighteenth century France experienced at least sixteen nation-wide famines, as well as localised famines almost every year.[21] While Colley goes on to claim that famine was not as much of a factor within Britain, it is evident that the *fear* of starvation was very present in the British mind. From the late eighteenth century to the early nineteenth century, scarcity was a real threat to the working classes, either through poor harvests, or through prices being too high for the working classes to afford. It was as much out of the fear of starvation as actual clemming that the Chartist movement arose, seeking a greater political voice in the nation. Wright acknowledges the radical tradition within Britain, but he connects what he calls the 'prehistory of the Chartist movement' much more closely to the French politics of the 1790s.[22] While I agree with John Stevenson that there is not a stark contrast 'between the calm of the eighteenth century and the years which followed the upheaval in France,'[23] it is evident that within the Victorian imagination at least, the French Revolution of 1789 held this pivotal historical role. It is this form of narrative—that demonised and elevated the inspirational role of the Revolution, as well as the parallels drawn with mid-nineteenth-century Britain—that interests me here. By perpetuating the precedence of the Revolution, Britain could deny its own heritage of hunger and violence. As a result, the revolutionary response to the British conditions of crop failures, Poor Laws, Corn Laws, and Encroachment Laws—to name a few—is repeatedly written in terms that echo the 1790s French Revolution's cry for 'Liberty, Equality, Fraternity, or Death.'

While the close cultural and historical relationships between Britain and France, and the terrifying hold of the French Revolution upon the British imagination, were entrenched well before the mid-nineteenth century, it is well established that Thomas Carlyle's *The French Revolution: A History in Three Parts* (1837) had a profound influence on the ways in which mid-century

---

19 Ronald Paulson, qtd in Kevin Gilmartin, *Writing Against Revolution: Literary Conservatism in Britain, 1790–1832* (Cambridge: Cambridge University Press, 2007), 2.

20 Gilmartin, *Writing Against Revolution*, 2.

21 Linda Colley, *Britons: Forging the Nation 1707–1837* (1992; London: Vintage, 1996), 39.

22 D.G. Wright, *Popular Radicalism: The Working-Class Experience 1780–1880* (London and New York: Longman Press, 1988), 21.

23 John Stevenson, 'Social Control and the Prevention of Riots in England, 1789–1829,' in *Social Control in Nineteenth Century Britain*, ed. A.P. Donajgrodzki (London: Croom Helm, 1977), 27.

writers and thinkers contended with the Revolution. In the first part of this chapter, however, I focus on Charles Dickens's *A Tale of Two Cities* (1859), which was heavily influenced by Carlyle's account, and volume 12 of Harriet Martineau's *Illustrations of Political Economy* (1832–34), *French Wines and Politics* (1833), which pre-dates Carlyle's work. Carlyle's account, according to Gareth Stedman Jones, positions the Revolution as an ideological war, 'born out of the loss of faith and habit.'[24] Indeed, when the Reform Bill was being debated in Parliament in 1831, many of the members against reform framed the Revolution as a seizure of political power, rather than motivated by social injustice and inequality. John Wilson Croker, for instance, acknowledges 'that frightful period—the dawn of that long and disastrous day of crime and calamity, bears some resemblance to our present circumstances,'[25] but rather than seeing the resemblance as a reason to beware of 'resisting the popular will,'[26] Croker positions the *Tiers État*, written in January 1789, as both a Reform Bill analogous to the one Britain was debating, and as a significant catalyst for the Revolution itself. In a similar vein, historian Sophia Rosenfeld argues that the French king's signing of the Declaration of the Rights of Man gave legitimacy to the Revolution by ushering in the 'legal protection of speech.'[27] Yet by positioning the Revolution as a political act in this manner, Croker is able to play on the fears of Revolution to justify rejecting Britain's Bill. He argues that the *Tiers État*, 'though veiled in all the sophistry of popular plausibility, was, in fact, the whole revolution,' and therefore that the nobility were 'justified in offering a firm, constitutional, and unanimous opposition.' In this way, Croker presents the *Tiers État* and Britain's Reform Bill as equally 'monstrous proposition[s].'[28] Likewise, speaking of the more recent 1830 uprising, Sir James Mackintosh argued, '[t]he dangers of Europe do not originate in democratical principles, or democratical power. They arose from those who conspired the subversion of all popular rights, however sanctioned by oaths, by constitution, and by laws.'[29]

Both Martineau and Dickens, however, focus more on the socio-economic causes of the Revolution: an event born out of physical hunger, a hunger that led to desperation and an awareness of being voiceless. Indeed, in *The Crowd in History* (1964), George Rudé asserts that the 'supply of cheap and plentiful food' was one of the 'great issues of the French Revolution. . . . It is therefore

---

24 Gareth Stedman Jones, 'The Redemptive Powers of Violence? Carlyle, Marx and Dickens,' in *Charles Dickens,* A Tale of Two Cities *and the French Revolution*, ed. Colin Jones, Josephine McDonagh, and Jon Mee (Basingstoke: Palgrave Macmillan, 2009), 41–63, 45.

25 *The Speech of the Right Honourable John Wilson Croker, on the Question that 'The Reform Bill Do Pass,' Tuesday, 22nd September, 1831* (London: John Murray, 1831), 4.

26 Ibid., 5.

27 Sophia Rosenfeld, 'On Being Heard: A Case for Paying Attention to the Historical Ear,' *American History Review*, 116.2 (2011): 316–34, 327.

28 *Croker, on the Question that 'The Reform Bill Do Pass,'* 6.

29 *Speech of the Right Hon. Sir James Mackintosh, Member of Parliament for Knaresborough, on the Second Reading of the Bill, to Amend the Representation of the People in England and Wales, On Monday, the 4th of July, 1831* (London: James Ridgway, 1831), 5.

hardly surprising that even in the most ostensibly *political* of these episodes the food problem should so frequently obtrude.'[30] Across the accounts of the French Revolution, there is a strong connection between being articulate and being rational; however, articulacy is often defined not by the quality of speech, but by how audible it is, or by who hears it. Unlike Carlyle's 'emphasis on silence and inarticulacy'[31] in describing the Revolution, Martineau and Dickens give rational voice to their revolutionaries through the history that the fictional narratives provide. Whereas Carlyle's account of the storming of the Bastille acknowledges 'Great is the combined voice of men,' he claims that 'the utterance of their *instincts*' is 'truer than their *thoughts*.'[32] In this way, while acknowledging the force of the revolutionaries, at this point Carlyle denies them rationality. Conversely, Martineau's and Dickens's revolutionaries, while still propelled by the instinct of hunger, are able to articulate their position through the space of the narrative, even if their voices are not heard by the authoritative figures within the text. Importantly, Martineau concludes *French Wines* with the signing of the Declaration of the Rights of Man, bringing the legitimacy that Rosenfeld suggests into her narrative. Stedman Jones pertinently observes that, 'although at certain points in [Carlyle's] narrative the people appear to be on the point of breaking into articulate speech, they never actually do so';[33] yet although the seeming inability to speak may arise from apparent lack of control, in Martineau and Dickens, this particular failure provides a statement regarding power relations between the privileged and the oppressed, rather than irrationalising the mob. While the violence is chaotic and excessive, it is perhaps even more disturbing that in the texts I examine, rationality married with desperate hunger lies at the core of revolutionary action.[34]

The other key disturbance in the texts is the way in which Martineau and Dickens deliberately speak to Britain's cultural and social condition through their presentations of revolutionary France. I have written elsewhere on the way in which Martineau uses the foreign setting as a means to translate English social issues into another cultural context in order to speak more freely about England.[35] Importantly, Sally Ledger writes that Dickens 'never regarded the 1850s with the equanimity of subsequent historians. . . . As in his other novels from the 1850s, Dickens's feeling is that British Culture could produce its own Terror if

---

30 George Rudé, *The Crowd in History: A Study of Popular Disturbances in France and England 1730–1848* (New York: John Wiley, 1964), 108.
31 Stedman Jones, 'Redemptive Powers of Violence?' 50.
32 Thomas Carlyle, *The French Revolution: A History in Three Parts* (1837; London: Chapman and Hall, 1857), vol. 1, 152. My emphasis.
33 Stedman Jones, 'Redemptive Powers of Violence?' 50.
34 Both Dickens and Martineau create a sense of a unified revolutionary voice in their narratives of the French Revolution, which bestows a limited privilege. In *Barnaby Rudge* (1841), however, Dickens does not privilege the English Gordon Rioters in the same way.
35 See *Translation, Authorship and the Victorian Professional Woman* (Farnham: Ashgate, 2011), 115. In 'The Anglo-French Alliance,' *Westminster Review* 63 (1855): 1–25, Martineau writes on the very close relationship between Britain and France historically, culturally, and intellectually.

the sufferings of the poor were not addressed.[36] Similarly, Mark Philp sees the historical setting of *A Tale of Two Cities* as more of a 'background for the more fundamental theme' of 'relations of privilege and subordination, of power and domination against impoverished weakness and sullen resentment,'[37] a theme that was just as pertinent to mid-century Britain in the aftermath of Chartism. For as much as '[r]adical opposition to the state had receded from public view since the suppression of the Chartist mass rally on Kennington Common in April 1848,'[38] the discontent remained hauntingly close to the surface, emerging a few years later and leading eventually to the Reform Act of 1867. For both Dickens and Martineau, the genre of historical fiction provides a translational distance to speak directly to the cultural conditions of Britain. However, while both texts take up the English obsession with France's revolutionary heritage, they crucially break down the distancing divide between England and France, a division that worked to remove England from revolutionary accountability, by emphasising the close economic relationship between the two nations during the revolution. By implicating England in the Revolution, both Dickens and Martineau challenge the idea that the terror of a French-style revolution is Other to Britain: even if Victorian Britain attempts to deny its own domestic revolutionary heritage, focusing instead on the potential terror of Continental revolutionary movements seeping across British shores, it still must face its dark, fundamental investment in the very Continental Revolution it fears.

Both Dickens and Martineau wrote their French tales with a French readership in mind. The translations of *A Tale of Two Cities* were reasonably popular, perhaps more readily accepted given the relative political stability of France in the 1850s. Although France had experienced riots in 1848, as had much of Europe, these uprisings were not of the scale of earlier revolutionary movements. In Dickens's narrative, it is also more evident that he wrote of Britain's escape from a similar revolutionary fate as a matter of circumstance, while Martineau was deliberately provocative in expressing moral superiority. Martineau's tale produced a volatile response from a France that had just experienced the July Revolution of 1830, which saw the abdication of Charles X and the ascension of Louis-Philippe, and the failed June Rebellion of 1832. While set historically in the 1788 lead-up to the most famous French Revolution, *French Wines and Politics* speaks explicitly to the tempests of hunger and revolution that converged in the more recent Parisian riots.

Given that *French Wines* was published as a part of a series, it is reasonable to assume that Martineau intended the novellas to inform and speak to each other.

36 Sally Ledger, 'From the Old Bailey to Revolutionary France: The Trials of Charles Darnay,' in *Charles Dickens,* A Tale of Two Cities *and the French Revolution*, ed. Jones, McDonagh and Mee, 75–86, 77–78.

37 Mark Philp, 'The New Philosophy: The Substance and the Shadow in *A Tale of Two Cities*,' in *Charles Dickens,* A Tale of Two Cities *and the French Revolution*, ed. Jones, McDonagh, and Mee, 24–40, 24.

38 Jones, McDonagh, and Mee, Introduction to *Charles Dickens,* A Tale of Two Cities *and the French Revolution*, 1–23, 8.

French Wines in many ways parallels volume 19 of the *Illustrations*, also published in 1833, *Sowers Not Reapers*, which I will examine in the next chapter. Although set in France and England respectively, these two novellas engage specifically with the social and psychological ramifications of scarcity and starvation, both on individuals and on the community. The parallels between the two texts of irrational destruction of food sources by violent mobs, punctuated by the actual violent revolution in the first and its constant underlying threat in the second, bring to light the implications of strategic localised hunger on an international stage. By publishing the two narratives within a few months of each other, the threat of the French Revolution breathes through the chaos of the later, English setting, potentially reinforcing the narrative of French revolutionary influence. Yet Martineau's intent was invariably global. She deliberately engages with contemporary debates on what was perceived as the newly globalised market and its effects on the nation-state; yet her apparently 'rational' voices—the characters that espouse political economy's ideals—are plagued by the volatility of the natural environment and its effect on economic structures. In *French Wines* the natural world produces a hurricane and a series of storms, while *Sowers Not Reapers* opens in the midst of a drought.[39] While these two events are significantly different in their mode of impact, both have extreme effects on crops, and therefore on food production. Furthermore, given the geographical proximity of Britain and France, the potential to share weather events and their devastating effect is implicit in the texts.

When Martineau published *French Wines*, she was fully aware that the French monarch would read it. Indeed, her *Autobiography* records the seemingly providential progression, as just as the novella was going to print, Martineau heard from her friend and economic predecessor, Jane Marcet, that the French monarch was intending to have Martineau's *Illustrations of Political Economy* translated into French and disseminated through the school system.[40] Marcet admonishes Martineau for not altering her tale, fearing for her friend's reputation, but Martineau is adamant: 'I wrote with a view to the people, and especially the most suffering of them; and the crowned heads must, for once, take their chance for their feelings.'[41] It is crucial that the crowned heads are plural, perhaps suggesting the other intended readerships: other imperial European rulers, especially Britain, and their people. In regard to provoking France, Louis-Philippe was of the House of Orléans, so as much as Martineau claimed, 'it was from history, and not from private communication, that I drew my materials; and I had no

39 In *The Physiology of Common Life* (1859), George Henry Lewes draws an important distinction between hunger and thirst in that hunger can be a pleasant sensation, while thirst cannot (30). In this way, he raises the idea of appetite, connecting it to ambition and social progress; however, this is only a positive sensation when the appetite or hunger can be answered by possible satiation.
40 Harriet Martineau, *Autobiography*, ed. Linda Peterson (1877; Toronto: Broadview, 2007), 186–87.
41 Ibid., 188. The French monarch's response was not favourable; the Emperor of Russia, however, had an even more violent response when his empire received similar treatment in the following month, ordering all Martineau's books to be delivered up and burned.

doubt that Louis Phillippe and his family thought of his father very much as I did,'[42] there seems little chance that he would not have taken very personally the ridiculing, impotent characterisation of the Duke of Orléans in Martineau's tale, little more than six months after the 1832 rebellion. The connection with and repetition of the past is a crucial element of Martineau's narrative, in which she constructs a fluid vision of history:

> Throughout Guienne, the Orleannois, and other provinces, not a score of revolutions could efface the recollections and traditions of the hurricane of July, 1788. Perhaps it may be still a subject of dispute a century hence whether it was charged, in addition to the natural agents of destruction, with a special message to warn the French nation of their approaching social convulsion.[43]

From the opening of the text, the preternatural noise of the hurricane is inseparable from the hungry uprising of the people, and contrasts eerily with the pregnant silences in the eyes of the political and actual storms. The storm thus operates as a deliberate motif of the volatile, self-destructive power of hunger, and acts as a persistent response of the natural world to the trauma of the nation.

While Dickens does not specifically acknowledge the particularly bad harvest of 1788 in *A Tale of Two Cities*, *French Wines and Politics* catalogues the crop destruction caused by the hurricane:

> The corn-fields were one vast morass. The almond groves were level with the ground; and of the chestnut woods nothing remained but an assemblage of bare poles. The more exposed vineyards were so many quagmires, and many dwellings were mere heaps of ruins. All who witnessed were horror-struck at the conviction of general, immediate, pressing want; and the more thoughtful glanced forwards in idea to the number of seasons that must pass away before all this damage could be repaired. (12–13)

Importantly, Martineau does not focus just on the immediate destruction of food by nature, but also on the broader issue that the crops are necessary to the economy. Without produce to sell, many people will not be able to participate in the market. In this way she is able to suggest economic, rather than political, inequalities as a form of injustice that contributes to the unrest. One of the key characters Charles, a winemaker, while espousing the ideals of rational political economy, is shown to be able to hold to this philosophy because he comes from a position of luxury due to his investment in foreign markets, his wealth, and his consequent ability to diversify his role within the market. Charles is able to exchange wine for fruit from Italy and the Levant, and further purchases large quantities of grapes from the English businessman Steele, for

---

42 Ibid.
43 Harriet Martineau, *French Wines and Politics* (London: Charles Fox, 1833), 18.

the demand for fruit in London being at present insignificant in comparison with that for claret, and the direct reverse being the case at Paris, it was
Steele's interest to transmit more wine and less fruit, and Charles's to take
fruit in exchange for his wine. It was therefore settled that, in addition to
their standing bargain for first-rate wine, Steele should have a large choice of
second-rate claret, in payment for chestnuts from Spain, oranges and citrons
from the Madeiras, olives from the Levant, and almonds from Italy. (31)

The network of trade in foodstuffs throughout Europe is central to Martineau's
vision, which is understandable given that she was a well-known proponent of
free trade. Charles is able to import these fruits and sell them in Paris, where
there was a desperate need for food, while finding an added market for his wine in
Britain. Not only is Charles able to survive through this kind of market flexibility,
it is important to note that he and Steele actually prosper out of the hurricane's
devastation. It is from this position that Charles is permitted the luxury of holding
to the belief that the devastation will ultimately promote the good of the nation.
He 'eagerly' tells his wife, Marguerite, of the great progress being made in society through the character-building nature of starvation and hardship: 'I see every
day, not only splendid instances of intellectual effort . . . but moral struggles and
self-sacrifices which dispose me more than ever to bow the knee to human nature'
(41). Marguerite challenges Charles's optimism, though, asking, 'But why should
the corn-owners be enriched by the scarcity of bread, and you by the destruction
of vineyards? You tell me that your gains by this storm will nearly compensate the
losses it has cost you. Is this fair?' (36–37)

Charles gives seemingly rational, logical explanations to justify his personal
prosperity as an essential contribution to national social and economic stability.
In this way he buys into what Regenia Gagnier refers to as the 'manifold irony'
of Adam Smith's narrative of political economy in *The Wealth of Nations* (1776),
'that selfish individuals could make an altruistic society; that the pursuit of profit
could be an ethical failing in an individual but lead to the wealth of all.'[44] Charles,
then, becomes a figure of critique for the convenience of Smith's assumption,
partly in the way Martineau counters his voice with Marguerite's, thus giving
voice to those disadvantaged by individual selfishness, but also by blurring the
lines of rationality. Charles disturbingly conflates luxury items, such as harps,
with the basic essentials of food in his economic argument, which reinforces his
privileged position. Marguerite, however, draws attention to corn growers—those
who produce bread, which made up approximately 50 per cent of the French
diet.[45] Marguerite's example crucially reasserts the fundamental issue of necessity
and hunger into the debate. In this way, her argument works to renegotiate what

---

44 Regenia Gagnier, 'The Law of Progress and the Ironies of Individualism in the Nineteenth
    Century,' *New Literary History*, 31.2 (2000): 315–36, 316.
45 Jeffry Kaplow, *The Names of Kings: The Parisian Laboring Poor in the Eighteenth Century* (New
    York: Basic Books, 1972), 72.

Simon Dentith refers to as 'the highly charged and volatile boundary between the economic and the moral.'[46] Britain becomes implicated in this seemingly unjust prosperity through Steele's participation and success with the French market in the wake of the hurricane.

While Martineau emphasises the more natural causes of unrest in the lead-up to the Revolution, the hurricane is initially written as exacerbating the silenced sense of injustice among the people, as though the violence of the storm enables the resilience and up-cry necessary to revolutionary determination. The day before the hurricane, there is widespread passive acceptance of the damage wreaked by a party of boar hunters, hosted by the Marquis de Thou, which trampled the vineyard of Antoine, Charles's brother, who also engages with Steele in business. Steele questions Antoine regarding his inaction when his vines are destroyed by the Marquis' party. Antoine replies: 'It is the only way to keep what we have left. . . . There is no use, but much peril, in complaint. Redress there is none; and ill-will towards the lord's pleasure is resented more deeply and lastingly than injury to his property' (9). Martineau's slip into the British title of 'lord' rather than 'marquis' draws attention to the parallels between the nations, as does Antoine's reminder to Steele of the British laws that give unreasonable privilege to the aristocracy: '[h]e was answered by a reference to the cruel old forest laws of England, and certain national blemishes of an analogous character which still remained' (10). From the outset of her tale, Martineau, as Dickens would go on to do, reminds her readers that the conditions that enabled the French Revolution are just as heavily entrenched within Britain.

The taste of wine, black bread, and death

To some extent it could be argued that Martineau's economic solutions in the *Illustrations* conveniently circumvent some of the complexities of political agendas and inequalities. Dickens, however, provides more space for questions of political agency within his socio-economic account of the French Revolution, in a way that links the people's physical hunger more explicitly with their social want. Stedman Jones writes of the conditions of the Revolution: 'it was not solely poverty that fuelled their anger. Something even stronger also drove their hatred: their abuse, the gross inequalities of unequal laws and uncontrolled punishment, being treated with contempt, being socially excluded and sexually abused.'[47] Thus it was not just physical hunger, but having to see others living in abundance while one was starving, that motivated the Revolution. In this way, physical hunger mingles with social hunger, creating the political articulation of unrest. In *A Tale of Two Cities*, Dickens portrays the inequalities between starvation and luxury within France with explicit violence, but more subtly shows the ways in which

---

46 Simon Dentith, 'Political Economy, Fiction and the Language of Practical Ideology in Nineteenth-Century England,' *Social History*, 8.2 (1983): 183–99, 198.
47 Stedman Jones, 'Redemptive Powers of Violence?' 55.

Britain is implicated. Apart from the obvious economic investment of Tellson's Bank, which operates as a narrative device to link the cities of London and Paris, a more nuanced investment is shown through the seeming innocuous culinary endeavours of Miss Pross, the Manettes' English housekeeper:

> Her dinners, of a very modest quality, were so well cooked and so well served, and so neat in their contrivances, half English and half French, that nothing could be better. Miss Pross's friendship being of the thoroughly practical kind, she had ravaged Soho and the adjacent provinces, in search of impoverished French, who, tempted by shillings and half-crowns, would impart culinary mysteries to her. From these decayed sons and daughters of Gaul, she had acquired wonderful arts, that the woman and girl who formed the staff of domestics regarded her as quite a Sorceress, or Cinderella's Godmother: who would send out for a fowl, a rabbit, a vegetable or two from the garden, and change them into anything she pleased.[48]

For Dr Manette, a Frenchman who had been imprisoned in the Bastille, being able to enjoy the tastes of France from the safety of London reinforces a sense of newfound privilege for him and his daughter, Lucie. The presence of the poor French immigrants in London, however, suggests the terror of France is seeping across national boundaries, bringing their trauma into Britain. They fail to escape that trauma through migration, shown through Miss Pross's 'ravag[ing]' of the poor French in Soho, which resonates with the way the French aristocracy were bleeding the peasants dry within France.

In positioning Miss Pross as engaging in the imperialist exploitation of French immigrants, I do not seek to lessen the heroic aspects of her character. However, her role, particularly in the way it parallels Madame Defarge, is more complicated, in that these two women, more than just operating as foils, work dialogically with each other. Theresa Magnum pertinently suggests that Madame Defarge's 'legacy lives on' in Miss Pross, raising the question as to '[w]ithout the respectable, all-consuming outlet of loving Lucie, how like Madame Defarge Miss Pross might be.'[49] Magnum goes on to suggest that Madame Defarge's destruction is due in part to the fact that, 'despite all her experience of dangerous women, she underestimates her English counterpart.'[50] While Miss Pross 'embod[ies] the self-sacrificing love and honour' associated with mothers and daughters,[51] the darker side of her nature is overshadowed by the masculinisation of Madame Defarge, while similarly Madame's lack of adherence to conventional (British middle-class) femininity perhaps leads her to be read in a more evil fashion than she deserves. Magnum points

48 Charles Dickens, *A Tale of Two Cities* (1859; London: Penguin, 2003), 103.
49 Theresa Magnum, 'Dickens and the Female Terrorist: The Long Shadow of Madame Defarge,' *Nineteenth-Century Contexts: An Interdisciplinary Journal*, 31.2 (2009): 143–60, 155.
50 Ibid., 156.
51 Grace Moore, *Dickens and Empire: Discourses of Class, Race and Colonialism in the Works of Charles Dickens* (Aldershot: Ashgate, 2004), 153.

out that the battle between these women is essentially one 'between two resourceful women, who are absolutely dedicated to a belief in the justness of their causes.'[52] This understanding forces an acknowledgement of the investment of both sides in revolutionary behaviour that is predicated on hunger, primarily social hunger in this instance. While neither woman is physically starving, they both fight—to the death—for a kind of social and political dominance that resonates with imperial conquest. Miss Pross's triumphant role is a reminder that history is written from the perspective of the victors, which often requires a blindness—or deafness—to the narrative of the other side. Miss Pross's deafness to the approaching carts, then, reflects the mid-century British approach to their historical investment in the revolution, suggesting a deafness to what is uncomfortable. The language of scarcity comes into play, alongside narratives of the need to adapt in order to survive, and Miss Pross's approach to the French recipes she gains in Soho can be read in terms of her resourcefulness, initiative, and ability to adapt. It remains, however, that rather than empathising with the poor French, the Englishwoman exploits their knowledge and their poverty, giving them a few coins in exchange for learning how to create culinary delicacies that the poor had no hope of being able to partake in themselves. 'These decayed sons and daughters of Gaul' in Britain are in little better position than their counterparts at home, who are described as 'miserable beasts' who rarely 'know the taste of wine, or of anything but black bread and death.'[53]

While the narrative does not detail what the French immigrants eat, the stark contrast between the choices available in Miss Pross's kitchen and that of the French peasants within France is worth noting, for it emphasises the imperialist thrust of Britain. Writing of the 1750s, sensory historian Mark M. Smith notes:

> The discovery of new foods and tastes did not, in the English instance, always lead to a diversification of the diet and the incorporation of different foods . . . instead, the initial English reaction was to emphasize the Englishness of their national cuisine. In effect, the English wrote nationalism into consumption, foodways, and taste. Food was tied intimately to the emergence of national identity in eighteenth-century Britain and international trade, imperial ambitions, and the workings of political economy cannot be properly understood outside of that process.[54]

While it could be argued that Miss Pross is cooking for an Anglo-French household, the fact that an Englishwoman is appropriating French tastes into her cooking speaks to her dominating the French. While the French themselves are restricted to the taste of black bread, Miss Pross can cook a variety of tastes associated with the nation of France. Jack Goody argues that '[l]uxury is a focus for discontent, particularly in regimes where the ideology (or one among the ideologies) is egalitarian,

---

52 Magnum, 'Dickens and the Female Terrorist,' 156.
53 Dickens, *A Tale*, 36.
54 Smith, *Sensory History*, 81.

where the premise of inequality . . . is challenged by other assumptions about the distribution of resources,'[55] yet in times of scarcity, 'luxury' itself becomes redefined. What was once of the every day becomes a rarity. Crucially, it is the ability of a nation to access the taste of its culture, and the way the resources necessary for that access are distributed, that reveals social inequality. Miss Pross's access implicitly challenges France's national identity, for many of the French cannot access their own tastes, which speaks to their lack of political and social power as much as their physical starvation. It is therefore also crucial that the recount of Miss Pross's culinary skills is followed quickly in the narrative by a shift back to Paris, where the Monseigneur's excesses of luxury and taste are described, set in 'his inner room, his sanctuary of sanctuaries,' in which he 'take[s] his chocolate':

> Monseigneur could swallow a great many things with ease, and was by some few sullen minds supposed to be rather rapidly swallowing France; but, his morning's chocolate could not so much as get into the throat of Monseigneur, without the aid of four strong men besides the Cook. (108)

While the meals in the Manette household are written in terms of modesty in contrast to this kind of excess, it remains that in both cases France is being exploited.

The Monseigneur plays no other function in the narrative apart from this scene, and in this way he serves as a tableau of his aristocratic class, a class that lives an existence wholly unaffected by its starving compatriots' plight. The juxtaposition of the performance of serving the Monseigneur's chocolate with the violent death of the child due to the Marquis' carriage, and the Marquis' careless response, heightens the connection between luxury and indifference, as well as that crucial narrative separation that permeates Dickens's account. Where they intersect, however, is when Dickens marries aristocratic cruelty to the hunger of the people. In this instance, he seems particularly inspired by Carlyle, who refers to the old French law 'authorising a Seigneur, as he returned from hunting, to kill not more than two Serfs, and refresh his feet in their warm blood and bowels.'[56] Importantly, it is written in terms of restraint—one might say moderation—that the Seigneur would kill only two; and that the law is no longer practised could also suggest that the aristocracy, as seen in Dickens's narrative, no longer shows such restraint. In *A Tale*, after the Marquis responds to his coin—the poor recompense for the death of a child—being thrown back into his carriage with 'I would ride over any of you very willingly, and exterminate you from the earth' (117), the narrative vision returns to the landscape:

> A beautiful landscape, with the corn bright in it but not abundant. Patches of poor rye where corn should have been, patches of poor peas and beans,

55 Jack Goody, 'The High and the Low: Culinary Culture in Asia and Europe,' in *Taste Culture Reader*, ed. Korsmeyer, 57–71, 68.
56 Carlyle, *French Revolution*, vol. 1, 12.

patches of most coarse vegetable substitutes for wheat. On inanimate nature, as on the men and women who cultivated it, a prevalent tendency towards an appearance of vegetating unwillingly – a dejected disposition to give up, and wither away. (118)

The dejection of the people, personified in the scarce crops, is later echoed in Defarge's despair that it is taking so long to carry out their revolutionary plans. His wife engages metaphorically with the nourishment of food, speaking of an 'earthquake . . . swallow[ing] a town,' and then telling Defarge that he must '[s]ustain [him]self without' the 'need to see [his] victim and [his] opportunity' (185–86). Madame Defarge continues to knit as she tells her husband that he must be sustained by his hunger, allowing that to define his sense of purpose.

Madame Defarge's knitting is a compulsive demonstration of physical and revolutionary hunger. The narrative explicitly states:

> All the women knitted. They knitted worthless things; but, the mechanical work was a mechanical substitute for eating and drinking; the hands moved for the jaws and the digestive apparatus; if the bony fingers had been still, the stomachs would have been more famine-pinched. (193)

However, while the physical act of knitting is described as a substitute for eating, it also exemplifies the translation of physical hunger into social and political hunger. John Bohstedt observes the crucial role of knitting, as 'women knit the networks of neighbourhood . . . , networks that were forms of social regulation,'[57] and in *A Tale*, the knitting can be seen as a more productive form of social networking and political organisation than the men drinking the watered-down wine in Defarge's shop. Yet it is also productive in that it creates and marks history in a material way that, although coded, cannot be denied. The hunger of the knitters is channelled into making a record of those who would be punished when the Revolution came, disguised in the seeming worthlessness of the objects produced. These objects actively contribute to the furtherance of the Revolution. The knitting motif becomes increasingly prominent in Dickens's narrative, climaxing at the advent of the guillotine: 'So much was closing in about the women who sat knitting, knitting, that their very selves were closing in around a structure yet unbuilt, where they were to sit knitting, knitting, counting the dropping heads' (194). This increased repetition suggests not that the hunger of the people was sated, but that it only increased as the revolution took hold: an insatiable hunger, devouring the perpetrators as much as it consumed their victims. Apart from the description of Charles's 'bloated gaoler' (291)—certainly not an image of starvation, but of the revolutionaries bloated on the blood that has been spilled in order to 'slake . . . [the] devouring thirst' of *La Guillotine* (285)—the vicious,

---

unbending demands of hunger remain: 'All the devouring and insatiate Monsters imagined since imagination could record itself, are fused in the one realisation, Guillotine' (384).

Although both Dickens and Martineau articulate the merging of physical and social hunger through the hunger for blood, one of the key differences in their narratives of hunger is that, where Dickens portrays the revolutionary hunger as insatiable, in *French Wines*, the greater the momentum of the Revolution, the less the revolutionaries focus on their physical starvation. In fact, although the text still speaks in terms of rations, they appear to have enough food. In the blood-thirsty climax outside the Tuileries, where the rioters viciously behead one of the king's soldiers with the king watching from an upper window, the 'fierce women' are described as 'gathering around, munching their suppers as if his [the soldier's] life-blood was the draught they looked for to wash down the last mouthful'; and after the beheading takes place, the executioner 'tosse[s] the headless body to a little distance, so that his friends might sit on it to finish their meal' (106–07). The brutality of the crowd, looking for small moments of victory such as making a sofa out of a fresh corpse, creates a sense of pregnant, dangerous consumption; but it is a consumption that is being sated. Their satisfaction in violence becomes completely enmeshed in the satisfaction of relieving their physical hunger.

Breaking bread; breaking wine

There remains an ironic yet powerful connection between the decivilising effects of hunger and the rational agenda of democracy. Idealistically, democracy is designed to be civilising, but the revolutionary transition that enables it is tumultuous, which raises questions regarding the extent to which order can be birthed out of chaos. The democratic inspiration of the French Revolution was both denied and challenged in the British Parliament, from Mackintosh's claim that it was not based on democratic principles, to John Wilson Croker arguing that the 'popular will' must be resisted, that it was, in fact, the bowing 'to an injudicious and obstinate resistance to popular opinion' that was the cause of France's continued instability.[58] Democracy is positioned as dangerous and destabilising because it potentially enables the people to think or determine their own tastes, overturning the universal vision of feudalism, but it is also dangerous because 'popular opinion' appeals to the self-serving element of capitalism. It must also be noted that the voice of this opinion is generally restricted to those who can vote, and they will vote according to their own gain, which reveals the flaws of democracy in a society without universal suffrage. Karl Marx posited that, if 'turbulence and strife will bring a profit, it will freely encourage both'; thus 'capital comes dripping from head to toe, from every pore, with blood and dirt.'[59]

58 Croker, *on the Question that 'The Reform Bill Do Pass,'* 5.
59 Karl Marx, *Capital: A Critique of Political Economy, Volume 1* (1867; trans. Ben Fowkes, London: Penguin, 1976), 926.

The corruption of democratic ideals by capitalism can be likened to food adulteration, while democracy itself speaks to a destabilisation of social order. In *The Presence of the Word*, Walter J. Ong closely connects the eighteenth-century rise of democracy with an obsession with taste:

> As feudal society finally bowed out, the individual and even a whole society were being forced to make decisions which an older, more tradition-bound culture used to provide ready-made. With democracy, the concern with taste wanes, as 'public opinion' is formed to take over regulatory functions.[60]

Ong usefully draws attention to the connection between democracy and changing concepts of taste, yet I would argue that rather than taste waning with the advent of democracy and public opinion, it actually becomes more crucial: 'taste' is no longer a seemingly universal aesthetic, but something that is culturally constructed and intrinsic to identity—with the rise of democracy, a somewhat fractured identity. David Howes and Marc Lalonde observe that the more destabilised a society, the more important the proximate senses (taste and olfaction) become:

> as long as social divisions remain clear and unambiguous, the distance senses [sight and hearing] suffice to monitor the boundaries of class. However, when social boundaries are cast in doubt, and finer discriminations become necessary, then the emphasis shifts to the proximate or 'affective' senses.[61]

Therefore, rather than causing taste to wane, the rise of riot, rebellion, and revolution leading to democracy, becomes intimately tied to the sense of taste. Within the idea of popular opinion, possibilities arise of acquired tastes, speaking to social ambition, as well as corruptive or dangerous tastes, the manipulation of people and classes through appealing to their tastes, and, importantly, the adulteration of taste, which connects metaphorically to disorder, to impure motives. The rumours and actual cases of food adulteration in the late eighteenth century led to food riots; yet food adulteration continued through much of the nineteenth century and, arguably, haunts current narratives around foods that are good or bad, as well as nourishing or unnourishing. In the context of social hunger, the quality of food enjoyed continues to register one's social class. The destruction of food rumoured to be spoiled or adulterated provides a persistent motif of protest against the lack of social agency.

The perversion of food destruction punctuates the violence of revolution in both Dickens's and Martineau's narratives. Bread and wine dominate this motif,

---

60 Walter J. Ong, *The Presence of the Word: Some Prolegomena for Cultural and Religious History* (1967; New York: State University of New York Press, 2000), 5.

61 David Howes and Marc Lalonde, 'The History of Sensibilities: Of the Standard of Taste in Mid-Eighteenth Century Britain and the Circulation of Smells in Post-Revolutionary France,' *Dialectical Anthropology*, 16 (1991): 125–35, 130.

partly because they were staples of the French diet, but also because of their broader symbolic interpretation of the Eucharist, and the central role of Holy Communion within church liturgies, and therefore within the community. The way the Eucharist was defined becomes significant in terms of social identity and taste. Given that France was a Catholic nation, and Catholicism held to the transubstantiation of the elements, Protestant England could link the Catholic sacrament to a French taste for blood. For Dickens and Martineau, both influenced by Unitarianism, the decreasing role of Holy Communion within dissenting circles creates a further distance from the belief that Eucharistic participants were consuming the actual blood and flesh of Christ. Therefore, even beyond the Catholic/ Protestant debate over blood or wine, within Protestantism the perceived *spiritual* quality or benefit of partaking in the bread and wine was questionable. This concept of quality links closely to ideas of adulteration and the quality of food, and therefore to perceived social equality, but also to social morality and communal trust. A pamphlet from 1855, *How to Detect Adulteration in Our Daily Food and Drink* (a title that alludes to the Lord's Prayer and 'our daily bread'), sees food adulteration as an affront to the 'moral dignity of our people, [who] have all deteriorated under a steady action of impure food, impure water, and poisonous preparations.'[62] Food adulteration challenges the stability of the community because it is an act of fraud—of deception; and in this way, it impacts the moral and spiritual health of the community. Given that the staples of bread and wine, as spiritual symbols as well as daily sustenance, were two of the most commonly adulterated products, it would seem that the very foundations of civilisation cannot be trusted. Apart from the spectrum of religious connotations, taking the Eucharist can be seen as an equalising act, as well as a central ritual in the community. Everyone had equal access to God through Communion. Yet the seeming equality was fictional. As Smith writes, 'Bread, wine, taste: all served to establish the immediacy and intimacy of Christ's presence,'[63] yet the crucial addition here is 'taste.' Taste is what separates—what the people *can* taste, as well as the quality of the product. The fragmented understanding of the spiritual meaning of Communion reflects the fracturing of society, for there are implications in terms of how close that intimacy with Christ becomes through the act—actually Christ, a symbol, or a memorial—in the same way that quality of taste can speak to political and social inclusion. In both Dickens and Martineau, much emphasis is placed on the quality of the bread and wine the starving people have access to: accounts of the wild rye taking over the wheat crops; of watered down wine; and rumours of corrupted flour. Breaking the bread resonates with the broken body of Christ, but in the destruction of bread, as in the destruction of wine, another interpretative layer is added to the destruction of the Revolution: it breaks down the foundations of community.

---

62 Qtd in Rebecca Stern, '"Adulterations Detected": Food and Fraud in Christina Rossetti's "Goblin Market"', *Nineteenth-Century Literature*, 57.4 (2003): 477–511, 482.
63 Smith, *Sensory History*, 78.

Given the devastation of crops by the July 1788 hurricane that dominates *French Wines*, it is not surprising that by September there was a sharp rise in bread prices in France. Rudé observes,

> in September 1788, when Parisians were celebrating the *parlement*'s second return, a sharp increase in the price of bread transformed the scope and nature of the riots. In the following April, the Réveillon riots in the Faubourg St. Antoine were probably due as much to the high price of bread as to the manufacturers' attacks on wages: in fact, food shops (but no others) were broken into, and the lieutenant of police himself believed that the insurgents had the twofold aim of settling accounts with Réveillon and of compelling authorities to reduce the price of bread.[64]

Early in his narrative, Dickens reveals the potential for destruction through the people's hunger. He subtly connects the hurricane to scarcity through metaphor:

> And now that the cloud settled on Saint Antoine, which a momentary gleam had driven from his sacred countenance, the darkness of it was heavy—cold, dirt, sickness, ignorance, and want, were the lords in waiting on the saintly presence—nobles of great power all of them; but, most especially the last. (32)

The physical hunger is implicitly tied to political powerlessness through the personification of the attributes of poverty as aristocratic figures, but it is the cloud of the hurricane that overwhelms with darkness and heaviness. When there is no more corn to grind, the suggestion is that the people are milled instead:

> Samples of a people that had undergone a terrible grinding and re-grinding in the mill . . . shivered at every corner, passed in and out at every doorway, looked from every window, fluttered in every vestige of a garment that the wind shook. The mill which had worked them down, was the mill that grinds young people old; the children had ancient faces and grave voices; and upon them, and upon grown faces, and ploughed in every furrow of age and coming up afresh, was the sign, Hunger. (32)

This passage inevitably evokes reference to the rumours of human bones being ground up to supplement and expand scant flour supplies. The reference to children evokes the image of the children Want and Ignorance in *A Christmas Carol*:

> Yellow, meagre, ragged, scowling, wolfish; but prostrate, too, in their humility. Where graceful youth should have filled their features out, and touched them with its freshest tints, a state and shrivelled hand, like that of age, had pinched, and twisted them, and pulled them into shreds. (71)

64 Rudé, *Crowd in History*, 108.

Not only do the ghostly children similarly suggest premature aging and decay, but the way in which they are pinched, twisted, and pulled suggests a similar mechanical destruction. Within these images of English and French poverty, Dickens draws the two nations into each other. In *A Tale*, that the hungry poor are themselves being consumed in this time of scarcity links back to the excess of the Monseigneur, who believes 'that the world was made for [him]' (109). Later his appetite becomes more explicitly turned on consuming the people, describing his treatment of the nation in terms of implements of torture, and those implements as devouring, ravenous creatures: 'the last drop of blood having being extracted from the flints, and the last screw of the rack having being turned so often that its purchase crumbled, and it now turned and turned with nothing to bite' (236). This insatiable desire to devour and destroy mingles with the Monseigneur's vicious desire for pleasure:

> For scores of years gone by, Monseigneur had squeezed it and wrung it, and had seldom graced it with his presence except for the pleasures of the chase—now, found in hunting the people; now, found in hunting the beasts, for whose preservation Monseigneur made edifying spaces of barbarous and barren wilderness. (236–37)

The conflation of the people and wild animals speaks to the cold perspective of the Monseigneur as a representative of the aristocracy, yet it also addresses the decivilisation of the people: the metaphorical hungry human mill (which parallels the insatiable guillotine) reflects and increases the physical and social hunger of the starved. Their decivilisation is marked through the limitations placed on the tastes to which they have access, and so it is crucial that Dickens emphasises not just the scarcity of bread, but its poor quality: 'Hunger was the inscription on the baker's shelves, written in every small loaf of his scanty stock of bad bread' (32–33). Their decivilised anger and desperation is marked early on in the way their quest for food is imagined in animal-like and violent terms. Consuming hunger occupies every space in which the people seem to hover, as if stalking a meal that is not there:

> In the hunted air of the people there was yet some wild-beast thought of the possibility of turning at bay. Depressed and slinking though they were, eyes of fire were not wanting among them; nor compressed lips, white with what they suppressed; nor foreheads knitted into the likeness of the gallows-rope they mused about enduring, or inflicting. The trade signs (and they were almost as many as the shops) were, all, grim illustrations of Want. (33)

The suppressed chaos of this scene, and the intrinsic connection between hunger and violence, suggest the dangerous potency of the people's rage that will arise into revolution.

Martineau more explicitly uses the destruction of food as an illustration of the decivilising hunger of the people. In *French Wines* the mob violence and destruction of food is instigated not just by the scarcity of food, but by the increased prices of what is available, in a way that revisits the Flour Wars of the mid-1770s, often seen as pre-revolutionary uprisings. In Martineau's account, the taxes are rising, as well as the price of food:

> the more gold was carried to the treasury, the more bread was bought up before the eyes of those deprived of it from its increased price . . . the people were rendered unable to purchase it, and furnished with the plea of want, wherewith to make the streets of Paris echo. (86)

This echo resonates with Dickens's echoing revolutionary footsteps throughout *A Tale of Two Cities*. In both texts, the reverberation of an echo affirms the way in which the rumble of hunger, as of revolutionary discontent, rolls through the nation, and also through Europe. In *French Wines*, the hungry rumble is intensified first by being taunted by seeing food that cannot be accessed, and then by a rumour that 'the bread furnished by court charity was of a bad quality' (87). Martineau is unclear as to whether the 'bad quality' means that the flour is adulterated, or merely that it is of a lesser quality than that which the court are presumed to eat. Both interpretations can be equally insidious, given that the restriction of quality of taste can be read as just as dehumanising as corrupted flour: it reinforces that the starving people are not equal to the aristocracy, not worth feeding with the same quality of food. Yet the flexibility in interpretation is also necessary for it allows for the ways in which rumours grow into extremes; and as the narrative of the rumour becomes extreme, so does the violent response:

> the consequence was that an anomalous and melancholy sight was seen by as many as walked in the city. Clamorous, starving crowds besieged the bakers' shops, and carried off all the bread from their ovens, all the flour from their bins; while the discontented among the mob politicians of the Orleans faction were on the way to snatch the food from the mouths of the hungry and throw it into the river, and to cut the sacks, and mix the flour with the puddles of the streets. Want and waste, faction and delusion were here seen in their direct extremes. (87)

Importantly, Martineau refers to the political factions of the Duke of Orléans infiltrating the starving 'pitiless mob' (91) in order to incense the crowd to further destruction. Their role is a perversion of hunger, as they promote waste and violent excess. After the bakeries have been ransacked, it is one of these factions that initiates cutting the sacks and throwing the flour into the river. Presumably, as a part of the Duke's party, they will not themselves suffer as a result; however, they lead the crowd to participate in this waste, exacerbating the hunger for which they, as agents of the aristocracy, could already be held responsible.

The nameless, faceless rioters are contrasted with Maigrot the baker. Not only is Maigrot allowed his name, he is known to Charles and Charles's family, lending him a greater sense of connection and purpose in the community, whereas the rioters are disconnected and dehumanised. He is profiled, significantly, because he is a baker: his profession stands immediately between the people and their bread. He is introduced into the narrative 'in a state of desperate anxiety,' standing in the doorway of his bakery with the destructive mob bearing down on him. Maigrot tries to escape through the mob, but is prevented, and then disappears into his store, which is, importantly, attached to his home: the economic violence infiltrates the sacred space of the hearth. There is no recourse. The threat of violence is narrated through Charles's perspective, as he observes to himself that 'it might depend on whether there was a way of exit at the back of the house, whether [Maigrot's] head would presently be carried on a pike, between two loaves of his own bread, or whether he would be kneading and baking in peace ten years hence' (88).

The provocative juxtaposition of Maigrot's life and livelihood in this image, just as his domestic and business spaces are juxtaposed, depicts the pervasive nature of the violence. This factor in some way mitigates Maigrot's subterfuge, as he 'escaped and actually joined in with the mob in time to see his own flour cast into the Seine' (89). In this way, Maigrot contributes to his own destruction, also leaving his wife, 'sinking and trembling,' to face the rioters. Charles rallies her, compelling her to help him in 'emptying the flour bins and distributing the bread' with empty reassurances 'to fear nothing, and all would be well' (89). From Martineau's moral perspective, it is perhaps justice, then, that Maigrot is then forced to bake bread from his own flour and give it to the mob by way of proof of its goodness. He is 'compelled to listen to these falsehoods [of the spoiled flour] in silence,' and then not only has to sacrifice his stock and income, but also his labour, in order to pacify the rioters (89–90). However, Maigrot's position is also drawn into contrast with Charles's own. Charles challenges the people in their destruction of flour, arguing that 'the grievance will not be removed by feeding the fishes with that which [their] children are craving' (95). However, Charles himself displays the same kind of irrationality when he first deliberately contaminates some of his own wine so that the Marquis will not want to buy it, and then refuses to sell wine to anyone because they might be agents of the Duke of Orléans, purchasing wine to feed to the mob, thereby adding inebriation to the already chaotic situation. As the violence increases, Charles goes further, locking himself in the cellar with his wine, prepared to blow himself up with the stock rather than allow the mob to raid it. This perversion of waste is emblematic of the broken community, where sustenance is destroyed before starving faces. Both Maigrot and Charles are simultaneously self-preserving and self-destructive, embodying the tensions between the individual and the community. Martineau favours Charles with his rationalising role: his fixation on alcohol as instrumental in the violence allows him to claim a moral upper hand while preserving his stock, evidently seeking to contain the violence, while Maigrot's self-preservation at the expense of his family leads to him having to sacrifice his bread. Yet in both cases, the abuse of bread and wine becomes emblematic of social violence and the destruction of the community.

The hungry brutality of the mob in Martineau's narrative is little mitigated in the horror and excess of destruction. They compel passers-by to eat the flour and pass judgement on it. If they declare the flour good, they are deemed 'parasites of the court,' while those who '[make] mouths at it [are] the friends of the people' (90). The taste of the flour determines the test. The Marquis de Thou is made a mockery of: he gives an indecisive verdict, depending on his interpretation of the looks received from the Duke and from the crowd, unable to choose a side. He reveals his foolishness further by telling the mob that he cannot eat any more of the flour because he 'shall presently dine,' so to do so would spoil his appetite (91). This statement is a cruel reminder of the luxury of moderation, for he can refrain while the people are driven to an excess of starvation and violence. Empathy thus rests with the mob, until their excess leads them to focus their abuse on Julien, Charles's young son. Julien's response, not formed by political conviction or understanding of the chaos, reflects the expected innocence of childhood: 'As soon as he had gulped down his share and could speak, he said he had never tasted raw flour before, but it was not so good as the hot cakes that were made of it sometimes' (92). Within the violence of the scene, the mob evokes the desired support; but as Martineau observes, this was 'likely to happen without too much dishonesty, when the raw flour was crammed into the mouth by foul and sometimes bloodied hands' (90). The child's nostalgia for hot cakes contrasts starkly with the taste of raw, bloodied flour; and within this scene, the loss of innocence in the wake of revolutionary trauma is written on the nation, as violence determines the tastes of the people.

In contrast to Martineau's wilful waste of flour and Charles's willingness to destroy his wine stores, the waste of the broken wine cask at the beginning of Dickens's narrative is an accident, and the event leads to rare revelry among the starving; however, just as Martineau's scenes of food destruction mark violence and revolution, Dickens uses this moment of revelry to foretell the revolution to come. Indeed, the connection between revelry and revolution can be seen in Brian Harrison's claim about the 1855 Sunday Trading Riots that 'the festive mood *is* the revolutionary mood.'[65] These riots, which would have been fresh in Dickens's mind when writing *A Tale of Two Cities*, highlighted the limitations still in place in working-class England. Harrison argues that the riots represented 'not an absolute gain for working-class influence in politics, but rather a change in the means through which that influence was exerted.'[66] In this sense, the riots, which took place in Hyde Park where over 150,000 people assembled to protest against Lord Grosvenor's bill to ban Sunday trading, legitimated violence in a political and cultural context where there is no civilised recourse to social discontent. Like Martineau's bloodied and muddied flour, Dickens's wine forms puddles between the 'rough, irregular stones of the street,' and as there 'was no drainage to carry off the wine, . . . not only did it all get taken up, but so much mud got taken up along with it.'[67]

65 Brian Harrison, 'The Sunday Trading Riots of 1855,' *Historical Journal*, 8 (1965): 219–45, 233. Harrison's emphasis.
66 Ibid., 219.
67 Dickens, *A Tale*, 31.

The connection of the red wine to revolution is made explicit in that 'one tall joker . . . scrawled upon a wall with his finger dipped in muddy wine lees – BLOOD' (32). Dickens then belabours the metaphor: 'The time was to come, when that wine too would be spilled on the street-stones, and when the stain of it would be red upon many there' (32). The repetition of the stain of wine, like the stain of blood, reinforces the haunting power of revolution within the community's collective memory, but this stain is also a reference to the haunting memory of starvation. Before the stain becomes evident—which only occurs after the flow has stopped—the 'jostling . . . crowd' is absorbed in sating physical want, attempting 'to sip, before the wine has all run out between the fingers,' or dipping 'little mugs of mutilated earthenware' in the muddy wine puddles (31). Next to those who desperately squeeze wine from their handkerchiefs into their infants' mouths are those who seek to look forward, attempting to redirect the flow of the wine to their own benefit (31). The scene written in frivolity is underwritten by a muddied narrative of scarcity, desperation, and a desire to survive. It is difficult not to read both Dickens's and Martineau's accounts back through Marx's 'flow of blood and dirt';[68] yet the key aspect in the relationship between food and destruction in Dickens is the 'special companionship' that is found in it.[69] Joseph Butwin observes that, in the context of riots, the 'fellowship which draws the raucous crowd together excludes an enemy who is marked out for revenge and ridicule. A taste for comedy and violence cannot be excluded.'[70] This fusion of comedy and violence is evident in both Dickens's and Martineau's accounts of the French Revolution, with a new understanding of community being formed in light of the persistent memory of the Terror mingling with the changing (and initially tenuous) social organisation of democracy. The people's hunger oscillates between the physical and the social, but as it moves corporately, an eerie sense of community is formed.

In *A Tale of Two Cities*, when the people hear that Foulon has been captured, who apocryphally 'told the starving people they might eat grass' (232), the people forget every hunger but that for 'the body and soul of Foulon,' to 'rend Foulon to pieces, and dig him into the ground, that grass may grow from him' (232). Yet this passion exacerbates hunger. The frenzied torture and assassination of Foulon is followed by an account of the consequent neglect of their children:

> Not before dark night did the men and women come back to the children, wailing and breadless. Then, the miserable bakers' shops were beset by long files of them, patiently waiting to buy bad bread; and while they waited with stomachs faint and empty, they beguiled the time by embracing one another on the triumphs of the day, and achieving them again in gossip. . . . Scanty and insufficient suppers those, and innocent of meat, as of most other sauce

---

68 Marx, *Capital*, 926.
69 Dickens, *A Tale*, 31.
70 Joseph Butwin, 'The Pacification of the Crowd: From "Janet's Repentance" to *Felix Holt*,' *Nineteenth-Century Fiction*, 35.3 (1980): 349–71, 352.

to wretched bread. Yet, human fellowship infused some nourishment into the flinty viands, and stuck some sparks of cheerfulness out of them. (235)

The sense of community is uncanny, discordant with the preceding violence; yet it is perhaps marked by the lack of meat, first because they cannot afford it, but also because they have already consumed their share of meat for the day in the death of Foulon. It is telling that the regurgitation of violence is seen as a kind of temporary sustenance, and 'human fellowship' a nourishment: their humanity is called into question through their seeming unaffected by their acts of violence, especially at the expense of their children. However, the replacing of physical sustenance with words at this point is a recapitulation of the sense of solidarity found earlier in Defarge's wine shop, where the wine gradually becomes thinner and sourer. The taste of the wine reflects the bitterness of Defarge's customers: 'A sour wine, moreover, or a souring, for its influence on the mood of those who drank it was to make them gloomy' (171). More significant, though, are the men who 'glided from seat to seat, and from corner to corner, swallowing talk in lieu of drink with greedy looks' (171). These men cannot even afford the watered-down wine. Their 'greedy looks,' then, speak to their growing social hunger: a desire to bring about the revolution so that they will no longer have to starve.

'Those were drinking days, and most men drank hard'[71]

The thinning wine in France contrasts with the apparent abundance and strength of wine and spirits in Britain in Dickens's tale. The narrative speaks of the excess of drink in London, saying that 'a moderate statement of the quantity of wine and punch which one man would swallow in the course of a night, without any detriment to his reputation as a perfect gentleman, would seem, in these days, a ridiculous exaggeration' (89–90). Furthermore, the unlikely hero, Sydney Carton, and his employer, Mr Stryver, seem constantly in a state of semi-inebriation, and depend on spirits to get them through long nights of work. Just before this revelation, Sydney takes Charles Darnay to an English tavern to 'strength[en]' him with 'a good dinner and good wine' (87). Importantly, Sydney himself claims to have already eaten, and instead drinks from 'his separate bottle of port' (87). That it is a 'separate' bottle speaks of Sydney's disconnection from community, especially in that it is port, often used as Eucharistic wine, perhaps expressing his lack of desire to participate in Britishness. For Darnay's meal is quintessentially British, and 'to eat British food was to affirm one's participation in the British nation in a more resolutely self-conscious way.'[72] This moment foreshadows the exchange of Sydney for Darnay: Darnay becomes the Englishman, while Sydney chooses the French taste of blood and wine in his Christ-like sacrifice—with a difference, for his wine is strong.

---

71 Dickens, *A Tale*, 89.
72 Howes and Lalonde, 'History of Sensibilities,' 128.

The suggestive penetration of Georgian London tastes self-consciously evokes the past of Dickens's mid-nineteenth-century audience, and begins to suggest the repression of Britain's own chaotic revolutionary heritage that is mirrored in much of *A Tale of Two Cities*. Crucially, the narrative moves back to Paris at the time when the Gordon Riots occurred in London, enabling the narrative repression of that historical moment. Book Two starts in London in March 1780, three months before the riots broke out, but the following chapter returns to France. In his introduction to *A Tale of Two Cities*, Richard Maxwell suggests that, as a consequence of this silence in the text, 'Londoners are able to pursue private lives characterized by tranquillity and happiness, as well as by those polite repressions necessary to any civilized society.'[73] But while Dickens mirrors the national repression, he refuses to allow his British readership to displace the terror of the French Revolution wholly onto the Continent. The mid-century readership remains haunted by this telling absence and the displacement onto the Continent. However, through historical narratives set wholly within Britain, the repressed domestic chaotic and violent past rises closer to the surface, revivifying Britain's own revolutionary heritage.

As historical fictions, *Barnaby Rudge; A Tale of the Riots of 'Eighty* and George Eliot's *Felix Holt, the Radical* (1866) use British violence of the past to speak to current issues of reform. Dickens began writing *Barnaby Rudge* in 1839 and published it in 1841, at the height of Chartism's volatility and only a few years after the First Reform Bill was passed, while Eliot's novel, set just after the passing of the 1832 Reform Bill, was written and published during the debates and unrest surrounding the Reform Act of 1867. By reimagining British riots of the past, Dickens and Eliot refocus the political climate of a mid-century Britain engaged in repression and counterfactual, nostalgic narratives of the nation's cultural heritage by engaging with a spectrum of hungers that compel riotous behaviour, from literal starvation and social discontent to social ambition and greed, but also, importantly, the fear of starvation, grown out of the memory of seasons of scarcity. This last aspect becomes increasingly important throughout mid-century British narratives, reminding even the reader positioned in a time of relative abundance that scarcity can always come again. Through the chaotic, poorly defined purpose of their rioters, Dickens and Eliot challenge the need to rationalise and contain the fear of revolution in the British imagination. They depict respective ages of physical hunger—of failed crops, corn laws, and poor laws—but also of social hunger, in which the rumbling stomachs of the British people sought to gain an articulate voice, speaking through the desire to bring about social change. Social greed is brought into grotesque juxtaposition with very real want, challenging the way in which poverty and political voicelessness is rationalised. Rohan McWilliam observes in *Popular Politics* that 'hunger by itself does not spur action; politics is necessary to provide the idea that hunger

---

73 Richard Maxwell, Introduction to *A Tale of Two Cities* (London: Penguin, 2003), xiii.

is not something to be endured.'[74] In this sense, politics teaches the people to articulate their hunger, to rationalise it, and speak against it—an idea that goes against the common representation of the people as a hungry, angry, irrational, animalistic mob.

Even more than the violence of the mob, though, the British imagination feared that the violence was rational, calculated, and even perhaps a reasoned response to social injustice by those who could not otherwise be heard. This fear was complicated by the need to hold onto the idea of Britain's civilisation. As a result, two main narratives arose in newspapers, periodicals, and treatises: one of the violent, markedly non-British (French or European) style mob, and the other of the exaggeratedly civilised British demonstration. However, as Butwin provocatively observes, '[t]hose who praise a revolution for its solemnity and its orderliness tell less about revolution than their fear of it.'[75] In both *Barnaby Rudge* and *Felix Holt* civilisation is overthrown by chaos. In the former, an uncontrollable riot develops out of a seemingly orderly procession, while in the latter it develops out of an election, which ought to be an institution of civilisation. The explosion of disorder in both narratives speaks to the uncontrollable, irrational nature of excessive social hunger. As much as the hunger is articulated in political streams, both Dickens and Eliot confuse these streams, decivilising the rioters by dispersing any sense of a unified purpose. Yet to say that the riot lacks unity does not make it irrational; the rationalities of the riots are varied but clear, all desiring some kind of satiation.

The absence of the Gordon Riots in the narratives surrounding the Reform Bills is telling, given that, as Linda Colley points out, they were in the mid-nineteenth century 'the largest, deadliest and most protracted urban riots on British history.'[76] Indeed, in 'Prophesying Revolution,' Ian McAlman argues that the Gordon Riots were not merely 'an isolated eruption of disorder but . . . a failed revolution.'[77] Yet in spite of this significance, their absence from the continued discourse on revolution and unrest in Britain makes these riots seem marginalised. It is possible that this marginalisation was justified because the Gordon Riots were narrowly defined as an anti-Catholic movement, and thus irrelevant to the reform debates of the mid-century. This definition, however, is far from adequate, given that in the riots it was not the whole Catholic population of London that was targeted, but only the *rich* Catholics. Some wealthy Protestant houses were also attacked, and what is also significant is that, in spite of Lord Gordon's claims of belonging to 'the party of the people' and that this purpose was to repeal the Catholic Relief Act, he himself did not oppose the Act's passage through Parliament.[78]

74 Rohan McWilliam, *Popular Politics in Nineteenth-Century England* (London and New York: Routledge, 1998), 33.
75 Butwin, 'Pacification of the Crowd,' 351.
76 Colley, *Britons*, 352.
77 Ian McAlman, 'Prophesying Revolution: "Mad Lord George", Edmund Burke and Madame La Motte,' in *Living and Learning: Essays in Honour of J.F.C. Harrison*, ed. Malcolm Chase and Ian Dyck (Aldershot: Scolar, 1996), 52–65, 53.
78 Ian Gilmour, *Riot, Risings and Revolution: Governance and Violence in Eighteenth-Century England* (London: Pimlico, 1993), 347.

These aspects call into question the anti-Catholic placard as the root cause of the riots. Other significant causes—poverty and political voicelessness—continued to haunt Britain into the mid-nineteenth century.

Dickens's representation of the Gordon Riots in *Barnaby Rudge* explicitly challenges the centrality of anti-Catholic sentiment, which was the dominant interpretation of the riots in the nineteenth century. In his preface, Dickens states that 'what we falsely call a religious cry is easily raised by men who have no religion,'[79] and this hypocrisy is shown most clearly through the representation of Gordon's secretary, Gashford. When Gordon tells Gashford that he dreamed he was a Jew, Gashford ponders,

> 'He may come to that before he dies . . . provided I lost nothing by it, I don't see why that religion shouldn't suit me as well as any other. There are rich men among the Jews. . . . For the present, though, we must be Christian to the core. Our prophetic motto will suit all creeds in their turn, that's a comfort.' (307)

This pondering is followed by an ironic description of Gashford eating a meal with Gordon. While Gordon is 'no less frugal in his repasts than in his Puritan attire,' the even hungrier Gashford, 'more devoted to the good things of this world, or more intent on sustaining his strength and spirits for the sake of the Protestant cause, ate and drank to the last minute' before coming down the stairs 'wiping his greasy mouth' (307). Gashford's hunger is explicitly social, yet it is perverted by greed, evidenced in his devouring of food in a way that resonates with Dickens's later representations of the French aristocracy in *A Tale of Two Cities*. Gashford's hunger must be sated, even at the cost of Gordon's followers. He exploits the physical hunger of the poor, teaching them to articulate it through social hunger, specifically in anti-Catholic terms. As France was often the scapegoat of violence, the apparent drinkers of Christ's literal blood as well as that of their own nation, Catholicism is marked as the cause of deprivation within Britain. This move bought into the heritage of, in particular, anti-Irish sentiment, as well as the fact that the Gordon Riots were, arguably, stirred in part by Britain's economic and political losses of the American War of Independence. France and Spain, both Catholic nations, had joined the Americans in the war against Britain.

Social and physical hunger are explicitly intertwined in the text. When Joe Willet runs away from his father's tyranny at the Maypole and joins the military, the sergeant toasts, 'For king and country!' to which Joe responds, 'for bread and meat!' (260). Similarly, when Hugh, the ostler from the Maypole, signs the petition to join Gordon's campaign, Dennis the hangman cries, 'No Popery, brother!' to which Hugh responds, 'No Property, brother!' Gashford corrects Hugh, saying 'Popery, Popery,' but the hangman says, 'It's all the same! . . . It's all right. Down with him, Muster Gashford. Down with everybody, down with everything!' (316).

---

79 Charles Dickens, *Barnaby Rudge; A Tale of the Riots of 'Eighty* (1841; London: Penguin, 2003), 3.

What is evident in these moments is the varied narratives of purpose—the different hungers—of the characters involved. The homes of the rioters, such as Dennis's hovel, depict their poverty, while Hugh's tone of declaration when he says 'I'm a No-Popery man, and ready to be sworn in' (316) suggests that he wants to be a part of something, to feel as though he has some kind of political agency. Hugh has been shown to be ignorant and illiterate, so the rationality of his declaration is called into question. He does not have the capacity to have read any of the pamphlets dedicated to the cause, but he is seeking to belong, to have a voice. Hugh and Dennis are together when Gashford approaches Dennis's home, which is described as a squalid 'retreat':

> Poverty has its whims and shows of taste, as wealth has. Some of these cabins were turreted, some had false windows painted on their rotten walls; one had a mimic clock, upon a crazy tower of four feet high, which screened the chimney; each in its little patch of ground had a rude seat or arbour. (366)

The emphasis on falseness and pretension in tastes reflects the emptiness of the impoverished. There is a dark suggestion that their hopes for social agency will be proven to be as unsatisfying as false windows painted on rotting walls.

Even though Dennis and Hugh are deemed weak-minded, their conversational misdirections, like the false windows, are crucial to the connection Dickens makes between physical and social hunger. It is made clear that, as far as the people are concerned, the cry in itself is not the point; the point is that they are heard, and that they have an outlet for their unrest—even if that outlet is violence. The emphasis on poverty rather than Popery is suggested by Gashford himself when he observes to Gordon that he is not just 'the saviour of his country's religion,' but 'the friend of his poor countrymen, the enemy of the proud and harsh; beloved of the rejected and oppressed, adored by forty thousand bold and loyal English hearts' (300). The haunting presence of Barnaby's father in the text symbolises the nation's visceral hunger for revolution: 'His repast ended – if that can be called one, which was a mere ravenous satisfying of the calls of hunger' (145). Importantly the calls—the narratives—of hunger are pluralised; it is not one voice, but many types of hunger that then compete within the space of unrest.

Voices of hunger unified in violence

The plurality of hunger potentially suggests its inability to be defined as a political voice: it lacks a unified purpose. It is perhaps for this reason that in his unsigned review of *Felix Holt*, the Scottish journalist E.S. Dallas wrote:

> *Felix Holt, the Radical* is not, as its title would lead one to suppose, a political novel, though it necessarily touches on politics . . . the purpose of the author is not . . . to advocate and render palatable any constitutional doctrines—it is rather to exhibit the characters of men as they conduct themselves in a political struggle, here panting after some high ideal of what ought to be, there

floundering contented in things as they are, some seeking honestly for the general good, others selfishly grasping at power and pelf.[80]

While Dallas's metaphor of panting suggests thirst rather than hunger, it does speak to similar ideas of the tensions between self and the community, sacrifice and ambition, that are aroused by physical and social hunger. The conflict of motivations seen in *Barnaby Rudge* are also evident in *Felix Holt*, even though the structures for civilisation and political agency seem more developed in Eliot's re-creation of post-Reform Britain. There is a move away from religion toward politics, as radicalism becomes the religion of reform—at least in the mind of the eponymous character—and dissent rather than Catholicism becomes a central community-forming creed. Yet in a way that resonates with Gashford's hypocrisy, the creed of reform is as apt an enabler of violence as religion. Indeed, the irony of Eliot's text is that, in spite of the Reform Act being meant to increase political agency through wider suffrage, the reality of its limitations—including, for Eliot, the poor education of the people, which enables them to be manipulated easily—leads to the violence.

The concerns of hunger in Treby Magna are invariably parochial, and in this way Eliot overturns the assumptions of the potential dangers being located in France. Treby Magna 'had lived quietly through the great earthquakes of the French Revolution and the Napoleonic Wars,' had 'remained unmoved by the "Rights of Man",' and was only beginning 'at last to know the higher pains of a dim political consciousness; and the development had been greatly helped by the recent agitation about the Reform Bill' (49). However, it is more that 'prices had fallen, poor-rates had risen, rent and tithe were not elastic enough, and the farmer's fat sorrow had become lean' that caused Treby Magna to be 'prepared to vibrate' when 'political agitation swept in a great current through the country' (48). In this image, the people are shown to be ready to be moulded into a particular political voice—to learn to articulate their social hunger. Colene Bentley suggests that Felix operates as a vehicle for Eliot's scepticism 'about purely political measures serving as vehicles for positive social change' in the way that his 'desire to improve the lot of his fellow workers does not translate into support for formal freedoms through the extension of voting rights.'[81] However, Felix's concern is not so much about who gets the vote, but how the voting is manipulated by electioneering. The electioneers get men on side by treating them in the public houses—appealing to their taste for beer—rather than through intellectual or rational political arguments. Yet it is also crucial that Bentley observes that Eliot relies on Felix's 'charisma' to 'generate social consensus,' which 'seems perplexing precisely because the novel if nothing else is critical of artifice in public life.'[82] What Eliot shows, however, is that, in the complexity of unrest, charisma,

---

80 [E.S. Dallas], Review of *Felix Holt, the Radical*, in *The Times* (26 June 1866), 6.
81 Colene Bentley, 'Democratic Citizenship in *Felix Holt*,' *Nineteenth-Century Contexts: An Interdisciplinary Journal*, 24.3 (2002): 271–89, 277.
82 Ibid., 282.

regardless of its ultimate lack of substance, becomes an operating force of unity. Although Felix is set up as the morally upright character, his integrity holds no sway for the men in the face of sating their appetites. At the Sugar Loaf, the public house where Mr Johnson treats the men, the unnourishing name of which conjures the same kind of emptiness as Felix's charisma, Felix confronts selfish satisfaction. Mr Johnson asks, 'Will it do any good to honest Tom, who is hungry in Sproxton, to hear that Jack at Newcastle has his bellyful of beef and pudding?' Felix responds, interrupting Johnson's speech, 'It ought to do him good. . . . If he know it's a bad thing to be hungry and not have enough to eat, he ought to be glad that another fellow, who is not idle, is not suffering in the same way.'[83] Although both Johnson and Felix are speaking on behalf of Radicalism, and both centre their arguments on hunger, Johnson looks to the self-seeking motivations of men while Felix looks to the necessity of community.

Felix recognises that selfish hunger is insatiable, that it will find new avenues of craving and taste, for he earlier explains to Esther Lyon:

> 'Let a man once throttle himself with a satin stock, and he'll get new wants and new motives. Metamorphosis will have begun in his neck-joint, and it will go on till it has changed his likings first and then his reasoning, which will follow his likings as the feet of a hungry dog follow his nose. I'll have none of your clerkly gentility. I might end by collecting greasy pence from poor men to buy myself a fine coat and a glutton's dinner, on pretence of serving the poor men.' (64–65)

Not only does Felix acknowledge the compulsion to develop new hungers, he revisits the idea of moderation—not as a luxury, as depicted by Dickens and Martineau in regard to the French aristocracy, but as a self-sacrificing moderation. But Felix is not starved; he still has enough. Importantly, he frames economic hunger as a political motivator, aligning political motivations with economic gain. In regard to the men at the Sugar Loaf, however, Felix reflects sorrowfully on his inability to relay his message:

> 'Where's the good . . . of pulling at such a tangled skein as this electioneering trickery? As long as three-fourths of the men in this country see nothing in an election but self-interest, and nothing in self-interest but some form of greed, one might as well try to purify the proceedings of the fishes and say to a hungry cod-fish—"My good friend, abstain; don't goggle your eyes so, or show such a stupid gluttonous mouth, or think the little fishes are worth noting except in relation to your own inside."' (147)

It is significant that Felix recognises that hunger is a more powerful, fundamental dynamic than rational thought, for, as Carlyle observes, 'apart from exile, or

---

83 George Eliot, *Felix Holt, the Radical* (1866; London: Penguin, 1995), 137.

other violent methods, is there not one method, whereby all things are tamed, even lions? The method of hunger!'[84] Hunger's visceral power must needs be matched, either by sating it, or by appealing to another visceral response through charisma. It is not just that the men are hungry, but they have been taught to think about—to articulate—their hunger in a particular way. In this case, in the choice between serving themselves, or serving their community, the promise of satiation added through the treat of beer encourages them to follow the self-serving narrative of hunger.

After the Sunday Trading Riots in London in 1855, the need to allay fears of urban rioting rose to the surface. In the *Quarterly Review*, Andrew Wynter wrote:

> Those who shudder at the idea of an outbreak in the metropolis, containing two millions and a half of people and at least fifty thousand of the 'dangerous classes,' forget that the capital is so wide that its different sections are totally unknown to each other. A mob in London is wholly without cohesion, and the individuals composing it have but few feelings, thoughts, or pursuits in common. They would immediately break up before the determined attack of a band of well-trained men who know and have confidence in each other.[85]

This assessment, however, was blind to the extraordinary organisation of previous demonstrations in London. On 12 October 1831, after the First Reform Bill had been rejected, the demonstration was highly organised, parish by parish, and coordinated for how the parishes were to meet—this kind of organisation is reflected in the procession to Parliament seen in *Barnaby Rudge*. The *Morning Chronicle* gave an account of the demonstration, noting the thousands of participants from across London. They are described as a 'united procession,' but even more importantly in terms of civilisation befitting Britain:

> yet through the whole line the procession was conducted with regularity and good order quite unexampled, refuting at once the audacious calumnies of the boroughmongers, and showing that a people so respectable, peaceable, united, and firm, were entitled to, and would have, the constitutional privileges of Englishmen and freemen.[86]

Keeping in mind Butwin's argument that emphasis on the orderliness of a crowd can be due to the need to repress fear of revolution, it is also evident that the motive of the *Morning Chronicle* is to convey the respectability of the procession—that they are worthy of full citizenship, including suffrage. In both *Barnaby Rudge* and *Felix Holt*, however, as was eventually the case with the October 1831 demonstration,

---

84 Carlyle, *French Revolution*, vol. 1, 77.
85 [Andrew Wynter], 'The Police and the Thieves,' *Quarterly Review*, 99 (1856): 173.
86 *The Morning Chronicle* (13 October 1831), *Place and Papers* vol. 2, British Museum Add. Ms. 27790, folios 1–176, 28.

the crowd cannot be contained: orderliness inevitably overflows into violence and destruction. In both narratives the Riot Act is read, but falls impotent against the determined—if disunified in purpose—crowd.

In *Felix Holt*, the orderliness suggested by an election is threatened by violence from the start, with the non-voting crowd intimidating those going to the polling booth until the violence emerges enough to cause the booth to close (304, 312). The climax of destruction occurs after the Riot Act is read, when the crowd turns to food destruction. The use of food as weapons symbolises both the role of hunger in their unrest and metaphorically a growing taste for violence. This progression resonates with Carlyle's *French Revolution*, when 'Cholat the wine-merchant . . . become[s] an impromptu cannoneer,'[87] although it is displaced from a human being and their occupation onto the objects or weapons of revolt. In this way, Eliot confronts the broader structures and mechanisms of society, not just the moral or ideological motivations of a particular class. Mr Crow, the constable,

> instead of persuading the crowd, . . . appeared to enrage them. Some one, snatching a raw potato from a sack in the greengrocer's shop behind him, threw it at the constable, and hit him on the mouth. Straightway raw potatoes and turnips were flying by twenties at the windows of the Seven Stars, and the panes were smashed. (313)

This violence then becomes refined as the 'voices turn[ed] to a savage roar' and the crowd rushed toward 'the hardware store, which furnished more effective weapons and missiles than turnips and potatoes' (313). This move from potatoes to metal and wood shows a change in taste that reflects the changing hunger from physical to social, and a return to a taste for blood in the rejection of food, just as Madame Defarge's decision to put down her knitting in favour of weapons marks her abandonment to the revolution. Even more dangerous than the weaponry found in the hardware store, though, is that to be found in the breweries and wine vaults, 'where the property was of a sort at once most likely to be threatened and most dangerous in its effects' (314). As in Martineau's *French Wines and Politics*, the intoxicating influence of alcohol, a perverted excess in contrast to starvation, is seen as the most dangerous force within a riotous crowd. Indeed, even before the booth is closed, 'the majority of the crowd were excited with drink,' leading to hoots, shouts, and scuffling (311). However, even when Felix takes charge of the rioters, trying to lead them aside, he notices that they are 'half-tipsy' (315), which suggests not that they are drunk and therefore out of their senses, but merely encouraged by the alcohol to pursue their violence. Further, Felix uses the promise of more gin in Tillot's vaults to lead the men away, before the promise of violence toward one of the constables becomes a greater pull (315). The progression from violence toward food and property to violence against other

87 Carlyle, *French Revolution*, vol. 1, 150.

people reflects the revolutionary movement seen in the French Revolution narratives, and the development of the taste for blood over that for food.

In *Barnaby Rudge*, it is the homeliness of the Maypole public house that makes its destruction by the rioters even more devastating. John Willet's bar is described as 'the very snuggest, cosiest, and completest bar, that ever the wit of man devised,' with closets 'all crammed to the throat with eatables, drinkables, or savoury condiments' (168). It is the Maypole's ability to provide abundant sustenance and taste that makes it so welcoming to visitors. When John tells the cook to add fish, lamb chops, chicken, salad, potato and sausages 'or something of that sort' to Mrs Varden's order for dinner, in free indirect discourse Mrs Varden comments on the luxurious abundance of tastes: 'Something of that sort! The resources of these inns! To talk carelessly about dishes, which in themselves were a first-rate holiday kind of dinner' (168). Furthermore, the kitchen is described as a place in which 'nothing in the way of cookery seemed impossible; where you could believe in anything to eat' (168). The Maypole not only makes visitors feel at home, it is a luxurious home, where the tastes available to the wealthy become a seemingly natural part of the visitors' experience. Mrs Varden is, however, overwhelmed by the abundance because it is not a part of her regular existence. Her head becomes 'quite dizzy and bewildered' by the choice of taste available to her, for her own 'housekeeping capacity was not large enough to comprehend them' (169).

As with Maigrot in *French Wines and Politics*, attention is drawn to the fact that the Maypole is both John Willet's home and place of business. Yet unlike the destruction in *French Wines*, the destruction in the Maypole has no direct relationship to the stated causes of the riots. John is Protestant, and far from aristocratic. He is an employer, however, and there is a sense that Hugh in particular, who leads this facet of the rioting, is rebelling against his subservient role, much as Joe Willet had done by running away. The destruction of food is not because the men are physically hungry at this point, but because they are hungry for perceived social freedom. This freedom is marked by an ability to move into previously inaccessible spaces and take authority over them. In the Maypole, this space is the bar:

> Here was the bar—the bar that the boldest never entered without special invitation—the sanctuary, the mystery, the hallowed ground: here it was, crammed with men, clubs, sticks, torches, pistols; filled with a deafening noise, oaths, shouts, screams, hootings; changed all at once into a bear-garden, a mad-house, an infernal temple: men darting in and out, by door and window, smashing the glass, turning the taps, drinking liquor out of China punchbowls, sitting astride of casks smoking private and personal pipes, cutting down the sacred grove of lemons, hacking and hewing at the celebrated cheese, breaking open inviolable drawers, putting things in their pockets which didn't belong to them, dividing his own money before his own eyes, wantonly wasting, breaking, pulling down and tearing up: nothing quiet, nothing private: men everywhere—above, below, overhead, in the bedrooms, in the kitchen, in the yard, in the stables—clambering in at windows when the stairs were handy; leaping over the banisters into chasms of passages:

new faces and figures presenting themselves every instant—some yelling, some singing, some fighting, some breaking glass and crockery, some laying the dust with the liquor they couldn't drink, some ringing the bells till they pulled them down, others beating them with pokers till they beat them into fragments: more men still—more, more, more—swarming on like insects: noise, smoke, light, darkness, frolic, anger, laughter, groans, plunder, fear, and ruin! (450)

By positioning the violence within the domestic space against the lemons and the cheese and the waste of liquor as sacrilege, Dickens emphasises that the riots are not about religion but about excess. The repetition of 'more, more, more' describes the men as well as the ruin as they are overtaken by their appetite for destruction. It reflects the insatiability of the guillotine in Dickens's later narrative, where the women are 'knitting, knitting' as the heads fall, as the hunger of the people becomes a kind of addiction, an excessive greed for more once a taste has been received, either of food or of political power. The chaos is evoked by hunger becoming an uncontrollable, destructive ravenous beast, the ultimate larger force that ironically unifies the community. The desecration of the Maypole is, on a smaller scale, a mimicry of the attack on the Houses of Parliament, where the rioters flood into the lobbies of both Houses. The density of the mob is described as a 'swarm' within and without the Houses, the 'air filled with execrations, hoots, and howlings. The mob raged and roared, like a mad monster as it was, unceasingly, and each new outrage served to swell its fury' (406–08). However, the vast number of men are no more knowledgeable regarding the situation than Barnaby himself when he joins the crowd, when his mother pleads with him, "'You don't know . . . what mischief they may do, where they may lead you, what their meaning is'" (397). A few pages later, the mass assemblage is described as seemingly organised and subdivided, but 'the general arrangement was, except to the few chiefs and leaders, as unintelligible as the plan of a great battle to the meanest soldier in the field' (404). It therefore leaves the motive to the mass individuals, while the unifying factor is the hunger for blood and destruction.

During the unrest of 1831 and 1832, the unsigned *The Reform Bill for England and Wales Examined* made a provocative move by attributing riotous behaviour to the Members of Parliament debating reform: 'The conduct of the opposing parties resembled rather the violence of a wild revolutionary struggle, than the deliberate decision of a grave constitutional matter by a highly civilized and educated people.'[88] If the rationality of the MPs is questioned because of their uncivilised behaviour, the very civilisation of the nation is called into question; yet at the same time it suggests that perhaps those who are (albeit violently) acting against the irrational Parliament are actually the rational ones. Turning the tables on the MPs in this manner is crucial, potentially posing the legitimacy of riots. The *Morning Chronicle* adamantly held to the organisation of the protesters in London,

---

88 *The Reform Bill for England and Wales Examined* (London: Hatchard & Son, 1831), 49.

describing an incredible level of organisation as hundreds of thousands of men coordinated a march throughout London. The level of organisation and control in this movement was terrifying in itself because it created a powerful sense of unity. It also spoke of reason rather than irrationality, defying the attempts to define the protesters as animalistic, chaotic mobs: something unhuman, something Other. And this is the most significant element of terror. In both *Barnaby Rudge* and *Felix Holt*, the narratives describe a mystical level of organisation and unity in spite of discrepancies of purpose. In *Barnaby*, after the procession to the Houses of Parliament, which is described as being 'in perfect order and profound silence' (404), and the riot that follows the rejection of the petition, the narrative reflects, '[a] mob is usually a creature of very mysterious existence, particularly in a large city. Where it comes from or whither it goes, few men can tell. Assembling and dispersing with equal suddenness, it is as difficult to follow to its various sources as the sea itself' (429). In *Felix Holt*, the 'movement was that of a flood hemmed in; it carried nobody away' (312), persisting and growing in strength in spite of the belief, like that expressed by Wynter, that 'with this sort of mob, which was animated by no real political passion or fury against social distinctions, it was in the highest degree unlikely that there would be any resistance to military force' (317). In both texts the unifying factor is hunger—images of hunger are written on the faces and bodies of the people throughout the text—but not all for the same thing. Some hunger for food, others for political agency or reform, or for a sense of belonging, while for some, like Gordon's secretary, it is the hunger for power. And yet it is ravenous hunger that propels each mob into riots and destruction, while ironically binding them together into a starved community. Within a Britain that had been through the Angry Thirties and the Hungry Forties, the mid-century readership is forced to contend with their own history: that of a ravenous mob seeking to consume the nation.

2 Humanising the mob

Misery generates hate: these sufferers hated the machines which they believed took their bread from them; they hated the buildings which contained those machines; they hated the manufacturers who owned those buildings.

(Charlotte Brontë, *Shirley* (1849), 62)

It is not what a man outwardly has or wants that constitutes the happiness or misery of him. Nakedness, hunger, distress of all kinds, death itself has been cheerfully suffered, when the heart was right. It is the feeling of *injustice* that is insupportable to all men. . . . No man can bear it, or ought to bear it.

(Thomas Carlyle, *Chartism* (1840), 30)

In *The Hunger Artists* (1993), Maud Ellmann positions corporate or communal hunger as a catalyst for social progress. While the individual experience of hunger is subjective, relative, and socially impotent, Ellmann suggests: 'It is only in the unified collective . . . that the experience of hunger sheds its intonations of submission and clarifies itself as solidarity or insurrection.'[1] On the one hand, this perspective illuminates the way in which shared hunger can build a sense of community, potentially leading to social progress. This potential, however, cannot rule out the threat of self-interest—a factor that tends to be on the rise in times of real or perceived scarcity, creating a hardened climate of injustice. Ellmann's assessment seems to buy into the language of progress in early political economy, which, while claiming to seek to reconcile the needs of the individual with social interests, tended instead to avoid moral interference with the economic science, and be blind to individual human cost for the sake of a wider socio-political vision. As in Ellmann's construction, the individual's experience is subjugated beneath the communal, with Adam Smith's 'invisible hand' operating as a mythical force that rationalises and regulates society.

The first half of the nineteenth century was a time of transition between competing economic narratives, which can be described crudely as the increasing

---

1 Ellmann, *The Hunger Artists*, 6.

entrenchment of capitalist political economy in competition with the diminishing feudal paternalism. While a certain amount of social dynamism, freedom, and independence is promised by the former, it often means the loss of a coherent community. Furthermore, access to such freedom and independence remains limited to those possessing the luxuries of social, economic, and cultural capital. Kathryn Gleadle argues that '[w]hereas the new political economy was to privilege the values of independence and self-help, the moral economy was enmeshed in older ideals of mutuality,'[2] and goes on to show the ways in which individuals, families, and communities resisted the growing depersonalised (arguably dehumanised) macroeconomic approach to social structures. The powerful intervention of individuals against the empirical 'de-moralizing' (to borrow from E.P. Thompson) of economic systems acted as a necessary political, community-based response to the distancing 'model of a *natural* and self-adjusting economy, working providentially for the best good of all'—a belief in itself 'as much a superstition as the notions which upheld the paternalist model [of feudalism].'[3] Within this context, this chapter explores the complexities of social inclusion in relation to the demonisation of the rioting mob, and the key differences between *ownership within* the community and *belonging to* the community. In the first chapter, I discussed the way in which the inability of Dickens's poor French migrants to taste their national foods challenges their cultural identity, but focused more on the undercurrent of imperialism evident in Miss Pross appropriating those tastes. In this chapter I extend the relationship between the access, not just to food, but to tastes, to the sense of belonging—to ideas of citizenship and civilised society—by examining the decivilising effects on those who are denied the choice of taste.

In *The Insatiability of Human Wants* (2000), Regenia Gagnier begins with the question, 'Is freedom in market society anything more than the capacity to exercise choice in the marketplace,'[4] which effectively brings together the ethical and economic nature of hunger and access to taste in relationship to political and social agency. It is evident that, as much as Adam Smith, David Ricardo, and other early political economists sought to 'disinfest' their economic theories of 'intrusive moral imperatives,'[5] in practice, the legitimating narratives of economic stability and progress could not be separated from the chaotic counter-narratives expressing the violation of the moral economy. The language of ethics persists within economic discourse, and is articulated most fully in response to the 'perceived injustice' that arises when the moral economy defined by Thompson—'based on customary economic relations in open markets whereby

---

2 Kathryn Gleadle, 'Gentry, Gender, and the Moral Economy during the Revolutionary and Napoleonic Wars in Provincial England,' in *Economic Women: Essays on Desire and Dispossession in Nineteenth-Century British Culture*, ed. Lana L. Dalley and Jill Rappoport (Columbus: Ohio State University Press, 2013), 24–40, 26.
3 Thompson, 'Moral Economy,' 91. My emphasis.
4 Gagnier, *Insatiability of Human Wants*, 1.
5 Thompson, 'Moral Economy,' 90.

pure food, honestly measured, was sold regularly throughout the year at a fair price with preference being given to local markets'—is noticeably broken down in practice.[6] In spite of the seeming scientific approach of political economy, economic practice remained judged on moral terms. As Joshua Bamfield suggests, 'the "moral economy" concept was still available to society to evaluate the actions of economic agents.'[7]

This double rhetoric of scientific economic strategies and the expectation of moral economic practices arising out of industrialisation remains in contemporary twenty-first-century political debates, arising as it does from the challenging tension between the individual and the community. Yet what I seek to address in this chapter is the specific problem of the response of the community to the individual in the crowd who becomes disaffected through displacement, dispossession, and political voicelessness, all of which can be related in nineteenth-century Britain to problems of scarcity and starvation. Mark M. Smith argues that '[h]unger threaten[s] to catapult man back in space and time, rendering him more animal than human,' and further, that '[s]carcity of food peel[s] back civilized man's exterior and reveal[s] an animal that would eat anything to survive.'[8] As much as economic and social narratives seek moral acquittal through distancing the unhuman, animalistic, irrational corporate body, it is the fear of being forced to acknowledge connection to—and therefore responsibility for—that body that motivates the need for imaginative distance: 'they' are not 'us'; 'we' are not 'them.' However, while the idea of a mob suggests a dehumanised, demonised collective, the literature I engage with most closely seeks to give voice and individual agency—social and political—to characters that have been marginalised through economic want and, as a result, give in to the isolating effects of misery and hatred. Community, reintegration, and belonging operate to diffuse violence, yet at the same time, in a fractured social context, as seen in the historical revolutions and riots of Chapter 1, often that sense of community is gained through violent uprisings—in the collective unity of the mob. Community and belonging, therefore, takes on an ironic and problematic identity, ultimately being held up as the abstract state hungered after by human individuals, often regardless of how it is acquired.

David Hume's remarks on the othering nature of taste—that *we* call barbarous whatever departs from *our* tastes[9]—signifies that taste, like hunger, is communal as well as individual. Shared tastes, an extension of shared food, builds a sense of community and belonging; and thus the barbarism or dehumanisation of being denied tastes is countered by the act of sharing food and therefore sharing tastes. In a similar, darker way, being denied the same tastes can work to create

---

6 Joshua Bamfield, 'Consumer-Owned Community Flour and Bread Societies in the Eighteenth and Early Nineteenth Centuries,' *Business History*, 40.4 (1998): 16–36, 20.

7 Ibid.

8 Mark M. Smith, *The Smell of Battle, the Taste of Siege: A Sensory History of the Civil War* (Oxford and New York: Oxford University Press, 2015), 90–91.

9 Hume, 'Of the Standard of Taste,' 203.

a cohesive collective. This chapter begins, then, by looking at the dehumanising effects of collective hunger, moves through the complexities of othering hungry foreigners, to the other who attempts to be heard by emulating expectations of civility, and ends with the civilising effects of sharing food and tastes. Sharing tastes both creates community and bestows rank. As Smith notes, food choices are 'not simply about nutrition. In fact, the choice of what to consume reflect[s] refinement and civilization, the two touchstones of . . . social order. In this sense, "taste" bestow[s] status, interlacing consumption with aesthetic worth.'[10] Without the capacity to taste, one's social position becomes tenuous and difficult to define; thus sharing food, and sharing tastes, speaks to reincorporating the hungry into the communal body. Cross-class eating in particular speaks to the rehumanisation of figures within all participant classes through the recognition of communal belonging.

The key narratives I engage with, by Harriet Martineau, Charlotte Brontë, and Elizabeth Gaskell, each contend with the ways in which hunger and social or political exclusion operate together catalytically toward violent protest, and in each, the question of community and belonging is central. Martineau's *Sowers Not Reapers* (1833), Brontë's *Shirley* (1849), and Gaskell's *Mary Barton* (1848) and *North and South* (1854–55) display a complexity of narrative voices that reveal the conflicting nature of hunger, and the impact of hunger on the community. Martineau was vilified as a proponent of Smith, Malthus, Ricardo, and other key economists, but while she positions herself as illustrating the rational, practical outworking of political economy, what actually dominates these tales are the chaotic counternarratives of violence, rebellion, and social unrest, motivated in many cases by the overwhelming sensation of hunger. Gaskell takes a different tack, famously stating in the preface to *Mary Barton* that she knows nothing of political economy—although it is evident in her letters that she read political economy and greatly admired Adam Smith, and the tenets of the theory are evident in her texts. In many ways, Gaskell's fiction achieves, in a more fluid, convincing manner, the very thing that Martineau sought to do: it provides a narrative illustration of political economy in a way that challenges and critiques its application. Crucially, the fiction of both gives individual faces and voices to the devastating effects of hunger in a way that disallows a rational, theoretical dismissal of very real human suffering.

Brontë's *Shirley* inhabits a provocative historical space in relation to Martineau and Gaskell. Published the year after *Mary Barton*, *Shirley* has often been read, appropriately, as a comment upon Chartism, at its height in the 1840s.[11] It is set, however, in 1812, well before the 1830 Swing Riots that informed Martineau's machine-breaker narrative in *Sowers Not Reapers* (1833). The 1812 setting provides a crucial link between hunger, industry, and violence that haunts the later

---

10 Smith, *Smell of Battle*, 88–89.
11 See Terry Eagleton, *Myths of Power: A Marxist Study of the Brontës* (rev. edn, New York: Palgrave, 2005), 45.

historical spaces. E.P. Thompson argues that '[i]n 1812 traditional food riots over-lap with Luddism,'[12] and marks as a turning point a moment in Nottingham in that year when 'women paraded with a loaf upon a pole, streaked with red and tied with black crepe, emblematic of "bleeding famine decked in Sackecloth",' emphasis-ing the 'growing symbolism of blood, and . . . its assimilation to the demand for bread.'[13] While Thompson's choice of 1812 seems to an extent arbitrary—indeed, he goes on to give many more examples from 1816, and it is also clear that such connections go back to the French Revolution—it is evident that the early years of the nineteenth century, consumed economically and psychologically by the Napoleonic Wars, brought about an ideological conflation of industry and starva-tion that continued to impact the nation throughout the Victorian period. Just as Peter Jones claims that 'it was impossible to separate completely the function of protest from its form,'[14] as I discussed in relation to potatoes as weaponry in Eliot's *Felix Holt* in the previous chapter, Thompson shows how the combination of blood and bread acts symbolically upon the crowd to unify them in purpose. Therefore the conflicts portrayed by Martineau, Gaskell, and Brontë, while having distinct mid-century concerns, are undergirded by earlier cries for blood. They are held together in part—as was common in the mid-century—by their distrust of protest as an appropriate, or indeed effective, means to bring about social change. In each of the narratives, protests lead to violence, increased scarcity, and greater isolation for members of the working classes. Thus the narratives remain haunted by the alienating 'even tenor' of the lives of the rich in times of eco-nomic downturn, juxtaposed with 'the anguish caused by the lottery-like nature' of working-class lives.[15]

Collective hunger

The misery and hatred expressed by Brontë in *Shirley* (1849) and Carlyle in *Chartism* (1840) are, crucially, due not to hunger and scarcity alone, but to the perceived injustice visited upon the impoverished in times of scarcity. They are qualities akin to hunger, not just as a seemingly natural consequence of starvation, but, like Ellmann's construction of hunger, while isolating as an individual experi-ence, they become a powerful, unifying social force when they infuse the hungry collective. Peter Jones speaks of the moral economy as 'the essential, cohesive ingredient in crowd action,'[16] yet more specifically, the crowd is moved by the collective inference and acknowledgement that the moral economy has been violated. Gerard Delanty, writing of postmodern cosmopolitanism, refers to the role of 'violent conflicts' and 'political violence' in reinforcing 'group identities

12 Thompson, 'Moral Economy,' 128–29.
13 Ibid., 135.
14 Peter Jones, 'Swing, Speenhamland and Rural Social Relations,' *Social History* 32.3 (2007): 271–90, 274.
15 Elizabeth Gaskell, *Mary Barton: A Tale of Manchester Life* (1848; Oxford: Oxford University Press, 1987), xxxv.
16 Jones, 'Swing, Speenhamland and Rural Social Relations,' 273.

and values.'[17] Indeed, Andrew Tolson's analysis of the working classes in Henry Mayhew's *London Labour and the London Poor* (1851–52) positions the connection between subculture, criminality, and identity as a means for the working classes to 'become visible.'[18] Through collective acts of violence and protest, the transient vagrant and invisible poor gain voice and visibility, as well as substance. Importantly, though, while this kind of movement operates not necessarily out of instinctive desperation, but out of a rational desire for social progress through revolution and reform, it can also lead to decivilisation and destruction. As Sam Wright suggests, to 'enter into a crowd is to become part of the dynamics of a unique reality';[19] thus the crowd gives a sense of identity and belonging that has been lost in the sense of voicelessness—of not belonging, or of being a lesser-class citizen. But at the same time, as '[g]roups in collective behavior are seldom the highly formalized creations found in the institutional order,' but are instead 'emergent, ever evolving, relatively ephemeral entities,'[20] not only are the effects of belonging to the crowd bound to ultimately cause disillusionment, the shifting nature of the crowd dynamic can make it unpredictable, and therefore uncontrollable. While Royle and Walvin suggest a civilising movement amongst the working classes of the early nineteenth century, stating that the 'food riots of the immediate post-war period were among the last of their kind' and that '[s]trikes were replacing collective bargaining by riot, and organised political protest was taking the place of local demonstrations in favour of the just price,'[21] these new forms of protest very often crossed over into violent uprisings. Like hunger that remains unchecked, the unchecked hungry crowd is uncontrollable. Indeed, when seemingly civilised, rational protest is dismissed or ridiculed by those with political power, there remains the dark suggestion that violence is necessary to be heard.

Brontë's 1812 setting for *Shirley* situates her narrative within the broader contexts of the French Wars abroad and the growing impetus of Luddism at home; yet the historical continuity of hunger and violence is firmly positioned within governmental coolness and individual self-interest at the expense of a community-focused vision. Patrick Brantlinger has argued that Luddism is a mere 'backdrop of Gothic horror' to the romantic narratives of Robert Moore, Shirley, and Caroline, and that, unlike *Barnaby Rudge* or *Mary Barton*, in which the upper classes produce the 'chief villains,' the working classes in *Shirley* are positioned as 'form[ing] the mob against which the largely virtuous upper-middle class characters must contend.'[22] However, while Brontë does present some characters more

---

17 Gerard Delanty, 'Cosmopolitanism and Violence: The Limits of Global Civil Society,' *European Journal of Social Theory*, 4 (2001): 41–52, 41.

18 Andrew Tolson, 'Social Surveillance and Subjectification: The Emergence of "Subculture" in the Work of Henry Mayhew,' *Cultural Studies*, 4 (1990): 113–27, 115.

19 Sam Wright, *Crowds and Riots: A Study in Social Organization* (Beverly Hills and London: Sage Publications, 1978), 7.

20 Ibid., 9.

21 Edward Royle and James Walvin, *English Radicals and Reformers 1760–1848* (Brighton: Harvester, 1982), 109.

22 Patrick Brantlinger, 'The Case against Trade Unions in Early Victorian Fiction,' *Victorian Studies* 13.1 (1969): 37–52, 41–42.

akin to Austenian village philanthropy, there remains a strong mix of virtue and villainy across the classes, more so than Dickens, but not unlike Gaskell's later approach in *North and South*. What I want to focalise here in relation to *Shirley* is the way in which responsibilities for hunger become strained within the community in times of scarcity. Scarcity narrows the scope of community responsibility, intensifying the self-interest observed by David Gauthier, who suggests it is,

> neither unrealistic nor pessimistic to suppose that beyond the ties of blood and friendship, which are necessarily limited in their scope, human beings exhibit little positive fellow-feeling. . . . One of the problems facing human societies is the absence of any form of effective and mutually beneficial interaction among persons not linked by some particular bond.[23]

Gagnier critiques Menger and Jevons for 'excluding history from their analyses' in order to create 'a static picture of the economy as a locus of scarcity,' thereby justifying a false sense of hunger.[24] Yet while history shows that the economy is not static, but operates in seasons of abundance as well as privation, the *perception* of scarcity can be as destructive as actual famine in terms of community relationships. In my first chapter, I referred to Nunokawa's observation that the nineteenth-century British imagination was preoccupied with a fear of loss and a return to the past.[25] When there has been a time of famine, then, even after it has passed, there remains the memory of starvation in the collective mind; and the fear of that hunger returning leads individuals and communities to hoard and accumulate out of that fear, potentially leading to excess and addiction, but also providing the psychological conditions of famine: 'Given scarcity, self-interest dictates that each fights to secure her own requirements to the exclusion of others.'[26] Thus while extending the scope of responsibility to the British government and international trade politics, Brontë is most focused on the widespread destructiveness of the grasping, narrow selfishness that arises in response to the effects of war economics, technology, and poor harvests. Ironically, while examining a small social setting, Brontë reveals that the problem of self-interest that Gauthier observes is far from isolated. By beginning in the heart of the local community, Brontë suggests the global implications of self-serving ideologies.

Gaskell is similarly engaged in the international implications of her work, even though the setting of *Mary Barton*, like *Shirley*, is parochial. In her preface, she sets herself up as a kind of social prophet, emphasising that she was writing *Mary Barton* in 1847, after which time Europe seemed to explode in revolutions and riots, with the People's Uprisings of 1848 that seemed to sweep through every nation on the Continent. Gaskell delves deeply into the individual lives of her

---

23 David Gauthier, *Morals by Agreement* (Oxford: Oxford University Press, 1986), 101.
24 Gagnier, *Insatiability of Human Wants*, 47.
25 Nunokawa, *Afterlife of Property*, 7.
26 Gagnier, *Insatiability of Human Wants*, 47.

working-class characters and their community, but in prefacing her work with reference to Europe's uprisings, Gaskell provides an outward vision, claiming that the hunger and political voicelessness that destroy the community of her imagined Manchester were commensurate with that which caused the uprisings in Europe. Importantly, Brantlinger argues that Gaskell is 'more interested in presenting the conflict between workers and masters in moral and psychological terms than economic ones,' and 'the inadequacies of trade unionism are the result more of failures of human sympathy than of the law of wages.'[27] I would suggest, though, that rather than minimising economic issues, Gaskell, like Brontë, seeks to overcome them, arguing for a human sympathy that surpasses political agendas and economic theories in order to acknowledge the humanity of the starving.

The setting of Brontë's novel pre-empts trade unionism, and her William Farren, like Gaskell's John Barton, functions as the voice of the starving populace. William's fate, singled out as he is as an individual, is different from John's, who stands for the suffering of his class. Even in these two representations, their masters' acknowledgement of the workers' humanity is central to their success: Robert Moore seeks help for William privately as an individual he respects, but Mr Carson does not recognise John until it is too late and they have both suffered too much for Barton's redemption. The dark picture that emerges is that it is perhaps William's willingness to speak for *himself*, in contrast to Barton's sacrifice of self for the sake of the community, that allows for his success. William's voice is heard because he distances himself from the rest of the starving bodies while coming to their defence. When the group of machine breakers approach Robert Moore, and after Moore takes Moses Barraclough under civil arrest, Farren speaks in his own defence:

'I've not much faith i' Moses Barraclough,' said he; 'and I would speak a work to you myseln, Mr Moore. It's out o' no ill-will that I'm here, for my part; it's just to mak' a effort to get things straightened, for they're sorely crooked. Ye see we're ill off,—varry ill off: wer families is poor and pined. We're thrown out o' work wi' these frames: we can get nought to do: we can earn nought. What is to be done? Mun we say wisht! and lig us down and dee? Nay: I've no grand words at my tongue's end, Mr Moore, but I feel that it would be a low principle for a reasonable man to starve to death like a dumb cratur':—I will not do't. I'm not for shedding blood: I'd neither kill a man nor hurt a man; and I'm not for pulling down mills and breaking machines: for, as ye say, that way o' going on 'll niver stop invention; but I'll talk,—I'll mak' as big a din' as ever I can. Invention may be all right, but I know it isn't right for poor folks to starve. Them that governs mun find a way to help us: they mun mak' fresh orderations. Ye'll say that's hard to do:—so mich louder mun we shout out then, for so much slacker with t' Parliament-men be to set on to a tough job.'[28]

27 Brantlinger, 'The Case against Trade Unions,' 50.
28 Charlotte Brontë, *Shirley* (1849; London: Penguin, 1974), 156–57.

Farren's plea is for non-violent cooperation; he asserts humanity for the starving, while also acknowledging the need for social and technological progress, but most importantly, his opening statement is a rejection of the crowd's leader. While Robert initially responds negatively, he is ultimately forced to recognise William's humanity. Farren claims his own voice, his own identity, apart from the perceived leader of unrest, before speaking for his class. He claims his reason and moral justice; yet while Robert seeks alternative employment for Farren, his opinion of Farren's class as a whole, of the hungry collective, does not change. He stands firmly against the humanity of his 'hands,' continuing to 'relish' in practice what appeals to his 'intellectual palate'—the 'haughty speech of Caius Marcius to the starving citizens' in Shakespeare's *Coriolanus*—in spite of Caroline's criticism of his ideological stance: 'you sympathize with the proud patrician who does not sympathize with his famished fellow-men, and insults them' (116).

The figurative references to taste and eating throughout *Shirley* work to reinforce the lack of food, and therefore the necessary lack of discrimination of taste amongst the starving poor. Gaskell also contends with this necessary loss of taste when John Barton, representing the 'gaunt, anxious, hunger-stamped men,'[29] says at the Union meeting:

> 'We donnot want dainties, we want bellyfuls; we donnot want gimcrack coats and waistcoats, we want warm clothes; and so that we get 'em, we'd not quarrel wi' what they're made on. We donnot want their grand houses, we want a roof to cover us from the rain, and the snow, and the storm; aye, and not alone to cover us, but the helpless ones that cling to us in the keen wind, and ask us with their eyes why we brought 'em into th' world to suffer?' (220)

Barton's declaration here speaks to the role of hunger in determining taste: the men are not concerned about *what* they eat or what they wear, as long as they have food and clothes. They have therefore become dehumanised to an extent, in that they do not have the luxury 'to savor (to think about) their food,' which is one of the rationalising distinctions between humans and animals.[30] Yet Barton perceives that the masters, with their luxury of tastes, think that the workers want to take everything they have. This moment is particularly pertinent because Barton's speech is made after the London Union delegate has spoken to the Manchester men in a highly manipulative and theatrical way about what they can achieve. Gaskell introduces this delegate himself in terms of taste, and he perceives the men's literal tastes through their manners:

> He smirked in acknowledgement of their uncouth greetings, and sat down; then glancing round, he inquired whether it would not be agreeable to the gentlemen present to have pipes and liquor handed round, adding, that he would stand treat.

29 Gaskell, *Mary Barton*, 98.
30 Smith, *Sensory History*, 76.

As the man who has had his taste educated to love reading, falls devour-
ingly upon books after a long abstinence, so these poor fellows, whose tastes
had been left to educate themselves into a liking for tobacco, beer, and similar
gratifications, gleamed up at the proposal of the London delegate. Tobacco
and drink deaden the pangs of hunger, and make one forget the miserable
home, the desolate future.

They were now ready to listen to him with approbation. He felt it; and
rising like a great orator, with his right arm outstretched, his left in the breast
of his waistcoat, he began to declaim, with a forced theatrical voice. (218)

The idea of tastes being taught—as a matter of education—is very telling here,
as is the fact that Gaskell connects so closely the cultural capital of education and
physical sustenance. Smith argues that tastes '"may be trained" to distinguish
good food from a truly "exquisite delicacy." Regardless, man's tongue was not
suited to base foods, especially when those tongues occupied elite positions; eating base foods might well count as an act of decivilization.'[31] In this sense, the
suggestion that the men's tastes had been 'left to educate themselves' serves not
only as a reminder that they have not had access to a range of sustenance, but that,
as a result, they are socially disempowered. Far from distinguishing 'good' from
'exquisite,' the perceived tastes of these men express animalistic coarseness.

The proffered tastes of tobacco and beer are, significantly, cheap; and while the
delegate is being ungenerous in his provision, it is also telling that he is appealing
to what is familiar to those he wants to win over. Tobacco in particular is known
to dull the sense of taste, and it stands to reason that, if eating for the sake of taste
is no longer a consideration, the desire to eat will lessen. Furthermore, chewing
tobacco provides motion for the mouth in the absence of food, much as Madame
Defarge's knitting occupied women's starving hands. The deception of tobacco,
then—mastication promising a satisfaction to the belly that is never fulfilled—
reflects the emptiness of the delegate's promises of social agency to the men.
Appealing to physical taste is a key aspect in political manipulation, as seen with
the campaigners in *Felix Holt*, which undergirds the way in which 'taste and gustation [help] arrange social authority.'[32] By seeming to sate their hunger, which
dwells in tobacco and alcohol since it has given up on food, the London delegate
is able to get the Manchester men on side. As the one controlling sustenance, he
has the greatest social authority. Through this temporal satisfaction, then, the men
enter into a kind of unequal communion, with the delegate as priest providing
physical sustenance and the metaphorical sustenance of hope—regardless of how
empty that hope may be.

Throughout *Mary Barton*, what people are able to use or choose to sate their
hunger is just as crucial as the fact that they are hungry in the first place. There
is a distinct contrast, for example, between the hungerless, luxurious spread
not just at the Carsons' breakfast table, but at that of the Carsons' servants in

31 Smith, *Smell of Battle*, 90.
32 Smith, *Sensory History*, 76.

the kitchen, and the luxurious spread in Holborn that John Barton describes, laid out for the Union delegates, that remains uneaten because they cannot but think of their starving families back home. Engagement with food as a form of solidarity emerges, then, through both eating and not eating, revealing the dynamics of self-preservation and self-sacrifice as well as community feeling. The dark message of the self-destructive nature of self-sacrifice begins when George Wilson goes to John Barton to ask him to help the Davenports. The narrative voice prefaces his sacrifice with the breakdown of families, and there-fore of community—'There were desperate fathers; there were bitter-tongued mothers (O God! what wonder!); there were reckless children; the very closest bonds of nature were snapt in that time of distress'—but goes on to elevate the sacrifices of the poor for each other, for while the 'vices of the poor sometimes astound us . . . when the secrets of all hearts shall be made known, their virtues will astound us in far greater degree' (64).

John Barton is initially dismissive, telling Wilson, 'I han got no money, I tell ye,' but his hardness cannot be sustained:

> Barton tried not to be interested, but he could not help it in spite of his gruff-ness. He rose, and went to the cupboard. . . . There lay the remains of his dinner, hastily put by ready for supper. Bread, and a slice of cold fat boiled bacon. He wrapped them in his handkerchief, put them in the crown of his hat, and said—'Come, let's be going.' (65)

Yet his sacrifice goes further than giving his meal to the Davenports; once he sees himself the extent of the Davenports' poverty, with the children desperately tearing the bread from his hands for it to 'vanish in an instant,' he goes home and pawns his own possessions in order to buy food for them, even though the Davenports are strangers to him (67). Because he sacrifices in silence, Barton is perceived as being more well-off, and his sacrifice is compounded by his being referred to as, ironically, 'the moneyed man' (70). Yet his attitude of sacrifice con-tinues to his own destruction throughout the narrative, with his opium addiction gaining strength as he refuses to accept financial help from the Union, claiming that others require it more than him, even though he himself has nothing. It is important that Barton originally tries not to be *interested* in his neighbours' plight; yet he destroys himself through his extreme lack of self-interest.

Wilson, who survives individually more successfully than Barton, is more mixed in his view of community. Unlike Barton, he is willing to ask others for help, as he does for the Davenports, but he is also willing to consume food himself when it is made available to him. He goes to Carson to seek medical help for the Davenports, and is overwhelmed by the luxuries of the Carsons' kitchen:

> The coffee steamed upon the fire, and altogether the odours were so mixed and appetising, that Wilson began to yearn for food to break his fast, which had lasted since dinner the day before. If the servants had known this, they would have willingly given him meat and bread in abundance but they were

like the rest of us, and not feeling hunger themselves, forgot it was possible another might. So Wilson's craving turned to sickness, while they chatted on, making the kitchen's free and keen remarks upon the parlour. (75)

Smell and taste are alike in that they are proximate senses that invade the body, and are so closely related that they were once thought to be the same sense. Jean-Anthelme Brillat-Savarin wrote:

> I am not only persuaded that without the participation of the sense of smell, there would be no complete taste; I am also inclined to believe that taste and smell form but one sense, of which the mouth is the laboratory and the nose the chimney; or to speak more exactly, that one sense serves to taste tactile substances, and the other to apprehend their vapors.[33]

By placing olfaction as the secondary part of the sense—the laboratory's chimney—Brillat-Savarin's perspective draws attention to the problem of when the mouth and taste are removed from the equation—when food is not consumed, but smell remains. Immanuel Kant even more provocatively observes that '[s]mell is, so to speak, taste at a distance, and other people are forced to share a scent whether they want to or not,'[34] while Smith, referring to an 1852 article in *Harper's New Monthly Magazine*, asserts that, '[u]nlike the eye and mouth, which were "well defended"— eyes could blink and mouths could shut—the nose "can not close the gates." Smells are transgressive, punching their way inside, the only real defense being not to breathe at all.'[35]

Within this context, the denial of food reveals the cruel intensity and injustice of unsatisfied hunger in the face of others' satisfaction leading to waste and excess. There is discord between nose and mouth, as the nose promises a taste that will not be experienced. David E. Sutton describes this as the 'promise of the return of the memorable whole'—that is, the wholeness of mouth and tongue sharing the experience of food;[36] and for the starving, this subtle bodily disunity expresses their lack of social agency. In the case of the Carsons' barely touched breakfast, the food is recognised by the nose—it can be smelled, but its distribution is restricted to a few—while others, like Wilson, are relentlessly reminded of their lack by virtue of their unclosable noses: there is no escape from the consciousness of social inequality. For this reason, Smith argues, '[s]mell, more than any other sense perhaps, serve[s] to create and mark the "other," at once justifying various forms of subjugation and serving as a barrier against meaningful integration into host or dominant societies.'[37] In contrast to the mouth-wateringly

---

33 Jean-Anthelme Brillat-Savarin, 'On Taste,' in *Taste Culture Reader*, ed. Korsmeyer, 15–23, 19.
34 Immanuel Kant, 'Objective and Subjective Senses: The Sense of Taste,' in *Taste Culture Reader*, ed. Korsmeyer, 209–14, 211.
35 Smith, *Smell of Battle*, 67.
36 David E. Sutton, 'Synesthesia, Memory, and the Taste of Home,' in *Taste Culture Reader*, ed. Korsmeyer, 304–16, 309.
37 Smith, *Sensory History*, 59.

torturous odours of the Carsons' breakfast table lies the 'odor associated with disease and death' that Janice Carlisle notes in the Davenports' cellar,[38] in which the smell was 'so fetid as almost to knock the two men [Barton and Wilson] down.'[39] The smell is palpable, invasive, can almost be tasted. Instead of the smell of food, this is the smell of decay; yet in neither case can olfaction be avoided, and in both it is an assault that marks social inequality. For George Wilson, the simultaneous sensory exposure and deprivation is undergirded by the emphasis on breaking his fast. Unlike the Carsons' servants, who cannot remember what it is like to be hungry, Wilson has not eaten, so to 'break fast' would be literal. The contrast is even more defined as Wilson enters 'the luxuries of the library,' where the family 'lazily enjoyed their nicely prepared food' (76). There is no sense of urgency, more of complacency, as the Carsons are cushioned by their wealth, even though their mill has burned down. Harry Carson is casually able, for instance, to pull five shillings from his pocket to give Wilson for Davenport, the same amount for which Barton had had to pawn his valuable possessions in order to procure. The nonchalance of the Carsons is disconcerting and agonising in response to the preceding scene of desolation; however, what the narrative reveals most powerfully is how their wealth not only protects them from want themselves, but shields them from having to see and acknowledge the starvation of others.

A small possibility of hope arises after Harry rides off to gaze at the 'lovely Mary Barton,' when 'the cook, who, when she had had time to think, after breakfast was sent in, had noticed [Wilson's] paleness, had had meat and bread ready to put in his hand when he came out of the parlour; and a full stomach makes every one of us more hopeful' (79). This moment is the closest *Mary Barton* comes to representing cross-class eating; however, even in the compassion of the cook, what is made clear is that there was plenty left over to give to Wilson, which hints toward waste while others are starving—and also, if the cook has 'time to think,' then surely those who have time to lazily consume their breakfast also have time on their hands. Thus they not only have the luxury of wealth for food, they have the luxury to choose not to recognise the poverty around them—they do not have to think about such unpleasant things. However, the hopefulness of a full stomach, combined with the empathy of the cook, sustains Wilson in a way that Barton denies himself. While Barton's self-sacrifice and destruction does end up bringing about some changes—empathy and understanding—the dark necessity of self-violence and violence toward others is a cruel reminder of the force of hunger.

Hungry foreigners

The narrowing of the communal vision, as well as the breakdown of community due to the perceived necessity of self-interest, is reinforced by othering foreigners; and the idea of foreignness itself becomes increasingly broad, moving

---

38 Janice Carlisle, 'The Smell of Class: British Novels of the 1860s,' *Victorian Literature and Culture*, 29.1 (2001): 1–19, 2.

39 Gaskell, *Mary Barton*, 66.

beyond people from foreign lands to people from different regions within the nation. Communities batten down the hatches, with the idea of connection itself becoming more and more scarce, to the point that even the immediate family at times is no longer recognised as a shared interest. In her reading of George Eliot's *Romola* (1862–63), Ilana M. Blumberg raises necessary questions in regard to human sympathy and community connection in economic terms: '[w]hat sort of exchange relation might match an ethical position that imagines oneself in debt to others who are not one's family but are also not sheer strangers? What sort of exchange relation would enact an authentic and appropriately measured sympathy?'[40]—questions that ultimately ask for the boundaries of community to be defined. The increasing restriction of foreignness is closely related to questions of whom the community is socially and economically responsible for, especially in times of scarcity. Against the seeming encroachment of foreignness, perceived foreignness is blamed for want, for the destructive force of self-interest, and for the continual breakdown of society, much as Dickens's *Barnaby Rudge* explores in the anti-Catholic element of the Gordon Riots. Just as mid-century Britain could face more clearly the threat of Continental revolutions but homegrown unrest was an incomprehensible, unspeakable horror, it was easier to blame others for starvation—from the Irish, to Continental migrants, to the itinerant English people who moved to look for work. The Poor Laws reinforced the closed community on the one hand, for the poor could only seek assistance from their home parish while the local community could deny any human responsibility for the poor stranger within their midst; yet on the other, as Lana Dalley and Jill Rappoport contend, the New Poor Law of 1834 'rejected traditional ideas of a parish's responsibility for its able-bodied destitute.'[41] This rejection is enabled through creating unions of parishes, thus removing the sense of *local* community in the distribution of welfare. The result is a double abdication of responsibility, first of the 'foreigners,' and then of the local, by creating distance through amalgamation. It is no longer individual parishes caring for their individuals, but an increasingly faceless body distributing without personal sympathy.

Another foreign dynamic lay, however, in the prosperous foreign migrant who could not empathise with the local poor. Fears of foreign investment, of the local community being milked dry to compound the wealth of those who are not committed to the life of the people of the community, arises alongside concerns of being overwhelmed by impoverished foreigners straining the already beleaguered labour market. In the next chapter I examine the perspective of the itinerant and the poor migrant; here, I am concerned with the inability of the foreigner (using the term loosely) to buy into the *community*, as much as they may economically engage with produce and the market in the geographical area in which they have invested. This lack of communal engagement is another form of luxury, as seen in the opening of Martineau's *French Wines and Politics*, in the conversation between

---

40 Ilana M. Blumberg, 'Beyond the Cash Nexus in George Eliot's *Romola*,' in *Economic Women*, ed. Dalley and Rappoport, 60–74, 69.
41 Lana L. Dalley and Jill Rappoport, Introduction, in *Economic Women*, 1–21, 4–5.

the business associates Steele, who is English, and Antoine, a French winemaker. Their relationship speaks to the fluidity between England and France in terms of travel and business, reminding Martineau's English readership that what happens in France has a direct impact on England's economy. Steele, Antoine, and Antoine's brother, Charles, provide the voices of rational political economy in the text, yet what becomes evident in their respective situations is that all three do so from a position of luxury. Steele has the luxury of being a foreigner—he can pass uninformed judgement on the French peasantry, casting them as lazy and careless. It is one thing, however, for the foreigner to make such an assessment on a business trip, but the injustice is heightened when the foreigner relocates and makes such assumptions about the locals. The implications of ownership and national identity come into play in a similar vein as colonisation—the foreigner is able to buy property and move to the new land, but does not possess the cultural heritage of the area: *that* belongs to the local community. In *Shirley*, this lack on the part of the 'foreigner' is most evident in Robert Moore's opinion of the English workers, whom he consistently refers to as the 'hands' as though they might be machines in his factory, but it is also evident in the young clergymen who have moved to the region, and is contrasted by Shirley's determined and deliberate investment in the community as a greater priority than her own property.

Shirley opens with the clergy's excess and abuse of hospitality being interrupted by news of the starved desperation of the machine breakers. This juxtaposition of abuse on one hand and violence on the other nuances the locus of moral violation in a way that persists throughout the novel. However, at the same time, the luddites can be seen as (albeit unlawfully) defending their local rights, whereas the curates' excess and carelessness disconnects them further from the community they have entered. This distinction is crucial because it supports E.P. Thompson's view of 'crowd action' containing 'some legitimating notion . . . the men and women in the crowd were informed by the belief that they were defending traditional rights or customs; and, in general, that they were supported by the wider consensus of the community.'[42] The 'foreigners' are also, then, the moral outsiders in contrast to those in the community who are positioned as maintaining social heritage. The rudeness of the curates reinforces their lack of belonging in a way that isolates them from empathy:

> Mr Sweeting is mincing the slice of roast beef on his plate, and complaining that it is very tough; Mr Donne says the beer is flat. Ay! that is the worst of it: if they would only be civil, Mrs Gale wouldn't mind it so much; if they would only seem satisfied with what they get, she wouldn't care, but 'these young parsons is so high and so scornful, they set everybody beneath their "fit"; they treat her with less than civility, just because she doesn't keep a servant, but does the work of the house herself, as her mother did afore her: then they were always speaking against Yorkshire ways and Yorkshire folk,' and by

42 Thompson, 'Moral Economy,' 78.

that very token Mrs Gale does not believe one of them to be a real gentleman, or come of gentle kin. (41)

The rudeness or incivility regarding the meal is measured against the distance of the men's origin, suggesting a direct correlation between the remoteness of their right to belong in the community and their manners. Mr Malone, the 'native of the land of shamrocks and potatoes,' is presented as the most hateful of the curates in the arrogant manner in which he first demands 'More bread!' and then commands Mrs Gale, 'Cut it, woman' (41–42). Malone is doubly displaced in terms of community and heritage, linking him to the Anglo-Irish gentry who were commonly despised as abdicating their landowning responsibilities. However, Sweeting, Donne, and Malone are equally included in the self-serving definition, exercising their 'good appetites' around their insults of the provision, their style of devouring compared to 'leaves before locusts' (42). The ironic reference to a biblical plague, figured through a raucous meal, positions the narrative in terms of disinterested colonisation, and offensive excess in the face of starvation.

Allusions to unequal distribution and want figure through much of the narrative, with the 'glutted' foreign markets and the trade restrictions due to war alliances to which Brontë attributes much of the scarcity in her novel:

> The 'Orders of Council,' provoked by Napoleon's Milan and Berlin decrees, and forbidding neutral powers to trade with France, had, by offending America, cut off the principal market of the Yorkshire woollen trade, and brought it consequently to the verge of ruin. Minor foreign markets were glutted, and would receive no more: the Brazils, Portugal, Sicily, were all overstocked by nearly two years' consumption. (61)

Brontë adds the technological developments and bad harvests to the complexities of the national economic situation, but what becomes particularly evident is that, in spite of the uneasy relationships between the community and 'foreigners,' it is necessary to maintain these relationships with other nations in order to survive as a community. As much as the community experiencing scarcity narrows in its parochialism, it must be acknowledged that what happens beyond the borders of the village or town impacts the people within: they cannot escape the foreignness they seek to shut out. The desire to distance oneself from unrest or discontent resembles the relegation of violence to history; protest is diffused by foreignising the places where it takes place. Brontë writes:

> [t]he throes of a sort of moral earthquake were felt heaving under the hills of the northern counties. But, as is usual in such cases, nobody took much notice . . . some local measures were or were not taken by the local magistracy . . . newspaper paragraphs were written on the subject, and there the thing stopped. (61)

Like the luxury the Carsons have to not see the poverty of their workers, by this kind of apathetic distancing, the northern counties become in a sense foreign, as though what happens there does not impact the rest of the nation. This is an extension of the displacement of unrest onto the Continent, but a way of rationalising home unrest that cannot be so easily geographically displaced. More importantly, if the starving are considered 'foreign,' they are less the responsibility of the home community. Even so, these psychological tricks are overturned by the crucial fact that foreign markets and situations—regardless of how 'foreign' they actually are—do impact the home community, and the desired separation is therefore ultimately impossible.

Gaskell's *North and South* contends with similar concerns regarding foreignness and community impact. The Crimean War, which was occurring when Gaskell wrote *North and South*, had astonishing effects in terms of breaking down longstanding lines of national division, such as through England's alliance with France against Russia. Stefanie Markovits argues that while it does not talk directly about the war, Gaskell's text is highly influenced by it.[43] The civil unrest Gaskell represents reflects, and is perhaps exacerbated by, the greater international crisis England was facing. There was a growing discourse in which the external war and the threats of civil unrest spoke to each other, worsened by the breakdown of community due, to a large extent, to poverty and forced mobility. Within the need to hold fiercely to a sense of parochial identity, the internal unrest was written in terms of war. In 1864, Matthew Arnold would write:

> the provincial spirit . . . does not persuade, it makes war; it has not urbanity, the tone of the city, of the centre, the tone which always aims at a spiritual and intellectual effect, and not excluding the use of banter, never disjoins banter itself from politeness, from felicity. But the provincial tone is more violent . . . it loves hard-hitting rather than persuading.[44]

In Gaskell's text, provincial warfare dominates the entire geography of the nation, causing the conflict to seem even more localised. Alongside this move, the term 'foreigner' is used repeatedly, not just for the imported Irish 'knobsticks,'[45] but also for those who move from the South of England to the North. Indeed, *North and South* seems overrun with domestic foreignness, with most of the mobile characters being termed foreign at some time or other. Although the South is part of the same nation, it is written in terms of a different country, with different cultural values, social and political systems, and language. Gaskell's vision of national reconciliation, ironically in the depersonalising, foreignising industrial town of Milton-Northern, is perhaps stated somewhat sentimentally through Nicholas Higgins's comment to Margaret Hale: 'And yet, yo see, North and South

43 See Stefanie Markovits, 'North and South, East and West: Elizabeth Gaskell, the Crimean War, and the Condition of England,' *Nineteenth-Century Literature* 59.4 (2005): 463–93.

44 Matthew Arnold, 'The Literary Influence of Academies' (1864), in *Lectures and Essays in Criticism*, vol. 3, ed. R.H. Super (Ann Arbor: University of Michigan Press, 1986), 249.

45 Elizabeth Gaskell, *North and South* (1854–55; London: Penguin, 1995), 233.

has both met and made kind o' friends in this big smoky place' (73). Neither Nicholas nor Margaret is originally from Milton—both are, in a sense, foreigners, although it is Nicholas who calls Margaret foreign because he is, at least, from the North—yet Milton is the place of connection, and ultimately where foreignness is left behind for community investment.

The fluidity of foreignness in both *North and South* and *Shirley* is at once problematic and productive because it enables greater possibilities of cultural and national hybridity. In Gaskell's text, hybridity is ultimately positive. Thornton and Nicholas are both described in terms attributable to monstrosity or hybridity in Darwinian evolutionary terms, with their individual abilities to adapt linked to the progress of the community. Nicholas describes Thornton as 'two chaps . . . bound up in one body,' while Nicholas speaks of Thornton staring at him 'as if [he] were some strange beast newly caught in some of the zones' (331). They therefore resonate with Darwin's ideas of natural selection and variety:

> As many more individuals of each species are born than can possibly survive; and as, consequently, there is a frequently recurring struggle for existence, if follows that any being, if it vary however slightly in any manner profitable to itself, under the complex and sometimes varying conditions of life, will have a better chance of surviving, and thus be *naturally selected*. From the strong principle of inheritance, any selected variety will tend to propagate its new and modified form.[46]

Within the context of political economy, this reading creates an uneasy alliance between self-interest and the community. Patricia Ingham observes that Thornton focuses on 'the "intra-species" struggle,' which is more Malthusian than Darwinian,[47] when he talks of employers being 'trampled down by his fellows in their haste to get rich';[48] yet a significant part of Thornton's development in the novel is the way in which he begins to look across classes to recognise and empathise with his workers. Nicholas shows his willingness to adapt by planning to move to the South in order to find work, although Margaret talks him out of it, as well as in his determination to find equal footing with Thornton. As hybrid characters, Thornton and Nicholas are at the centre of adaptation, and therefore play significant parts in overcoming conceptions of foreignness.

Yet the difference with Thornton's relationship to Higgins is that they are both from the North. Brontë's Robert Moore is in many ways like Thornton in the earlier parts of Gaskell's narrative: both men see themselves as having struggled to gain their current positions, and take the liberal approach that it is therefore possible for anyone to achieve that position, if they choose to work toward it.

---

46 Charles Darwin, *On the Origin of Species by Natural Selection* (1859; Mineola, New York: Dover, 2006), 3.
47 Patricia Ingham, Introduction to *North and South* (London: Penguin, 1995), xxi.
48 Gaskell, *North and South*, 151.

Thornton speaks of his sacrificing his education in order to overcome poverty in harsh terms that reflect the intensity of his determination: 'I was too busy to think about any dead people, with the living pressing alongside of me, neck to neck, in the struggle for bread' (86). Both Thornton and Moore lack compassion, then, for the poor, in favour of their own interests and that of their immediate families. Moore, however, is more definitively Other by being

> but half a Briton. . . . A hybrid in nature, it is probable he had a hybrid's feeling on many points—patriotism for one; it was likely he was unapt to attach himself to parties, to sects, even to climes and customs; it is not impossible that he had a tendency to isolate himself from any community amidst which his lot might temporarily happen to be thrown, and that he felt it to be his best wisdom to push the interests of Robert Gérard Moore, to the exclusion of philanthropic consideration for general interests: with which he regarded the said Gérard Moore as in a great measure discon-nected. Trade was Mr Moore's hereditary calling: the Gérards of Antwerp had been merchants for two centuries back. (60)

Both Thornton and Moore come from a background of poverty, and therefore contend with Nunokawa's memory of loss and the fear that times of scarcity will return. When Moore tells Caroline that poverty is 'necessarily selfish, contracted, grovelling, anxious' (99), it is important to note that he perceives himself on the brink of poverty, and is therefore justifying his own self-interest. However, Moore's response of self-isolation and not being willing to adapt to Yorkshire limits his progress in the community. Although he is a 'semi-foreigner' (62), he seeks to avoid starvation through distancing himself further from the locals. For him, the fear of poverty is very real, for he has speculations outstanding as well as having 'risked the last of his capital' in order to buy the machinery that the luddites destroy (64). He therefore looks for stability by aligning himself with his heritage that lies in Antwerp, not Yorkshire—a heritage of centuries of trade. Crucially he looks for stability through cultural heritage, even though he is physi-cally removed from it.

Moore's choice of Belgium is reinforced in the food choices of his house-hold, demonstrated through his sister's housekeeping. Both Robert and Hortense express their connection to their Belgian heritage through taste, holding onto national foods as well as food preparation. Carlisle observes the way in which country cooking—that is, tastes of home—can be read as 'nostalgia . . . [which] is clearly linked to abundance.'[49] For Robert and Hortense, it is evident that their need to hold onto the Belgian tastes as superior is imperative to their memories of abundance and desire to maintain their sense of prosperity, regardless of their economic instability. While Hortense's English maid Sarah serves the Belgian food with a facial expression suggesting 'I never dished such stuff i' my life

---

49 Carlisle, 'Smell of Class,' 9.

afore; it's not fit for dogs' (105), Hortense's pride in the meal is such that had Caroline 'evinced any disrelish thereof, such manifestation would have injured her in Mademoiselle's good graces for ever; a positive crime might have been more easily pardoned than a symptom of distaste for the foreign comestibles' (106). However, even amidst this pride there is a sense of lack, for Hortense has to substitute 'dried pease' [*sic*] for her soup with 'bitter lamentations' because 'in this desolate country of England no haricot beans were to be had' (105). To an extent, the loss of choice in taste that Hortense experiences reveals her own sense of displacement and a kind of cultural impoverishment; but at the same time, it is an unpalatable shadow of the decivilisation of the Yorkshire poor for whom taste is not even a consideration—they are fortunate to receive that which is provided in William Farren's home: 'it was only porridge, and too little of that' (158).

Self-othering through the rhetoric of foreignness, as seen particularly in Hortense's idealisation of Belgian food and disdain for anything English, is used to promote self-interest. While Adam Smith saw the limits of self-interest, the ideal of political economy was that if human beings pursued their 'rational self-interest' (with the critical emphasis on 'rational'), it would lead to 'economic optimality and market equilibrium for society in general.'[50] Gordon Bigelow has shown the way in which *North and South* expresses the development of this kind of equilibrium in the midst of industrialised selfishness,[51] but at the same time, the poverty and scarcity of Gaskell's Milton refuses to ignore the competitive, often destructive, angst necessitated by the 'survival of the fittest' construct. Similarly, Brontë calls rationality into question through the way in which Caroline questions Robert in regard to his attitude toward the Yorkshire poor, significantly educating him through readings of the iconically English Shakespeare. Gaskell and Brontë bring to the fore the most powerful tension within social progress: utilitarianism and the future growth of the community, city, and nation, versus the value of the immediate individual. The broad desires set within an international context become focalised through narratives of specific voices, competing for conflicting agendas. Within this understanding, then, the power of the voices, and their capacity to be heard, become central in the hunger for belonging.

Civilised voices unheard

While Ellmann addresses self-starvation and protest, her study does not fully address the limitations of choice: self-starvation is complicated by prices and having to choose what is affordable; parents choosing to feed their children but not having enough to also feed themselves; and also guilt preventing people from being able to eat, even when there is food in front of them, because they

---

50 Gagnier, *Insatiability of Human Wants*, 25.
51 Gordon Bigelow, *Fiction, Famine, and the Rise of Economics in Victorian Britain and Ireland* (Cambridge: Cambridge University Press, 2003), 174.

cannot help their consciousness of those who are going without. Kathryn Gleadle addresses these concerns, looking at the food shortages at the turn of the century, focusing particularly on the diaries and records of Katherine Plymley. Plymley, as a member of the gentry, belonged to a family that, unlike the portrayal of the wealthy in *Mary Barton*, dared to face their relative prosperity within a community that was in want. She recognised the 'implications of the moral economy for personal consumption,' was horrified by 'what she perceived to be the shocking waste of food in elite households,' and was inspired by William Paley's *Principles of Moral and Political Philosophy* (1785) to hold to the edict that 'the poor had a right to basic levels of subsistence, and that the rich had a duty to limit their diet so as to provide for them.'[52] However, alongside Katherine Plymley's moderate approach, she recounts her niece, Jane, literally starving herself to death out of guilt for the starving poor:

> 'Her idea . . . was that the poor were obliged to live upon very little, yet they not only did live but work'd. She believed herself undeserving of more than wou'd support nature in health, and she thought from the example of the lower orders that a very little would do that.' Jane, recorded her aunt, 'thought very highly of the general character of the poor and very lowly of herself.'[53]

The Plymleys were perhaps rare in their social consciousness, a remnant of feudal paternalism, yet they also represent the sense of moral responsibility that existed within the national consciousness, perhaps lost to a greater degree by the 1840s through the entrenchment of political economy's macroeconomic approach. Gleadle's research draws out the social counternarrative that resisted the extreme interpretations of political economy in an attempt to reinstate community consciousness and responsibility. While Jane Plymley's death seems extreme and a waste of life, it also 'register[s] an engagement with the economic crisis unfolding around her,'[54] regardless of how disturbing the result may be. It is perhaps even more disturbing to note the loss of this sense of communal responsibility in the wake of the entrenchment of capitalist liberalism in the middle of the century, leading to the self-interest so prevalent in Gaskell's Manchester tale.

One of the recurring images of self-starvation, as an alternative to Ellmann's construction, is that of the poor feeding others out of their own want, to their own detriment, as John Barton does. While this kind of sacrifice works to re-create broken communities, both Harriet Martineau and Elizabeth Gaskell critique the necessity for this kind of sacrifice to take place within the context of political economy, as well as the inevitable self-destruction that still occurs. Sacrificial self-destruction stands in opposition to the conditioned passivity, even apathy, in the face of oppression and abuse, growing out of the fear of repercussions if one

52 Gleadle, 'Gentry, Gender, and the Moral Economy,' 34–35.
53 Qtd in Gleadle, 'Gentry, Gender, and the Moral Economy,' 36–37.
54 Gleadle, 'Gentry, Gender, and the Moral Economy,' 36.

retaliates. The silencing of characters reinforces their powerlessness; and so when the mob gains some power, they reinforce it by silencing others. For example, in Martineau's *French Wines and Politics*, the impact of the revolutionary voice is dependent on being heard by those holding political authority. Although the king, residing in Versailles, has been told that the Bastille has been taken, he does not comprehend the seriousness of the situation because he cannot hear the rebellion himself. He can still 'sleep the whole night without hearing the drums and larums which kept all Paris awake; and could not therefore believe that all would not come right.'[55] Gaskell directly addresses the importance of being heard, expressly stating in her preface to *Mary Barton* that her explicit purpose in writing the novel is to give voice to the starving. In *Mary Barton*, Gaskell very deliberately privileges the voices of the workers in the narrative—that is, for the readers—but it is crucial in the text that she emphasises, through those figures, that their voices are not heard by those in authority. Indeed, although John Barton's voice is privileged in the text, he is not properly heard until the end of the novel when he confesses to Mr Carson that he is the one who murdered Harry. It is at this point that the dialogue is finally opened between classes, providing a dark suggestion, put forward in much of the literature of riots and revolution, that brute force is necessary to being heard, thereby providing a kind of rationale for violence.

In *Mary Barton* this violence comes as a last resort after a delegation of starving men go to London to take a petition to the House of Commons, unsuccessfully pleading for reform. Not only are the men refused entry into the House, they are stopped *en route* by a procession of carriages on their way to have tea with the Queen. The men are turned into a spectacle, a form of entertainment, as they are ridiculed and whipped for getting in the way of the Queen's guests' pleasure. This response is all the more poignant, given that many of the starving men, being provided with the meal in Holborn to gird them on their way to Westminster, found that they could not eat any of it. Gaskell deliberately juxtaposes these two meals—the untouched meal of the men and the delayed tea with the Queen—by having John tell Mary that theirs was 'such a spread for a breakfast as th' Queen herself might ha' sitten down to. . . . There were mutton kidneys, and sausages, and broiled ham, and fried beef and onions; more like a dinner nor a breakfast' (114). For these men, 'such a set of thin, wan, wretched-looking chaps as they were' (115), this was a feast beyond comprehension; yet the unspoken suggestion of the narrative is that the Queen's guests would be dining on—and actually eating—unimaginable delicacies.

The procession of delegates begins as a rational response to reports that 'the very existence of their distress had been denied in parliament,' and that 'they could not believe that government knew of their misery: they rather chose to think it possible that men could voluntarily assume the office of legislators for a nation who were ignorant of its real state' (97). The narrative suggests that the Manchester men are irrational only in that they naïvely think the best of Parliament. Unlike the protesters and revolutionaries in other texts, these men exemplify civilised

---

55 Martineau, *French Wines and Politics*, 100.

behaviour. Barton recounts: '"Well, we could na get on for these carriages, though we waited and waited. Th' horses were too fat to move quick; they never known want of food, one might tell by their sleek coats; and police pushed us back when we tried to cross"' (116). Yet let alone the revelation that the horses are better fed than the men of Manchester, the brutality of the police and coachmen places the men lower than the animals. Barton tries to reason with the police:

> 'And why are we to be molested,' asks I, 'going decently about our business, which is life and death to us, and many a little one clemming at home in Lancashire? What business is of most consequence i' the sight o' God, think yo, our'n or them gran' ladies and gentlemen as yo think so much on?' (116)

Yet he speaks without effect: '"But I might as well ha' held my peace, for he only laughed"' (116).

Even Barton's account gives a sense of distance to this event, the delegates presented as a group of starving men in contrast to an unseen monarch. The tone of narrative reflects the removed view of Parliament. Although the men seek to articulate their hunger to Parliament in a rational, reasoned manner, rather than being heard, they are turned into an amusing display. The visual impact of hunger on their bodies, when removed to the South, is not recognised with compassion and sympathy, but rather with a sense of annoyance and inconvenience. However, earlier in the text, the realities of starvation are presented very intimately in the death of Barton's son:

> Every thing, the doctor said, depended on good nourishment. . . . Mocking words! when the commonest food in the house would not furnish one little meal. . . . Hungry himself, almost to an animal pitch of ravenousness, but with the bodily pain swallowed up in anxiety for his little sinking lad, he stood at one of the shop windows where all edible luxuries are displayed; haunches of venison, Stilton cheeses, moulds of jelly—all appetising sights to the common passer-by. And out of this shop came Mrs Hunter! She crossed to her carriage, followed by the shopman loaded with purchases for a party. The door was quickly slammed to, and she drove away; and Barton returned home with a bitter spirit of wrath in his heart, to see his only boy a corpse! (25)

The devastating helplessness of Barton's situation, juxtaposed with the prosperity of the Hunters, provides a cruel explanation for Barton's future demise. The co-existing worlds of the wealthy and the workers remain separate until Barton's violence penetrates the divide by assassinating Harry Carson. Yet at the point of Barton's son's death, the wealthy are able to remain oblivious to the suffering around them—it is not a part of their world.

In order to maintain that distinction from the poor, social narratives arise that marginalise and blame the working classes for their situation, a functional narrative that persists beyond the nineteenth century. In the late twentieth century, looking back at the nineteenth, historian Val R. Lorwin referred to 'the sense of injustice' that grew 'out of the qualities of economic growth: the character of entrepreneurship, the distribution of income, and—even more—the nature of employer authority.'[56] However, this perspective does not account fully for the very real effects of economic inequalities on individual human beings and families. Within liberal ideologies, it is convenient to determine that all have the potential to achieve success and prosperity, and that it therefore follows that all are responsible for their current position. This perspective, though, does not fully appreciate the unevenness of privilege at the starting point. Gaskell's John Thornton revels in a liberal hard line, stating that

> 'some of these early manufacturers did ride to the devil in magnificent style—crushing human bone and flesh under their horses' hoofs without remorse. But by-and-by came a re-action; there were more factories, more masters; more men were wanted. The power of masters and men became more evenly balanced.' (84)

He goes on to say:

> 'It is one of the great beauties of our system, that a working-man may raise himself into the power and position of a master by his own exertions and behaviour; that, in fact every one who rules himself to decency and sobriety of conduct, and attention to his duties, comes over to our ranks: . . . one on the side of authority and order.' (84)

Essentially Thornton's faith in this self-regulating market proves ineffectual and he himself is reformed. Higgins is permitted to make this transition to an extent, but the mobility between classes is very limited and rare. However, it is important to note Thornton's claim that such progression is predicated on sobriety. Apart from the fact that Bessy Higgins remarks to Margaret Hale that she worries when her father, Nicholas, drinks too much, thereby overturning the apparent need for sobriety, Thornton's view buys into the idea that the working classes are poor because they spend their money on alcohol. Mr Hale also notes that they live hand-to-mouth, and yet they seem to have luxurious homes relative to their poor counterparts in the South: 'I see furniture here which our labourers would never have thought of buying, and food commonly used which they would consider lux-uries' (158). Mr Hale's inability to understand the manner in which the working class live works to reinforce the marginalisation of the poor as abusers of alcohol and other substances as a way of deflecting social injustice—they are set apart as uncivilised, not truly members of society, and, most importantly, not rational.

The political significance of wine is made evident in the title of Martineau's *French Wines and Politics*—wine is a part of France's national identity, something

---

56 Val R. Lorwin, 'Working-Class Politics and Economic Development in Western Europe,' *The American Historical Review*, 63.2 (1968): 338–51, 342.

that is explored in more detail decades later in Dickens's *A Tale of Two Cities*, in which Defarge's wine shop is the centre of community and political scheming, much like the public house in Britain. In George Eliot's *Felix Holt*, it is crucial to defend the breweries, wine vaults, and public houses during the riot, while in Dickens's *Barnaby Rudge*, one of the key events is when the Maypole, a public house, is invaded by the rioters. This kind of invasion speaks to the breakdown of community—it is a sacrilegious attack on a meeting place. However, the connection to alcohol goes further in two key directions: first, it speaks to alcoholism, and the fact that, like opium abuse, alcoholism became rife amongst the poor because alcohol was cheaper than food, and had the added benefit of dulling hunger pains. Its intoxicating effect provided a cheap escape. This is an aspect that both Martineau and Gaskell explore, Martineau in *Sowers Not Reapers*, in which Mrs Kay has become addicted to laudanum in order to save food for her children (although she says that this addiction is a return to her infancy, when her mother had given her laudanum to dull her hunger), and Gaskell through John Barton, who ends up not being able to eat, only taking opium, even after food becomes available, believing strongly that others need the food available more than he does. In both these cases, the memory of childhood hunger comes into play, becoming a type of hunger within itself.

Second, however, inebriation was seen to add courage to destructive, violent behaviour; and while not denying this power, there was a sense of blaming the alcohol for social chaos, as a way of rationalising it—it was a way of protecting the idea of civilisation, rather than having to face the fact that human members of society chose to behave in a riotous or uncivilised manner. John Barton is necessarily under the influence both when he murders Harry, and when he confesses to Carson. What is really crucial, though, is that in many of the texts that address alcohol and riots, the narrative describes the rioters as 'half tipsy' or the like—therefore, not completely out of their senses, clearly able to make decisions, and often with a very precise, uninhibited aim. Furthermore, the demands of the crowd tended to be complex, showing a rationality of thought. Peter Jones comments on protesting crowds in the 1830s in particular, stating that they 'rarely, if ever, requested higher wages or set out to destroy threshing machines alone. Instead, they expressed a series of interrelated demands which can only be properly understood when taken together.'[57] It is more dangerous to suggest that there is a rationale behind both the violence and the alcoholism, an idea that is expressed throughout Gaskell's and Martineau's work, because rational claims made by thoughtful men and women are not so easily dismissed as the shouting protests of a demoniac inebriated crowd. The addiction to violence and alcohol becomes another form of hunger, however, a physical need to consume; and indeed the opening context of drought and thirst in Martineau's *Sowers Not Reapers* brings thirst—a desire closely connected to hunger—to the fore of devastation.

After dealing with the nature and power of hunger in *The Physiology of Common Life*, George Henry Lewes goes on to discuss thirst as 'a disturbance far more

---

57 Jones, 'Swing, Speenhamland and Rural Social Relations,' 275.

terrible than that of starvation.'[58] He argues that 'the sensation of Thirst is never agreeable, no matter how slight it may be, and in this respect is unlike Hunger, which, in its incipient state of Appetite, is decidedly agreeable.'[59] In this sense, thirst takes on a character of an extreme greater than hunger with no redeeming qualities; and it is within this despairing context that Martineau's text is framed. The publication of *Sowers Not Reapers* emerges in the wake of the 1830 Swing Riots, which began with machine breaking, and intensified into the destruction of any objects of perceived oppression, including workhouses, barns full of grain, rick burning, and even the maiming of cattle. In this text, the communities that the rioters belong to are marked not just by hunger, but by 'the more urgent evil of thirst.'[60] The opening scene is one of dislocation and a fragmented community, as

> [o]thers were also abroad, with the view of relieving their hardships instead of seeking to avenge them. The dwellers on high grounds were so far worse off than the inhabitants of the valleys, that they could not quench their thirst, and lost in sleep their weariness and their apprehensions of hunger. (297)

The devastation due to lack of rain is intensified by Mrs Kay's memories of abundance: 'When I used to have my fill of meat every day, I little thought that the bread I ate with it would grow scarce among us,' an account she gives to her sister-in-law, Mary, as they trespass onto the property of Warden, the miller, in order to take water from his spring (299). Barriers of laws and boundaries of property are broken down in this community that has been devastated by drought, but the sympathetic response to trespassing is what prevents the ultimate devastation of this community's spirit.

The tragedy of Mrs Kay's situation is exacerbated by her alcoholism. It is telling that, while there is no water to drink, let alone replenish the fields, there is access to alcohol. She confesses to her husband that she drinks to dull the pain of hunger, but like John Barton, her addiction overtakes her: even when food is offered, she is unable to eat. Her husband tries to rally her, suggesting that with 'good food' she will recover, and offers to watch over her to prevent her drinking, but she responds: '"I shall never relish food more; but I will try; and do you as you said. I am not sure how I shall mind it in such a case; I never can tell any thing beforehand now. But you know your part; and if I fall back, you must all mind me as little as you can"' (354). Mrs Kay succumbs to her addiction in the end; and her hopeless *ennui* in this conversation reveals the desolation of unquenchable thirst, displayed with bitter irony through the liquid more readily available than water. Along the lines of Lewes's view of thirst, in many ways *Sowers Not Reapers* portrays the most lethargic, hopeless state of society; but at the same time

---

58 Lewes, *Physiology of Common Life*, 31.
59 Ibid., 40.
60 Harriet Martineau, *Sowers Not Reapers* (London: Charles Fox, 1833), in *Illustrations of Political Economy: Selected Tales*, ed. Deborah Logan (Toronto: Broadview Press, 2004), 295–382, 297.

it offers a very human approach to community restoration, one that is founded on recognising the humanity of others, empathising with the poor, and working in a practical sense to restore a sense of belonging and cohesiveness to the community.

Cooperatives and compassion

The mid-nineteenth century's intellectual push toward communism in the wake of the demise of feudalism, the rise of mercantile capitalism, and the hard lines of political economy, failed to resist the reign of self-interest, and as such fell short of the expectations of public intellectuals like George Henry Lewes and John Stuart Mill. In his *Principles of Political Economy* (1848), Mill sets up a strange kind of democratic communism as the ideal social organisation, arguing for a 'Communist association' in which 'every member of the association would be amenable to the most universal, and one of the strongest, of personal motives, that of public opinion,' but acknowledges that the re-education of society would be necessary to bring about such order.[61] Lewes contends with this kind of ideal:

> the systems of Communism so confidently promulgated attract the attention of most thinkers. But can any system of Communism yet devised be accepted as an efficient solution of the social problem? . . . Communism is simply a *political* solution of a problem which embraces far deeper and higher questions than politics.[62]

Even more strongly, he adds, 'Just where man most obviously rises above the bee, Communism leaves him to the care of *Priests and Teachers*, who cannot agree among themselves!'[63] Both realise the impracticability of applying such a doctrine to the dynamics of society. While neither Gaskell nor Martineau is a proponent of communism, their narratives explore the practical possibilities available through cooperatives between classes, simultaneously recognising humanity across the classes. While they both write of economic inequalities in terms of class, their literary narratives have the scope to bring individual humanity to the classes, rather than statistics of poverty and starvation, or theory-based arguments over the production and distribution of wealth. In this way, they both critique the agenda and potential outcomes of political economy through their fictions.

It is not until Mr Carson recognises his likeness to John Barton—that they both grieve for a lost son—that he can forgive his son's murderer. It is crucial that he prays with Barton, 'Forgive *us* our trespasses,'[64] acknowledging his own fault,

61 John Stuart Mill, *Principles of Political Economy with Some of their Applications to Social Philosophy* (1848; 7th edn, 1871; Oxford: Oxford University Press, 1994), 12.
62 George Henry Lewes, *Comte's Philosophy of the Sciences: Being an Exposition of the Principles of the Cours de Philosophie Positive of Auguste Comte* (London: Henry G. Bohn, 1853), 11–12.
63 Ibid., 12.
64 Gaskell, *Mary Barton*, 438, emphasis added.

wrapped up in the fault of his class. This is a difficult moment in the narrative, as Gaskell navigates between justification for violence and sympathy for why the crime was committed. Crucially, Carson recognises the poverty and hunger of Barton, relating to it from his own impoverished childhood, but also realising that it was so much more dire than anything he had experienced. Up to this point, Carson was entirely unaware of the extent of the poverty amongst his workers; the effects on him had merely been to cut back on a few luxuries, and he was essentially rewarded with more leisure to spend time with his family after his mill burned down. Rather than rationalising poverty by claiming that everyone had had to make cuts, he is forced to acknowledge that his wealth protected him from despair. In this way, Carson can be seen as a redeemed version of the Marquis in Martineau's *French Wines*, who is brought into compelling contrast with the starving 'pitiless mob' who try to force-feed him the soiled flour.

The moment of recognition for Carson, although occurring too late in the text, is similar to Thornton's acknowledgement of Higgins's manliness in *North and South*. Thornton shakes Nicholas's hand after offering him work. Their earlier exchange had been fuelled by animosity and the disdain of the other's respective class, yet when Thornton hears of Nicholas's determination to see him, his humility, and his resolve to care for Boucher's children, he gains respect for Nicholas. He recognises his own spirit of determination in him, and it is through relating to him, by beginning to recognise sameness, that cross-class understanding and appreciation begins. Neither of them can be 'gentlemen' in the Southern sense of the word, but nor would they wish it. They are both 'men' according to Thornton's definition. For Thornton, manliness is to do with character—endurance, strength, and faith—rather than appearance, reputation, or social position.[65] In this sense, it is possible for one of any class to be a man; manliness is based more on merit and personal achievement than on heredity. He recognises this kind of manliness in Nicholas. Thornton and Nicholas are, therefore, equal, which marks the changing times within England's social structure. Their handshake is a sign of mutual understanding, of mutual respect, as they make their agreement between men, rather than as master and worker.

By bringing together Thornton and Higgins, the animosity between the two classes in the North is effectively mediated. From the moment of their handshake, Thornton and Higgins's relationship only grows in respect and appreciation, shown in that, when Thornton has to close his mill, Nicholas is at the forefront of getting the names of the men who would be willing to work for him, should he at any stage be a master again. The importance of their relationship to the progress of the entire community is shown when together they come up with the idea of the dining room co-op for the factory workers so that they have better quality food. Thornton himself eats with the workers in the dining room, which reinforces the sense of communion and equality between them. He gets to know them as men, rather than as enemies. As Mr Bell states, there's 'nothing like the act of eating

---

65 Gaskell, *North and South*, 163.

for equalizing men' (354). While possibly seen as a breakdown of social structure, which could be chaotic, this communion is necessary to social progress. Separation had led to misunderstanding and animosity, strikes, and starvation, while communion leads to understanding and productivity. Yet the encounter is not only important for economic productivity; the sense of humanity, of human interest—of the individual amid the mass—is brought to the fore, through the change in both Thornton and his workers:

> He and they had led parallel lives—very close, but never touching—till the accident (or so it seemed) of his acquaintance with Higgins. Once brought face to face, man to man, with an individual of the masses around him, and (take notice) out of the character of master and workman, in the first instance, they had each begun to recognize that 'we have all of us one human heart.' (409)

It is this adaptation that is necessary for the survival of the manufacturing species in the North. Unlike the requirement in *Mary Barton* of a violent murder to break down the barriers between classes, Thornton and Higgins find a cooperative way to effect the same change.

In neither text, however, is the transition to understanding and empathy smooth. While Carson individually has a change of heart, it cannot be ignored that the wealthy business and landowners problematically cry poverty and decivilisation at the cutbacks to luxuries as though for them to be deprived in this way is a threat to the stability of the nation. Similarly in *North and South*, the Thorntons still have their banquet in spite of the strike in order to maintain the narrative of stability amongst their business associates. Gleadle, for instance, remarks that the socially conscious Plymleys economised 'so that they could continue to display a certain level of financial well-being in other regards' because this 'gave them authority and status within the community.'[66] Thornton's dinner allows him to perform social authority, while at the same time giving him the opportunity to discuss the crisis with the other factory owners, and it is crucial that he does so with hospitality in order to create as affable an atmosphere as possible, given the tense situation and differences of opinion. Margaret Hale does not understand this motive, finding 'the number of delicacies oppressive'; but 'it was one of Mrs Thornton's rigorous laws of hospitality, that of each separate dainty enough should be provided for all the guests to partake, if they felt inclined,' and 'her son shared this feeling' (159). By providing for their alimental wants with abundant equality, psychologically the guests would be less likely to feel the need to push forward their own economic agenda in the business discussions. And while in the context of the business relationship this kind of narrative is important, Robert Moore also raises the vital point in *Shirley*, 'would my bankruptcy put bread in your hungry children's mouths?'[67] The destruction of businesses by

---

66 Gleadle, 'Gentry, Gender, and the Moral Economy,' 31.
67 Brontë, *Shirley*, 157.

luddism or by strikes evidently only creates more devastation and starvation. In *Mary Barton*, though, Gaskell powerfully draws out the injustice that the starving working classes see in the comparable luxury in which the mill-owning class is able to continue, while most potently contrasting such luxury with the self-destruction of the poor.

In *French Wines and Politics*, Martineau gives a voice of empathetic rationality to Marguerite—she possesses a different voice of reason, one that has the courage to acknowledge the personal, individual losses and devastation. There is an understanding of immediate pain and chaos, rather than being wilfully blinded by the bigger picture of overall, depersonalised, social progress in her husband's vision. In spite of my wariness of Charles's perspective, though, he does make a crucial point, similar to Moore's and Thornton's, when he asks the mob, 'when did a tyrannical government inflict upon you such evils as you are this day inflicting upon yourselves?' He continues, 'will you throw away what is in your hands, that others may reduce you to crave the small pittance that will remain theirs,' and then suggests that the mob is being manipulated by those who seek to cause trouble, but will not be adversely affected themselves.[68] His argument is valid, but lacks moral substance because of Charles's personal benefits that result from the rebellion—he cannot be removed from self-interest, which fits his character as a representative of political economy. In *Sowers Not Reapers*, Chatham presents similar arguments to Charles's in *French Wines*, but Chatham is more convincing because he does not himself benefit from the riots—rather he is imprisoned because of his association with them, even though there is no suggestion that he actually takes part in the destruction. Like Charles, Chatham seeks to be 'a good friend to all parties,' and speaks out on behalf of both sides.[69] In defence of the hungry, and to his own detriment, Chatham consistently argues, 'How should they be champions of the right while they are victims of the wrong? They must be fed before they can effectually struggle for perpetual food' (329). It is Chatham's willingness to sacrifice himself, as opposed to his French counterpart's self-preservation, that sets him apart as the humane voice of reason. It is this motive of self-preservation in tension with that of preserving the community that is drawn into focus in both texts. This idea is explored in Friedrich Salomon Perls's psychoanalytic study, *Ego, Hunger and Aggression* (1947), in which he positions hunger in relation to the evolutionary needs for self-preservation and species survival, two hungers that do not always coalesce. This connection is crucial in trying to contend with this challenging tension between the needs of the individual and the stability or progress of the community.

Just as *French Wines* is complicated by the hurricane, and *Mary Barton* by fire and seasons of bad harvests, the effect of the Corn Laws in *Sowers Not Reapers* is complicated by the natural elements, although in the more prolonged and more

---

68 Martineau, *French Wines and Politics*, 96–97.
69 Martineau, *Sowers Not Reapers*, 329.

difficult to frame event of drought. In *Sowers Not Reapers*, the natural crop failure is more central to the community's concerns than political interference or selfish neglect, but the violence and food destruction is uncannily similar. The wheat that has arrived is rumoured to be spoiled—although in line with the more natural focus of *Sowers Not Reapers*, it has not been deliberately corrupted by the government, but has been destroyed by seawater. However, the rumour that inflames the crowd is that good grain has been hidden from them. Finding no good corn at the mill owner Kirkland's property, they move on toward Sheffield, 'to burn down a mill or two' (313). Some were expected to remain, however, and, in a much more civilised manner than Maigrot's customers, to 'ask bread' of Mrs Skipper the baker (313).

There is a sense of civilisation in the English mob, unlike the barbaric nature of the Continental one. Like Charles with Maigrot, Chatham warns Mrs Skipper of the approaching crowd, although they are not described in the same terms as the faceless mob seen in *French Wines*. Chatham's attitude is selfless, but also crucial is the agency that Mrs Skipper claims through her compassion. Rather than being demonised, the mob in *Sowers Not Reapers* are recognised as a part of the community, and are even given their names. It is, perhaps, the humanising of the mob that diffuses the threat of violence. Mrs Skipper calls them 'Poor souls!' and observes,

> 'They do not seem creatures to be afraid of, *when one comes close to them*;— so tired and lagging! I say, Dixon, won't you have something to eat after your walk? Smith, you look worse still, and I saw how early you were off to your work this morning, and you have a way to go before supper. Try a roll, won't you? Come, that's right, Bullen, set to, and tell me if it is not good bread; and you, Taylor,—carry it home to your wife, if you scruple to eat it yourself.—Bless you, make no speeches! I only wish I had more; but this is all, you see, except the dough that is laid for the morning, and that belongs to my customers, not to me.' (317, emphasis added)

The physical closeness of the men is particularly crucial: a mob at a distance appears as a massive, single entity, but here Mrs Skipper gives them each their own identity, ironically fragmenting the mob in order to reinstate the community. It is also important that their names are common English names—there is no hint of foreignness in this part of the narrative. Within the community where they are known, the rioters are not the demons *themselves*, as the French rebels are; rather they are 'men *possessed* by the demon of want'—while they may be *filled* with this demon, it is a separate entity from them (335, emphasis added). Because the community suffers with them, there is an effectual understanding, an empathy, as to why they take their violent approach, even by those characters who disagree with, or suffer because of, their method.

Yet while this threat is diffused within the community structure and Mrs Skipper is preserved, the movement of the rioters through other villages and towns acts as

a reminder that they are not necessarily known in those other places, and therefore the same kind of diffusion would not be possible. While Mrs Skipper could
acknowledge and remind them of their humanity, in towns where they are not
familiar, under the secretive mask of their midnight drills, the rioters would be as
much demonised figures of fear and destruction as the revolutionaries in France.
In a similar way, the delegation of Manchester men in *Mary Barton* are not seen
as individuals, as members of a community, but as a faceless spectacle. While
their protest and procession is comparatively civilised, contained, and polite, their
message does not connect on a human level. The movement in *French Wines and
Politics*, however, is chaotic and widespread, moving throughout the nation, from
Guienne to Paris to Versailles, and the hurricane that ushers in the social unrest
affects the entire nation. Similarly, the cloak of darkness in the English drills and
riots, along with the machine breaking in *Shirley* and even John Barton's murder
of Harry, is necessary in the desire to maintain anonymity. Yet this very anonymity
works against the disaffected and disenfranchised, reinforcing their dehumanised
state, rather than reasserting their place as citizens of the nation.

Shirley Keeldar attempts an economic alternative of relief for the poor across
three parishes. Like Robert Moore, she is technically a foreigner in Yorkshire,
not to mention a female landowner, thus doubly othered in her privileged position. However, unlike Moore, she is less interested in her own gains than she is in
maintaining the stability of the community. While it is true that she has the luxury
of funds to act, it is also notable that other wealthy figures do not attempt to do
the same. She argues, '[f]or those who are not hungry, it is easy to palaver about
the degradations of charity, and so on; but they forget the brevity of life, as well
as the bitterness.'[70] Shirley enlists the advice and assistance of respected locals
in order to administer her plan, including spinsters known for their philanthropy,
and the older parsons who were established in the community. She understands
the value of appropriating their positions within the community in order to establish herself. Her distribution of funds in the form of welfare goes some way to
mitigate the dire poverty of the district: the 'neighbourhood seemed to grow
calmer: for a fortnight past no cloth had been destroyed; no outrage on mill or
mansion had been committed in the three parishes,' thanks also to the fact that
others were inspired to follow her lead (288). But the fund cannot be sustained,
and so Shirley's optimism is ultimately misplaced. Without a long-term solution
to unemployment, the fear of ongoing starvation is too powerful, and too easily channelled toward the unfeeling foreigner, Moore. Even so, Shirley remains
committed to her cooperative approach, owning a 'herd of milch kine . . . for the
convenience of the neighbourhood' (345). On the morning after Moore's mill
is attacked, the crowd of cottagers at her house to collect their milk and butter shows that the possibilities for community remain in spite of the anonymous
violence. In some ways, Shirley is like Eliot's Romola, who 'does not invest her

---

70 Brontë, *Shirley*, 268.

money in enduring material possessions . . . she buys food, the least staying of all commodities.'[71] But where Blumberg would suggest that 'Romola does not invest at all,'[72] I would suggest that, rather than leaving a mark through an ancient, inaccessible library like her father, which is so easily sold off by her husband, Tito, Romola, like Shirley Keeldar, invests in the cultural heritage of the community. Blumberg goes on to observe that 'Romola's exchanges create new ties that uphold human obligations, particularly those the strong owe to the weak';[73] and in this statement, it is clear that Romola *does* invest: I would argue in something more longlasting than material capital—the ongoing communal body. In the same way, Brontë's Shirley, although the financial capital she invests in the community runs dry, is shown through her economic investment that she has invested her*self* in the community, becoming a part of it, and through that investment will maintain her heritage in Yorkshire. Shirley, unlike Moore, holds the respect of the community, and in this way she is able to exercise her influence over the crowd in a way similar to Martineau's Mrs Skipper, but with even more authority. Unlike the violent response to Moore's harsh words, Shirley is able to evoke the reason of the cottagers, such as William Farren, and, like Mrs Skipper, restore the sense of belonging to the community—notably through the distribution of food and familiarity with individuals in the crowd.

Linda Peterson points out that while planning her *Illustrations*, 'Martineau envisioned an English revolution—not one of regicide and lawless violence . . . but a war of ideas in which thinking men and women of all classes would usher in a new political era.'[74] Yet she was aware that, in practice, as Gagnier observes, 'the great system of wealth and social order is a delusion for most of society.'[75] Writing fifteen years later, Elizabeth Gaskell and Charlotte Brontë lived through a type of English revolution with the advent of Chartism, and the ever-constant threat of Continental violence inspiring the British workers to rise up *en masse*, like a storm that refuses to break. Martineau, Brontë, and Gaskell all depict social organisations in which a significant proportion of the community are brutalised by starvation through varying degrees of natural and governmental intervention. The self-sacrificing try to mitigate the destruction of their communities by giving out of their own small portions, believing, as John Barton suggests repeatedly, that only the poor are concerned with the plight of the poor. This narrative of neglect crosses over from the physical scarcity of food to the rehearsing and reinforcing of narratives of self-interest, in spite of attempts at intervention by figures like Shirley Keeldar and (eventually, and to a lesser extent) John Thornton. The 'locus of scarcity' that Gagnier critiques ferments revolution and social chaos, shouting

71 Blumberg, 'Beyond the Cash Nexus,' 69–70.

72 Ibid., 70.

73 Ibid.

74 Linda Peterson, 'From French Revolution to English Reform: Hannah More, Harriet Martineau, and the "Little Book",' *Nineteenth-Century Literature* 60.4 (2006): 409–50, 441.

75 Regenia Gagnier, 'On the Insatiability of Human Wants: Economic and Aesthetic Man,' *Victorian Studies* 36.2 (1993): 125–53, 128.

with violence to the broader capitalist discourse of social and economic progress, crippling communities even in times of prosperity with the belief that there will never be enough for all, even for those living in relative wealth. One's capacity to give is restricted more by the belief in one's own poverty, than by one's actual economic capital. Within Martineau's, Brontë's, and Gaskell's carefully con-structed narratives, the lens of chaotic hunger, figured through violence, looting, and community breakdown, disrupts the economic fictions they present, refusing to sanction illusions of progress.

3   Disenfranchised communities

London!—that great large place! . . . He had often heard the old men in the work-house, too, say that no lad of spirit need want in London. . . . It was the very place for a homeless boy, who must die in the streets unless some one helped him.

(Charles Dickens, *Oliver Twist* (1837), 57)

[The nation] is imagined as *community*, because, regardless of the actual inequality and exploitation that may prevail in each, the nation is always conceived as a deep, horizontal comradeship.

(Benedict Anderson, *Imagined Communities* (1983), 7)

Benedict Anderson's well-known definition of the nation as 'an imagined political community' goes some way toward revealing the deep divide between a harmonious national ideal, and the material difficulties raised through the very inequalities and exploitations that are implicit in this vision of nationalism.[1] The hunger for this ideal epitomises the convergence of physical and social hunger, where the starving are overwhelmed by their powerlessness to alter their state within the nation's economic and social structures. Beyond Anderson's claim that the nation's community is imagined because 'the members of even the small-est nation will never know most of their fellow-members,'[2] even more so the ideal is merely imagined because the disenfranchised are given little stake in that community, and are effectively exiled from it, even without crossing geographi-cal national borders. The gravitation of characters back to London, identified by Grace Moore in *Dickens and Empire* (2004),[3] can be read as a deep desire—a social hunger—to be integrated at the heart of the nation. Moore goes on to suggest that the ideological construct of 'an homogenous national identity' is predicated on 'promot[ing] unity where none exists,' and emphasises that this unity in the mid-nineteenth century is 'constructed around a myth of affluence.'[4] In this way,

---

1 Benedict Anderson, *Imagined Communities: Reflections on the Origin and Spread of Nationalism* (1983; London and New York: Verso, 2006), 6–7.
2 Ibid., 6.
3 Moore, *Dickens and Empire*, 13.
4 Ibid., 21, 24.

it becomes increasingly evident that the solidarity of the British Empire is tenuous at best, with the security of the British national identity being threatened by famine, and revolutionary and economic migration. When mobility is necessitated on physical starvation and political disempowerment, not only is the myth of stability broken down, but so is the cohesive rootedness of the local community: the faces are in constant flux, the familiar becoming unknown. This transformation has a dire impact on the ability to feel the visceral affinity to 'home'; and so the only option seems to be—if the luxury exists—to close one's eyes to the shifting surface. While Anderson claims that even without being heard or hearing these fellow members, 'in the minds of each lives the image of their communion,'[5] social history shows that such claims of communion require wilful blindness and deafness to the poor, the homeless, and the 'foreign,' a term incorporating foreign nationals as well as the domestic foreignness discussed in the previous chapter. Anderson's community is imagined, therefore, from his Marxist approach, by the bourgeoisie for the bourgeoisie; it is a locus of 'us' against a network of 'thems,' built to establish the political power of nationalism in spite of the 'philosophical poverty' of the visionaries.[6]

This philosophical poverty resonates with *Oliver Twist* (1837), in which members of the unfeeling workhouse committee are derided sardonically by Dickens as 'philosophers' and 'economists.' My concern in this chapter is the plight of those excluded from the national communal vision—the disenfranchised and broken; their social hunger to belong to that community; and their attempts to construct their own version of national belonging. In *After Chartism* (1993), Margot C. Finn argues that political radicalism in the mid-nineteenth century was inherently tied to a nationalist narrative as a way of trying to navigate a new national identity in the wake of disenfranchisement. Claiming to move away from a Marxist model of class against class, although her view is not that far removed from Anderson's Marxist communal nationalism, Finn extends the perspective of radicalism by asserting that it was the 'national idiom cherished by these radical leaders' that was most crucial to the progress of Chartist sentiment.[7] While class remains central, the national vision brings to the fore the necessity of belonging: if one is denied a voice within the community, citizenship is conditional and limited. Conditional belonging is bearable, and perhaps even invisible when one has enough to live, but once the means to live are restricted, the impact of physical hunger exacerbates the awareness of social impoverishment.

Chartism emerged from a desire to be considered full citizens—men (albeit gendered) who could vote, who had a stake in the local community and in the nation. It also spoke to the desire for the centralised London government to recognise and authorise the North in particular, but, in general, the rest of Britain. The gravitation toward London reflects a hunger for the authority the capital held,

5 Anderson, *Imagined Communities*, 6.
6 Ibid., 5.
7 Margot C. Finn, *After Chartism: Class and Nation in English Radical Politics, 1848–1874* (Cambridge: Cambridge University Press, 1993), 14.

as well as the economic affluence it was perceived to produce. This social hunger was largely born out of physical hunger—the need to feed one's family, and to be assured of continual provision. Yet the reality for many was that they needed to relocate or become itinerant in order to find work, to send one's children to other regions in order to find work, or even to migrate to other lands. Such mobility destabilises the understanding of home, and brings to the fore questions of community rootedness. The fragmented migrant identity threatened to challenge where one belonged politically, ideologically, and spiritually, in a material sense removing individuals from the place of their family, cultural heritage, and even language. Mobility thus strained local communities as well as families. The middle-class construct of the domestic hearth is less recognisable in a social context in which one rents property on short-term bases, or lives in boarding houses or other transitory lodgings while travelling between work opportunities. Arguably, the presence of European refugees in Britain—due to political exile, war, and famine—furthered the tensions of poverty and disaffection, but also provided a mirror to the displacement of the British within the domestic national space. The consequent disruption of local community, especially in times of poor harvests and unstable trade laws, contributes to social unrest, as well as an unwillingness to invest cultural or social capital into the community at times when economic capital is perceived as rare. The mobility of the child Oliver, then, who will die in the streets without help, speaks to the fraught state of communities that the Vagrancy Acts and New Poor Laws could do little to alleviate.

Disaffection among the disenfranchised poor persists as a social narrative into the twenty-first century. Between 6 August and 11 August 2011, the BlackBerry Riots, originating in London after the police shooting of Mark Duggan in Tottenham before spreading across other cities including Birmingham, Bristol, and Manchester, reminded the world of Britain's capacity to erupt in collective violence. While the estimated involvement of 13,000 to 15,000 individuals pales in comparison to the 40,000–60,000 participants in the 1780 Gordon Riots, or the estimated 120,000 protesters who, upon the House of Lords rejecting the first Reform Bill, marched to Parliament on 13 October 1831 before devolving into violence and destruction, the twenty-first-century international media, as well as the British nation, responded with shock and confusion at this seemingly sudden outbreak of lawlessness. On a superficial level, technology was blamed for enabling the extent of the riots (although the cyber technology was, arguably, still not as effective as the 1831 printing press in disseminating organisation to protesters), while political narratives sought to hold onto myths of racial disaffection and a juvenile criminal underclass. However, the Lambeth Council interim report on the riots notes: '[t]hese were not riots committed by children, but—largely—by young adults. We do not believe that these were race riots. Most convicted rioters were not gang members.'[8] Significantly, while the report

---

8 'Five Days in August: An Interim Report on the 2011 English Riots,' Riots, Community and Victims Panel (RCVP) (London, November 2011), 13, at http://socialwelfare.bl.uk/subject-areas/services-client-groups/young-offenders/riotscommunitiesandvictimspanel/5days11.aspx

states that there 'appears to be a link between deprivation and rioting,' the importance of belonging to the community is made clear: '[h]aving a stake in society is important. We spoke to many individuals from similar backgrounds who didn't riot. They told us that they had a place in society that they did not want to jeopardise. They showed an awareness of shared values.' In a similar vein, a direct correlation was asserted between the level of rioting and not just deprivation, but the 'amount of social capital people had invested in their local communities.'[9] While both Conservative Prime Minister David Cameron and Opposition Leader Ed Miliband referred to the selfishness and irresponsibility of the rioters, the interim report's recognition of both social and economic investment makes a crucial intervention in the analysis of the causes of rioting.[10] Miliband's question, '[w]hy are there people who think it's okay to loot, vandalise and terrorise their own neighbourhoods?' is answered through his own subsequent clause: '[w]ho seem to *owe no loyalty* to their communities?'[11] Without a sense of belonging, of ownership and investment within the community, moral restraint holds less meaning and value.

While these twenty-first-century riots emerge within a very different context and momentum, the narratives of broken, disenfranchised communities resonate with the social narratives of nineteenth-century Britain relating to poverty and social identity, the excess of self-interest in times of scarcity, and the attempt to deflect responsibility through othering, blaming, and questioning the legitimacy of the presence of those perceived not to belong to the community. However, as much as David Cameron would claim that '[t]hose thugs we saw last week do not represent us, nor do they represent our young people—and they will not drag us down,'[12] such rhetoric denies the inherent reality of internal conflicts within society: the 'thugs' referred to are British citizens, many of whom, by virtue of their age (and unlike their nineteenth-century Chartist counterparts), have the right of suffrage. The way in which history has shown that universal suffrage does not automatically instil effective cultural or social agency reveals the importance of other factors within the community that contribute to the sense of belonging and having a voice. Within the heritage of hunger and violence in British culture, this chapter continues my focus on dual physical and social hunger as the catalyst of protest, and the sources of responsibility that arise out of unrest. While the social condition of nineteenth-century Britain was blamed on diverse agents—from rifts between masters and workers, and the centralised government

---

9 Ibid., 13; 12.
10 It is telling that the final report from the RCVP reverts to the exclusionary narrative of a juvenile criminal underclass: http://webarchive.nationalarchives.gov.uk/20121003195935/http:/riots panel.independent.gov.uk/wp-content/uploads/2012/03/Riots-Panel-Final-Report1.pdf
11 Ed Miliband, 'Speech on the Riots,' Haverstock School, 15 August 2011, *New Statesman*, http://www.newstatesman.com/politics/2011/08/society-young-heard-riots (published 15 August 2011; accessed 22 August 2014; emphasis added).
12 David Cameron, 'Speech on the Fight-Back after the Riots,' Witney, 15 August 2011, *New Statesman*, http://www.newstatesman.com/politics/2011/08/society-fight-work-rights (published 15 August 2011; accessed 22 August 2014).

of London mismanaging scarcity and not understanding the rest of the nation, to immigration and myths of a criminal underclass—a central factor remains in the inability of the poor, whether English or migrants, to establish a stable home: a place in which they belong. As a result of being deprived of a home, the poor are effectively exiled in a domestic diaspora, evidenced, for example, in the itinerant workers leaving their regions of origin in order to find employment.

Oliver Twist, who has never known a stable home, travels to the mysterious-sounding place of London in hope that he will find a place to belong. In the narratives I address in this chapter, by Martineau, Dickens, Gaskell, and Henry Mayhew, the tensions of physical and social hunger are exacerbated through the need to be mobile, and the implications such mobility has on one's connection to society. The resulting transience of home necessitates a transformation in the way community and identity are formed. In *Portable Property: Victorian Culture on the Move* (2008), John Plotz examines the ways in which 'Victorian England . . . [became] a forcing bed from which portability emerged as a new way of imagining community, national identity, and even liberal selfhood';[13] and while Plotz deals more with British emigration, the instability of property and the 'opposition between fungible and relic object[s]' also speaks to the mobility of the poor within Britain, particularly in regard to forced mobility and the consequent changing perspective of property.[14] The need to have property that can be easily moved becomes increasingly important; and in this way, the connection between being physically hungry and hungering for particular cultural, social, or economic property becomes evident. Migrants and itinerants long both for foods and for objects from 'home' in order to remove some of the hunger for belonging. In their transience, these figures seek grounding within their access to familiar goods, including familiar flavours—tastes associated with home—to be able to remember, at least, that they have had that humanising connection of community, even if that memory in itself provokes another kind of hunger for what has been lost. In itinerancy, if others can be found who similarly appreciate those familiar tastes, a new sense of community can be formed, relocated in the food, although the problem of access remains as to whether itinerants can afford such foods, as well as if they are available. The possibility, then, for them to become doubly disenfranchised emerges. However, I do want to focus on the hope of a community that is not predicated on place. As Tim Cresswell suggests, culture—and I would add 'home'—'no longer sits in places, but is hybrid, dynamic—more about routes than roots.'[15] Home becomes more about a communal network of belonging than about a physical space in which one resides. Ironically, then, or perhaps of necessity, cultural identity can be reinforced and refined through hunger and loss, as well as through being removed from the place of belonging.

13 John Plotz, *Portable Property: Victorian Culture on the Move* (Princeton and Oxford: Princeton University Press, 2008), xiii–xiv.
14 Ibid., 15.
15 Tim Cresswell, *On the Move: Mobility in the Western World* (New York: Routledge, 2006), 1.

Criminals, vagrants, and exiles

Criminality permeates this chapter, informing the ways in which mobile people are perceived within the community. They are outsiders; they do not belong; and by extension, they are potentially dangerous. Yet at the same time, they are often vulnerable and hungry. Being mobile exacerbates both physical and social hunger, without necessarily having a parish to which to turn. Crimes such as theft, or homelessness designated as vagrancy, are marked by hunger; but the recognition of hunger tends to exacerbate social fear rather than lessening it—hunger is potentially contagious when food is scarce. Both vague and specific connections between poverty, mobility, and crime were at the fore of the nineteenth-century social and political consciousness. Political refugees from Europe were often defined as criminals in their home country, and then made the scapegoats for revolutionary activities within Britain; impoverished itinerants ran a risky path associated with vagrancy; and Heather Shore argues that the rising concept of the juvenile delinquent was inherently tied to the changing dynamics and fluidity of the home.[16] Cresswell expresses the dual nature of mobility, standing as a symbol for progress, freedom, and opportunity, but also figured 'as shiftlessness, as deviance, and as resistance.'[17] Historically, legislation surrounding poor relief, settlement, and vagrancy has been closely interrelated in Britain, establishing a longstanding near criminalisation of mobility that responds to a deep-seated distrust of those who seem rootless or disconnected from the community. Paul Ocobock makes a crucial observation about the tenor of vagrancy legislation in Western civilisation:

> [v]agrancy laws are unique; while most crimes are defined by actions, vagrancy laws make no specific action or inaction illegal. Rather the laws are based on personal condition, state of being, and social and economic status. . . . Through history, those so labeled and arrested for vagrancy have often been poor, young, able-bodied, unemployed, rootless and homeless. . . . In general, the primary aim of vagrancy laws has been to establish control over idle individuals who could labor but choose not to and rootless, roofless persons seemingly unfettered by traditional domestic life and free to travel outside the surveillance of the state.[18]

These legislated definitions are problematically and all too conveniently woolly, given the difficulties in determining legitimacy in mobility and unemployment. Alongside the change in poor laws, and within a political and economic climate

---

16 Heather Shore, *Artful Dodgers: Youth and Crime in Early 19th-Century London* (Woodbridge and New York: Boydell Press, 1999), 18.

17 Cresswell, *On the Move*, 1–2.

18 Paul Ocobock, 'Introduction: Vagrancy and Homelessness in Global and Historical Perspective,' in *Cast Out: Vagrancy and Homelessness in Global and Historical Perspective*, ed. A.L. Beier and Paul Robert Ocobock (Athens: Ohio University Press, 2008), 1–34, 1–2.

that exacerbated poverty and instability, such legislation merely made it more difficult to determine responsibility for those who found themselves unable to work.

Patricia Fumerton's *Unsettled* (2006) reveals the way in which criminality was entrenched in ideas of mobility from the time of the 1572 Vagrancy Act, which required, among other measures, legitimate travellers to carry on their person written authorisation for their movement. However, Fumerton points out the continuing difficulty in trying to define vagrancy within a nation that contained migrants and itinerants: 'the 1572 act . . . was deliberately broad in its scope, leaving considerable room for interpretation. As a result, the "legitimate" destitute traveler not only rubbed elbows with the "illegitimate" vagrant, but also risked at any moment being identified as such.'[19] The dangers of being tainted by association, alongside the fluidity and uncertainty of definition, undoubtedly impacted the sense of society and belonging by creating cultural aversions to geographic mobility, even within the British mainland. Due to expire in September 1824, the Vagrancy Act was repealed and overwritten in June 1824,[20] with the claim that it was 'expedient to make further Provision for the Suppression of Vagrancy, and for the Punishment of idle and disorderly Persons, Rogues and Vagabonds, and incorrigible Rogues, in *England*.'[21] Westminster's specific concern for England is politically telling, yet my focus here is on the role of the Industrial Revolution, famine, and Continental unrest in the desire to renew and redefine the Vagrancy Act: more people were necessarily on the move in search of economic security and employment, but such internal momentum was perceived as a threat to the stability of the nation. It stands to reason, then, that the Act sought to contain people— specifically the indigent poor—by preventing their movement within the nation. If individuals were perceived to be capable but unwilling to work, they would be removed from the parish (unless it was their parish of origin); and if they returned to where they were removed from, they would be incarcerated.[22] Searching abroad for work, then, could potentially be a criminal act, if work could not be found in that other place. Without an income and without connections in the parish, travellers faced being rendered homeless. Ocobock argues that '[o]ne of the chief aims of the 1824 act was to . . . criminalize sleeping out, effectively making homelessness an act of vagrancy,' while the 1834 Poor Law sought to 'standardize relief among the "deserving" and casual wards were created to give vagrants temporary overnight shelter. Casual wards were a response to the continual refusal of workhouse authorities of admitting vagrants and petty criminals.'[23] However, the lines

19 Patricia Fumerton, *Unsettled: The Culture of Mobility and the Working Poor in Early Modern England* (Chicago and London: University of Chicago Press, 2006), xi.
20 Robert Peel, as Home Secretary, oversaw the reformed Vagrancy Act, as well as the New Poor Laws in 1834.
21 'An Act for the Punishment of idle and disorderly Persons, and Rogues and Vagabonds, in that Part of Great Britain called *England*,' CAP LXXIII, 21 June 1824, I, www.legislation.gov.uk/ ukpga/1824/83/pdfs/ukpga18240083_en.pdf
22 Ibid., III.
23 Ocobock, 'Introduction,' 22.

between incapacity and unwillingness are not always easy to draw when work is scarce; parishes would work surreptitiously to support poor travellers by either hiding them or lying about their date of arrival, while at the same time vigilantism arose against perceived vagrants as communities felt the vagrancy laws were failing them,[24] further complicating the outworking of the vagrancy legislation. Parochial interventions, which can be seen in terms of altruism and compassion, but also as a resistance of central governmental control and the unionisation of parishes,[25] blur the lines of vagrancy, and therefore destabilise the relationship between mobility and criminality within the local community.

The vulnerability of Dickens's Oliver Twist is expressed most profoundly in that he is both determinedly mobile and always hungry throughout the novel. Birthed out of his mother's mobility, Oliver constantly shifts between home spaces, sometimes from choice and sometimes forced, ever looking for belonging and finding a weird community through the unlikely coincidences of connection within the broader London and national space.[26] When he finds his way to London, the young child is already a vagrant, although he would not know the word; and his immediate connection to Jack Dawkins causes Oliver to leave behind one unconscious criminal identity to take on another. That Oliver does not recognise his own vagrancy, or the criminal activities of Fagin's gang, reveals the slippage between poverty, criminality, and mobility that haunted the nineteenth-century consciousness. The figure of Oliver also reveals the power of hunger and satiation in creating a sense of belonging, and therefore stability, in that his sense of home in each place is defined through the food to which he has access. The satiation of physical hunger operates as a blind to criminality, which promotes empathy for the poor, so the provider of food is necessarily but problematically trusted and unquestioned. Through the motif of food provision, the provider becomes the master, enslaving the starved. As expressed by Alexandre Ledru-Rollin in *The Decline of England* (1850), 'The master looks upon his apprentice as his slave, and treats him as the caprice of brutal avarice may dictate. For the least fault the child is deprived of food, or has to perform a task heavier than his strength can support.'[27] Food is the mechanism through which this power is gained and maintained, by means of the strategic denial and giving of acceptance—of communion and belonging. Jack's provision of ham, bread, and beer, 'a long and hearty meal' in Oliver's experience, immediately earns Jack the title of Oliver's friend, even before Oliver knows his name.[28] This relationship seems innocuous, but Oliver is then taken to Fagin, where the abuse of the vulnerable is exacerbated through Fagin's provision: he seems to be constantly

24 Ibid.
25 Ibid., 11.
26 I use the term 'home' loosely here—arguably Oliver never finds a true sense of home or belonging. The very small world that Oliver exists within resonates with Anderson's national imagined community.
27 Alexandre Ledru-Rollin, *The Decline of England* (London: E. Churton, 1850), 271.
28 Charles Dickens, *Oliver Twist* (1837–38; London: Penguin, 2002), 61.

making food and drink, providing physical sustenance for the boys, and using that provision to manipulate them. If, as Smith suggests, taste '[gives] meaning to space and location' and 'the taste of a place hold[s] a great deal of sway over how people under[stand] themselves and their relationship to the larger society,'[29] in Oliver's interactions with Jack and Fagin, the extension of tastes means that his social space—and therefore sense of belonging—is also extended through these experiences of new foods. Not only do they provide an answer for Oliver's physical hunger, Jack and Fagin seem to provide for Oliver's hunger to have an identity and a community, even if it is, problematically, a criminal one. For Oliver, Fagin even more than Jack gives him access to tastes that he has never encountered—hams, sausages, gin, and coffee—and Fagin denies food to the boys when they do not please him.[30] In this way, Fagin exhibits his authority over the boys' identities, taming them through their stomachs.

Importantly, apart from the scraps of bacon he receives while at Mr and Mrs Sowerberry's, Oliver does not partake in meat until he is in London with Jack and Fagin. Mr Bumble ironically expresses the common belief of meat providing moral strength:

> 'Meat, ma'am, meat,' replied Bumble. . . . 'You've raised a [*sic*] artificial soul and spirit in him, ma'am, unbecoming a person of his condition. . . . What have paupers to do with soul or spirit either? It's quite enough that we let 'em have live bodies. If you had kept the boy on gruel, ma'am, this would never have happened.' (53)

Howes and Lalonde observe the traditional British belief in meat bestowing strength, while fruits and vegetables were 'thought to incite human weaknesses of every sort.'[31] In the case of Oliver, however, fruit and vegetables are not the remedy for this apparent excess of meat, but absolute starvation, followed by a diet of gruel. That Oliver and the children in the workhouse are restricted to gruel removes their humanity from them; and Oliver's iconic request for 'more' (15) speaks not just to the desire to sate his physical hunger, but his social hunger to have a voice and to belong. As Oliver gains access to meat, he begins to develop not just his physical strength, but his individual identity, although he must maintain his mobility in order to prevent being morally tainted by those who provide the meat for him. This necessity provides an ironic counterpoint to the connection between criminality and mobility, for without it Oliver would remain embedded within Fagin's criminal gang.

Essentially, it is Oliver's escape to London that enables him eventually to find a home. Due to the excess of numbers within the urban space of London (with Manchester a close second), the capital occupied the focus and imagination of much

29 Smith, *Sensory History*, 78.
30 Dickens, *Oliver Twist*, 66.
31 Howes and Lalonde, 'History of Sensibilities,' 126.

of the nineteenth-century concerns regarding overpopulation, under-employment, and seemingly heightened revolutionary and criminal behaviour. Shore argues that '[o]nly in London, with its comparative size and density, was the theory of the criminal class, the underclass, really tenable,' and that 'the omnipresence of London, its importance in popular perception, clearly justifies its central focus in this examination of urban juvenile crime.'[32] This position can be explained in that, as Sue Zemka points out, '[d]ensely inhabited space is contested space';[33] however, London is also crucial in being the economic, cultural, and political centre of the British Empire. As the thermometer of the Empire, London's social and economic positioning is essential to the stability of the nation. It is also the place of imagined stability, with the regional poor looking to the capital as a mythical oasis in times of scarcity. Fumerton notes that 'London bore the brunt of the problem with unsettled poor in early modern England,'[34] which reveals the historical extent of this belief, while 'between 1841 and 1851, London absorbed 330,000 migrants, a 17 percent increase in its population; in 1831, Manchester boasted a population of 142,000, having doubled in size since the census of 1801.'[35] This increase of migration included people from Continental Europe, Ireland, Wales, and Scotland, but also domestic migrants from rural England, who turned to the urban space in an attempt to find employment. London, therefore, becomes a kind of unofficial domestic colony, with its borders and capacity stretched by the unprecedented increase in the population of the poor. From another direction, though, Moore reveals the way in which these colonisers become the colonised, with both Dickens and Henry Mayhew 'adopt[ing] a process of displacement whereby the urban poor [come] to be aligned . . . with the colonized, both as a means of stimulating public interest in their less-than-exotic lives, and as a way of emphasizing their complete alienation.'[36] Within this vision, it becomes unclear to whom London actually belongs: it is no one's home. No one is legitimate, thus everyone is potentially criminalised. This perspective evokes Patrick Brantlinger's provocative observation that 'the Empire may intrude as a shadowy realm of escape, renewal, banishment, or return for characters who for one reason or another need to enter or exit from scenes of domestic conflict.'[37] Shore similarly presents an image of the colonised poor by referring to the way in which many Victorian commentators 'were outraged by immorality, ignorance, cunning, poverty, in the same way as missionaries exploring lost civilisations,' rather than petitioning for penal or governmental reform.[38] By being made an object

32 Shore, *Artful Dodgers*, 15.
33 Sue Zemka, 'Brief Encounters: Street Scenes in Gaskell's Manchester,' *ELH*, 76.3 (2009): 793–819, 795.
34 Fumerton, *Unsettled*, 12.
35 Zemka, 'Brief Encounters,' 794.
36 Moore, *Dickens and Empire*, 2.
37 Patrick Brantlinger, *Rule of Darkness: British Literature and Imperialism 1830–1914* (Ithaca: Cornell University Press, 1988), 12.
38 Shore, *Artful Dodgers*, 4.

of commentary in this way, the poor are distanced—again, 'not us', not 'our' responsibility. Seth Koven's *Slumming* (2004) reinforces this idea of distancing by examining the middle-class fascination with touring the impoverished areas of London as a cultural, ethnographic experience, like an anti-Grand Tour. Yet while this kind of tourism enabled a sense of distance, Mayhew's groundbreaking ethnographic study *London Labour and the London Poor* (1851–52) disturbingly penetrates the spaces of impoverished, criminalised London, inconsistently prosecuting and defending the capital's disenfranchised inhabitants in a way that destabilises the identity of the poor as the criminal Other.

From the outset of his study, Mayhew articulates a binary that situates people-movement in relation to civilisation: 'there are—socially, morally, and perhaps even physically considered—but two distinct and broadly marked races, viz., the wanderers and the settlers—the vagabond and the citizen—the nomadic and the civilized tribes.'[39] This binary is complicated by the foreigner's presence, either from another nation, or from another part of Britain. Mayhew buys into the popular angst regarding mobility by suggesting that people groups are civilised and moral to the extent that they remain in one place, while 'wandering and rootless men' are the 'potential ruin of London.'[40] John Scanlan describes Mayhew's London:

> In fact there was an aura of decay everywhere – on the streets, and inside homes – in the air that people inhaled and in the dust that was blown around and thereafter carried everywhere on clothes; the microscopic matter and trace of the city's greater decay . . . the most desperate of the poor were seen to be at one with decay, becoming a source of both dread and fascination.[41]

Decay and waste provide a figure for criminality, but also for poverty; and the preoccupation with decay offers a counterpoint to starvation, with the city seeming to devour and discard its own starving, wasted subjects.

While A.L. Beier suggests that not many historians 'give much credence to the threat of a teeming, organized, and dangerous criminal element' in their assessment of Victorian London, rejecting the concepts of a criminal underclass or 'sub-culture' that 'threatened to turn the respectable world upside down,'[42] cultural historians see the importance in acknowledging the power of such social narratives in the mindset of Victorian society. Indeed, as Andrew Tolson observes, it was ethnographic work produced by figures like Mayhew that legitimated ideas of subculture, providing a paradoxical rationalisation of poverty culture and criminal culture within London, and therefore unintentionally answering, to some extent,

---

39 Henry Mayhew, *London Labour and the London Poor* (1851–52; 4 vols, London: Griffin, Bohn, & Co., 1861–62), vol. 1, 1.

40 John Scanlan, 'In Deadly Time: The Lasting on of Waste in Mayhew's London,' *Time Society*, 16 (2007): 189–206, 191.

41 Ibid., 197; 199.

42 A.L. Beier, '"Takin' It to the Streets": Henry Mayhew and the Language of the Underclass in Mid-Nineteenth-Century London,' in *Cast Out*, ed. Beier and Ocobock, 88–116, 90.

the social hunger of the poor for a legitimate social identity.[43] Subculture becomes a means to find a cultural home when traditional home forms are inaccessible. Yet such subcultures can be seen as a threat to the imagined community because their very existence evidences the way in which the community operates by means of exclusion. William Augustus Miles, for example, in his presentation to the House of Lords, *Poverty, Mendicity and Crime* (1839), writes:

> There is a youthful population in the Metropolis devoted to crime, trained to it from infancy, adhering to it from Education and Circumstances . . . different from the rest of Society, not only in thoughts, habits, and manners, but even in appearance, possessing, moreover, a language exclusively of their own.[44]

The references to education, habits and manners, and most particularly language, speak to the definition of a discrete culture, lending legitimacy to the apparent criminal underclass. This legitimacy simultaneously reduces and increases the perceived threat: reduced because it is rationalised as a stream of legitimised culture, but increased through the establishment and entrenchment of criminality within the national body.

In terms of Mayhew, while he does not always display empathy for his impoverished subjects, he does arguably give them voice, albeit mediated by his own. Importantly, while Mayhew condemns criminality, he also condemns the poverty and oppression that cause it, manipulating the voices of his interviewees in order to achieve that end. Bryan S. Green notes the way in which Mayhew 'abandons' the 'impartiality' of the ethnographer to issue 'instructions' to his readers in order to motivate them to 'put an end "to . . . the degradation and demoralization of our fellow creatures."'[45] From this perspective, Mayhew seems to attribute citizenship and belonging to the disenfranchised poor by claiming them as fellow creatures. Although this idea is complicated by ideas of philanthropic charity, it does go some way to reinstating the distanced tourist attractions of the London slums to a place of belonging to the nation. This inclusion directly confronts the social narrative that seeks to position the poor as Other—as Foreign—and therefore unconnected with what it means to be British. It follows, then, that it is easier to focus on the crime, rather than the poverty that led to it; it is one thing to disenfranchise a criminal, yet it is morally compromising to turn away the vulnerable and starving. However, when there is a seeming proliferation of vulnerable people, that group as a whole can be perceived as overwhelming the nation. For that reason, the mobility of such a group is seen as a threat, which then lends itself to

---

43 See Tolson, 'Social Surveillance.'

44 William Augusts Miles, *Poverty, Mendicity, and Crime, Or, The Facts, Examinations, &c. Upon which the Report Was Founded*, ed. H. Brandon. Presented to the House of Lords (London: Shaw and Sons, 1839), 45.

45 Bryan S. Green, 'Learning from Mayhew: The Role of the Impartial Spectator in Mayhew's *London Labour and the London Poor*,' *Journal of Contemporary Ethnography*, 31 (2002): 99–134, 126. Qtd in Mayhew, *London Labour and the London Poor*, vol. 3, 272.

criminalisation: '[t]he respectable feared that, as Britain underwent rapid indus-
trialization and urbanization, a new breed of criminal threatened the social order.
They perceived the source of the problem to lie in moral decrepitude.'[46] Out of
fear and ideas of moral supremacy, the criminalisation of the poor conveniently
reconciles with self-interest.

John Binny's section of volume 4 of *London Labour* specifically addresses the
desire to separate 'criminal' and 'respectable' society by reinforcing the extent to
which these imagined worlds are enmeshed. In this way, Binny interrogates what
is means to belong, examining the children of London:

> The public streets of the metropolis are regarded by these ragged little felons
> and the children of honest industrious parents in a very different aspect. The
> latter walk the streets with their eyes sparkling with wonder and delight at the
> beautiful and grand sights of the metropolis. They are struck with the splen-
> dour of the shops and the elegance and stateliness of the public buildings,
> and with the dense crowds of people of various orders, and trains of vehicles
> thronging the streets. These little ragged thieves walk along the streets with
> very different emotions. They, too, in their own way enjoy the sights and
> sounds of London. Amid the busy crowds many of them are to be seen sit-
> ting in groups on the pavement or loitering about in good-humour and merri-
> ment; yet ever and anon their keen roguish eyes sparkle as they look into the
> windows of the confectioners', bakers', and greengrocers' shops, at the same
> time keeping a sharp eye on the policeman as he passes on his beat.[47]

While they may have 'very different emotions,' both types of children walk the
same streets, and both have eyes that sparkle with enjoyment in response to what
they see. In this sense, the groups inhabit the same space in a remarkably similar
way. However, the wide-eyed wonder of the 'honest' children gives the impression of foreignness, observing the sights as if they were tourists. Although the
'honest' children are Londoners, this space is not familiar to them and, importantly, they are mobile within it. The thieves, though, sit securely in merry groups,
overturning the assumption of which group is stable and which is nomadic: the
city-space belongs to them. Similarly, while Brantlinger and Ulin observe 'the
proliferating, eccentric, nomadic voices of [Mayhew's] street people, who refuse
to stay inside neatly constructed houses, classes, pigeonholes, stereotypes,'[48] the
conflict goes deeper: not only do the nomadic criminals refuse to be contained,
they actively invade spaces of respectability, and even originate from within
them. They are not a transient presence in London; rather they blend into the
middle-class social landscape: '[t]he most accomplished pickpockets *reside* at

46 Beier, '"Takin' It to the Streets,"' 90.

47 John Binny, 'Thieves and Swindlers,' in *London Labour and the London Poor*, vol. 4, 273–392, 274.

48 Patrick Brantlinger and Donald Ulin, 'Policing Nomads: Discourse and Social Control in Early
    Victorian Britain,' *Cultural Critique*, 25 (1993): 33–63, 59.

Islington, Hoxton, Kingsland Road, St Luke's, the Borough, Camberwell, and Lambeth, in quiet, respectable streets, and *occasionally* change their lodging if watched by the police.'[49] While living in apparent economic and social stability, the thief could be the respectable reader's next-door neighbour. On the surface of the city, in their secure dwelling places, thieves are established as part of the urban community. Importantly, Binny and Mayhew create narratives that re-enfranchise the deprived. Although they are on the one hand raising terror in regard to crime, they are on the other hand legitimating the poor as a part of the national social body.

'The exile is free to land upon our shores, and free to perish of hunger beneath our inclement skies'[50]

Alongside Britain's domestic mobility, the nineteenth century saw an increase in mobilisation across Europe, with Britain—especially London—being a major destination. The Great Irish Famine saw an estimated one million leave Ireland, while between 44 and 52 million people from Continental Europe migrated between the end of the Napoleonic Wars and the First World War.[51] With every nation on the Continent seeming engorged with revolution and battle, mainland Britain was effectively hedged in on all sides with an overwhelming number of starved people displaced by war, famine, and destruction. The effect of this international mobility reveals a deep irony in the vicious cycle of hunger: out of physical hunger and want, people banded together in protest in Ellmann's terms, yet were further exiled for their political and social hunger. In turn, having sought asylum on Britain's shores, they are led into a place of renewed physical hunger alongside social displacement. One of the paradoxes of British domestic and foreign policy in the nineteenth century is that while the British poor (which included the Irish) were often brutalised as a result of the vagrancy and settlement laws, foreign exiles were given free right of passage and settlement within Britain. Britain prided itself as a nation for being open to refugees, as expressed by the Conservative Foreign Secretary Lord Malmesbury in 1852:

> 'I can well conceive the pleasure and happiness of a refugee, hunted from his native land, and approaching the shores of England, and the joy with which he first catches sight of them; but they are not greater than the pleasure and happiness every Englishman feels in knowing that his country affords the refugees a home and safety.'[52]

---

49 Binny, 'Thieves and Swindlers,' 308. Emphasis added.
50 G.J. Harvey, *The Star of Freedom* (18 September 1852), 88.
51 Dudley Baines, *Migration in a Mature Economy: Emigration and Internal Migration in England and Wales 1861–1900* (Cambridge: Cambridge University Press, 1985), 1.
52 Qtd in Bernard Parker, *The Refugee Question in Mid-Victorian Politics* (1979; Cambridge: Cambridge University Press, 2008), 4.

This official national narrative constructed an image of England as a haven, under-girded by what Elaine Freedgood describes as the desire to banish danger from the domestic scene and relocate it 'in the world outside British boarders':[53] not only was England safe and secure, it was in a position to provide refuge to those vulnerable people from without. Britain is the nation of affluence. This social narrative was as important to mid-century Britain as the repression of Britain's violent heritage; however, in practice, the poor refugees arriving on England's shores found themselves in an unexpectedly vulnerable position. Refugees may have had right of passage and settlement, but they had no recourse to public fund-ing. Some French refugees even believed that the lack of access to welfare was a deliberate British plot to starve them literally to death.[54] The French exile and socialist thinker Pierre Leroux wrote of his wife and children living in a slum 'with no air to breathe' and 'almost no bread to eat.' He derided the British narrative of hospitable asylum, stating that Britain provided 'political liberty but also the liberty to die of starvation.'[55] Furthermore it should be noted, as Bernard Parker points out, that the freedom of asylum within Britain was 'maintained, not by law, but by the absence of laws,' and so therefore passively rather than by any active notion of international duty on the part of the British Parliament. In 1793 (until 1826) and in 1848 (until 1850) Alien Bills were introduced, linked, no doubt, to the terror raised by the French Revolution for the former and the Springtime of the Peoples in the latter; but it is also important to note that between 1826 and 1905, no foreigner was expelled from Britain under such legislation.[56]

The political exiles are seemingly punished for fighting to stave their hunger. It becomes a hopeless starvation, a hunger they no longer have the energy to fight. In English characters this kind of despairing hunger is represented through Gaskell's John Barton and Martineau's Mrs Kaye, but some of the most poignant figures are the nameless, transient foreign beggars, such as the Irish and Italian waifs in *Mary Barton* who are aided, respectively, by John Barton and Mary. Zemka goes as far as to describe these street encounters as 'parable[s] of mourning. Time and again, the novel presents us with characters who are lost, needy, or hungry children.'[57] The recognition of hunger, absence, and emptiness throughout the novel speaks to the lack of community connection, exacerbated by 'the unknowability, the inac-cessibility, of the poor.'[58] The European refugees were, of course, subject to the English vagrancy laws, and Parker observes that '[a]s well as not being of any positive benefit to Britain, the presence of refugees could be an irritant. Many of

53 Elaine Freedgood, *Victorian Writing about Risk: Imagining a Safe England in a Dangerous World* (Cambridge: Cambridge University Press, 2004), 1.
54 Sabine Freitag, 'Introduction,' *Exiles from European Revolution: Refugees in Mid-Victorian England*, ed. Sabine Freitag (New York and Oxford: Berghahn Books, 2003), 8.
55 *La Grève de Samarez, poème philosophique* (Paris, 1863), 237; 305, qtd in Fabrice Bensimon, 'The French Exiles and the British,' in *Exiles from European Revolution*, ed. Freitag, 88–102, 89–90.
56 Parker, *Refugee Question*, 3.
57 Zemka, 'Brief Encounters,' 799–800.
58 Ibid., 804.

them were poor, and were found begging and occasionally stealing and swindling to stay alive.'[59] John Barton's compassion toward the Irish child seems in stark contrast to the murder he has just committed, although from a cynical perspective, this could be an allusion to the perceived Irish influence on Chartism. However, the need for Mary to be compelled to help the Italian boy is a provocative foil: Barton's violence is repositioned as a sacrifice of his self, of his own position and morality, for the sake of desperately trying to aid such vulnerable creatures, particularly one of a similar age to his own dead son.

The Irish migrants deserve particular attention, not just because of their presence in the social narrative as particularly disruptive, or the impact of the Great Famine on much of Europe, but also because they were positioned in the social imagination in a particularly liminal space: they were not quite foreign, existing as the closest British colony to the mainland, but they were also not embraced as British. Furthermore, as Sabine Clemm notes, 'the Irish always appear outside the collective national identity . . . while the Welsh and Scottish occasionally merge with it.'[60] In this way, the Irish presence within mainland Britain disrupts the nation's imagined community, for as much as they may be in the space of the nation, the national narrative does not permit them to find a home there. Their presence on the mainland was particularly uncomfortable given that their emigration to Britain was politically unique, in that the Irish were migrating to the nation that many held accountable for Ireland's demise,[61] and at the same time, although Ireland was considered a colony, it could not be dismissed in the way more distant (geographically and culturally) colonies could be:

> Whereas it is possible to imagine Australia as empty and to dismiss India's population, although undeniably existent, as visibly 'Other,' pagan, savage, and in need of British influence, the Irish people and their culture and religion were all uncomfortably close to Britain's own. Furthermore, the Irish had a voice that is far less easily ignored than that of other, non-European colonial subjects—most Irish people in the mid-nineteenth-century were native speakers of English, and those who spoke Irish at all (up to a third of the population) were predominantly bilingual. Thus, they had the potential to talk back and resist the easy dehumanisation that the populations of other British colonies underwent in imperial discourse.[62]

Of course, talk back the Irish did, from protesting against the 1800 Act of Union to the rise of the Fenians. Yet the very desire of England to dehumanise a nation so closely connected with their own calls into question their own humanity; and

59 Parker, *Refugee Question*, 6.
60 Sabine Clemm, *Dickens, Journalism, and Nationhood: Mapping the World in* Household Words (New York and London: Routledge, 2009), 81.
61 Roger Swift, 'Thomas Carlyle, "Chartism", and the Irish in Early Victorian England,' *Victorian Literature and Culture*, 29.1 (2001): 67–83, 77.
62 Clemm, *Dickens, Journalism, and Nationhood*, 81.

so the focus of criticism centred on what was perceived as the uncivilised Catholic religion and, with significant links for many critics including Dickens, the abjection of famine, as a means to Other and barbarise the Irish foreigner. Apart from the horror of the proximity of the famine, though, some British camps felt a sense of responsibility, blaming British mismanagement as one of the major contributors to the extent and impact of the famine. Michael de Nie observes that '[w]ith literally hundreds of thousands of people dying only miles from England's shores, the British people needed self-justification. This was accomplished by projecting the blame for Irish suffering onto the Irish themselves,'[63] and, indeed, on their Catholic superstitions.

David Lloyd has suggested that the British perception of the Irish during the Great Famine was shaped by representations of 'the Irish as excess, as irrational and immoral, as a redundant surplus that threatene[d] to overwhelm England, as an abundance of wretchedness.'[64] In a similar vein, on 1 September 1846, a columnist for *The Times* wrote,

> they have come amongst us, but they have not become of us. They have earned our money; but they have carried back neither our habits nor our sympathies, neither our love of cleanliness nor our love of comfort, neither our economy nor our prudence. Is this distinctive character incapable of subjugation or change?[65]

As the Other, the Irish migrants are figured as an opaque force flooding the nation, not an assimilating group that blends or melts into Britain. They therefore remain terrifyingly visible, as does their hunger. Furthermore, unlike the European refugees, the Irish *were* expelled, by virtue of the settlement laws. Brantlinger and Ulin observe that the compulsion of the British to equate vagrancy with Irish migrancy was well in place even in the early 1840s,[66] and although paupers were meant to be taken back to their parish of origin, the Irish were 'not returned to their own union, but . . . unceremoniously dumped at the nearest port of entry.'[67] And indeed, the prejudice toward the Irish persists to some degree, with some twenty-first-century scholars reporting:

> [t]he 1851 Census reported 50,289 foreigners in England and Wales, in a total population of nearly 18 millions, which was a percentage of only 0.28. They were greatly outnumbered by the 520,000 Irish in England and Wales, who *did* present social problems, and by 130,000 Scots.[68]

63 Michael De Nie, 'The Famine, Irish Identity, and the British Press,' *Irish Studies Review*, 6.1 (1998): 27–35, 28.
64 Lloyd, 'Indigent Sublime,' 160.
65 Qtd in De Nie, 'Famine, Irish Identity, and the British Press,' 28.
66 Brantlinger and Ulin, 'Policing Nomads,' 41.
67 Christine Kineally, *This Great Calamity: The Irish Famine 1845–52* (Dublin: Gill & Macmillan Ltd., 1994), 25.
68 Parker, *Refugee Question*, 4, Parker's emphasis.

While the Irish migrants may have outnumbered the Continental European migrants, to single them out as a particular social problem seems to buy into the social myth predicated on nineteenth-century prejudice. Bernard Parker persists in his argument that, unlike the Irish, '[t]hose [Europeans] who did come to settle did not generally come in as cheap labour, and so were not resented for that, or not half so much as the Irish,'[69] yet Roger Swift points out that 'the poor Irish, who were the only visible Irish, became convenient scapegoats for environmental deterioration.'[70] While there were vast numbers of famine refugees fleeing Ireland, the visibility of the poor migrants was crucial to the British reception of migration; for although there were skilled, professional, and middle-class Irish migrants during the famine years, these migrants were invisible in comparison with the 'largely illiterate and unskilled' majority, who 'entered the lowliest and least healthy of urban occupations.'[71] Yet it is interesting that in terms of visibility the opposite was true for the European refugees, perhaps out of Britain's desire to maintain its position as a haven for European turmoil. Instead, figures like the Belgians Robert and Hortense Moore in Brontë's *Shirley* emerge, with the capacity to find hope and prosperity within Britain.

First published in the final years of the Great Famine, Mayhew's *London Labour and the London Poor* reinforces the spectre of the starving Irish presence. Mayhew focuses on the Irish migrants' domesticity as much as on their mobility, which emphasises not just that the starving were still coming to London (which challenged the official reports that the famine was over), but, more crucially, that they were coming to *stay*. Dickens reveals similar concerns in 'A Crisis in the Affairs of Mr. John Bull' (1850), when C.J. London is criticised by Mrs Bull for 'the encouragement [he] gave to that mewling little Pussy, when it strayed here.'[72] Although this reference is to Puseyism, and therefore to 'homegrown' Catholicism, it follows the description of Ireland, or Mr Bull's sister, 'Miss Eringobragh,' who has become immoveable from Mr Bull's hearth: she 'grovel[s] on the ground, with her head in the ashes. This unfortunate lady had been, for a length of time, in a horrible condition of mind and body, and presented a most lamentable spectacle of disease, dirt, rags, superstition and degradation.'[73] Therefore Dickens not only raises concerns regarding Catholicism, but, like Mayhew, seems to buy into the English fear of Irish entrenchment within the mainland. Also like Mayhew, Dickens reflects on 'the conspicuousness of the Irish' within London, 'draw[ing] on the English reading public's perception of the foreignness of the Irish experience'[74] in order to reveal the complex position of the Irish within the so-called United Kingdom. Andrew Tolson writes of social visibility in terms of agency

69 Ibid., 5.
70 Swift, 'Thomas Carlyle,' 77.
71 Ibid., 78.
72 [Charles Dickens], 'A Crisis in the Affairs of Mr. John Bull,' *Household Words*, 2.35 (23 November 1850): 193–96, 195.
73 Ibid.
74 Leon Litvack, 'Dickens, Ireland and the Irish, Part 1,' *The Dickensian*, 99.459 (2003): 34–59, 51.

and the 'recognition it gives to cultural diversity,'[75] and he celebrates the way in which Mayhew gives voice to the poor. Yet Mayhew's ambivalence toward the Irish presence simultaneously confronts and buys into the popular fear of the Irish influx, which was bound up not just in the economic practicalities of food shortages, but also in the established representation of the Irish as demonic Catholic mobs, infamous for inflaming the English poor to riots, protests, and mass destruction. The parallels between the representation of the Irish mobs and the French Revolution are quite poignant, especially in terms of the gothic language of terror and the sublime; yet the sublime in mid-nineteenth-century representations of the Irish is not the aesthetic of majestic, awe-inspiring mountains and castles, or even the oceanic waves of revolution, but the perverted excess of abject numbers—the overcrowded cities, the innumerable starving images in the popular press, and the sheer overwhelming casualty count.

While buying into the fear of both proximity and increased migration, Mayhew reinforces Britain's connection with Ireland, referring to Ireland, similar to Dickens, as 'the sister kingdom,' speaking of the Irish being 'driven over from "the sister Isle",' but he is more sympathetic toward their experience:

> First they were driven over by the famine, when they could not procure, or began to fear that soon they could not procure, food to eat. Secondly, they were forced to take refuge in this country by the evictions, when their landlords had left them no roof to shelter them in their own.[76]

Mayhew's text speaks to the very practical economic situation in Britain of overpopulation, food scarcity, and disease, matters that were exacerbated in the cities and industrial towns as the British moved around the nation. Locating the blame for the situation within the Irish community was as entrenched a narrative as this kind of movement itself, and indeed links back to the anti-Catholic rhetoric of the Gordon Riots: Irish migration and mobility within Britain were far from new phenomena. Two decades before the famine, Malthus wrote to David Ricardo that 'a great part of the population [of Ireland] should be swept from the soil,' while Carlyle's attitude in *Chartism* is even more militant: 'time has come when the Irish population must either be improved a little, or else exterminated.'[77] While these views seem extreme, they were rife in mid-nineteenth-century Britain. Christine Kineally points out that the 'idea of communities of Irish existing in many British cities, known as "Little Irelands", where poverty, disease, alcoholism, crime and children were endemic, was made popular as early as 1831,' and the people living in these ghettoes were perceived as 'dirty, lawless and drunken.'[78]

75 Tolson, 'Social Surveillance,' 114.
76 Mayhew, *London Labour and the London Poor*, vol. 1, 104–05.
77 Qtd in Lloyd, 'Indigent Sublime,' 158.
78 Kineally, *This Great Calamity*, 329–30.

Andrew Halliday's section on 'Foreign Beggars' in volume 4 of *London Labour and the London Poor* reveals Mayhew's desire, as editor, to portray the diversity of London's foreign vagrants and criminals beyond the Irish contingency, from the French swindler pretending that he cannot speak English, to 'the foreign political exile, the foreign political spy, the foreign fraudulent trades-man, the foreign escaped thief, and the foreign convict who has served his time,' finding refuge in Leicester Square as if it were 'what, in the middle-ages, sanctuary was to the murderer.'[79] Halliday argues that it is more difficult to identify a foreign beggar who is truly in need because they 'are generally so mixed up with political events.'[80] He therefore increases the doubt of their legitimacy by questioning how much their position is a result of misfortune, and how much is by active choice. The connection of foreignness to criminality (or at least suspect civil behaviour or activities) is most profound, though, in the far more extensive accounts of the Irish. Mayhew's section on the Street Irish in volume 1 is far more detailed, teasing out the complexities of prejudice and empathy concerning the poor Irish figure.

Given the spectre of the Famine, Mayhew's emphasis on the Irish diet is crucial. His account of the 'squabbles' in lodging houses in the times when the Irish staple diet was potatoes, 'as to whether the potato-pot or the tea-kettle should have preference on the fire,' uses national taste stereotypes to illustrate the tensions between English and Irish predominance.[81] The transition of the Irish diet toward coffee and bread for breakfast is therefore positioned as a means to bring about a type of cultural *détente*. However, it is in this conscious need to adapt that the Irish are again differentiated from their English counterparts: 'In such details I have found the Irish far more communicative than the English. Many a poor untaught Englishman will shrink from speaking of his spare diet, and his trouble to procure that.'[82] The need to articulate cultural transitions is linked to the expression of literal tastes. Furthermore, the willingness of the Irish to eat bread without butter, unlike the English Mayhew describes, reveals at once the necessity of having to do without butter, but also the crucial ability of the Irish to adapt to such circumstances. They are, essentially, able to find '[f]amiliar flavourings [to] make unfamiliar foods palatable.'[83] It is partly this adaptability that makes the Irish a threat in English eyes: adaptability in Darwinian terms designates the means to survive. The Irish ability to choose tastes and preferences within the narrow limitations of their impoverished income is necessarily tied to their ability to feel a sense of independence and social legitimacy. Disparity in diet was a way for both the British and the foreign migrants to differentiate themselves, with adaptation potentially designating cultural persistence: taste becomes a national issue.

79 Halliday, 'Foreign Beggars,' *London Labour and the London Poor*, vol. 4, 419–27, 419.
80 Ibid., vol. 4, 419.
81 Mayhew, *London Labour and the London Poor*, vol. 1, 113.
82 Ibid.
83 Carolyn Korsmeyer, 'Preface: Taste: Physiology and Circumstance,' in *Taste Culture Reader*, ed. Korsmeyer, 13–14.

The French exile Alexandre Ledru-Rollin, whose infamous critique, *De la decadence de l'Angleterre* (published in English under the title *The Decline of England* in 1850), alienated him from his host nation within weeks of his fleeing to Britain, directly connects the British with their feudal past in terms of taste:

> In the fourteenth century the serfs, their ancestors, sang:—
> 'The landholders are clothed in velvet and in purple, lined with vair and minever; they have meats, and spices, and good wines, and we—we eat the refuse of straw, and drink water. They have ease and fine manor; we have pain and toil, rain and wind, in the open air. Why do they keep us in slavery? we are all come from the same father and mother, Adam and Eve.'[84]

To an extent, Ledru-Rollin provides a French migrant perspective on England in the way that Mayhew examines London, through his use of interviews and narratives to give voice to the poor. While Sabine Freitag suggests that Ledru-Rollin was insulting the English nation for their inhospitable treatment of foreign exiles and their poor food,[85] Ledru-Rollin's critique goes much deeper and is much more complex than the kind of spiteful example of biting the hand that feeds him that Freitag claims. While Freitag argues that his criticism was an exception, Fabrice Bensimon insists that his work was largely derived from other readily available texts.[86] It is evident, then, that Ledru-Rollin enters a legitimate, well-established critical space on economic and philosophical terms, much as the British critiqued France and other Continental nations. His text critiques Britain's treatment of itself as well as foreigners. He does not declare, for example, that all British food is bad, but specifically says: '[t]hese workmen are really an intelligent body of men; but the *dishonourables* are degraded by their incessant labour, their miserable pay, their execrable food, and the unhealthiness of their dwellings' (149). Thus he confronts the distribution of wealth through the distribution of tastes, and defends the disenfranchised English as much as he stands for the vulnerable migrant. While he stands for his fellow exiles, '[t]hrown as strangers upon the English soil by the chance of revolutions' being marked 'as felons escaped from the galleys, as miserable bandits, as the filth of the sewers of Paris' (3), this introduction leads into his defence of the English:

> What then avails the skilful culture, which makes the earth yield all of which she is capable? what avail fruitful harvests, fat pastures, prize-flocks, with their long and fine wool, if the people of the country, the hirelings of the glebe, die of hunger? I speak not alone of Ireland returning to a savage state; of Ireland, where the animal!—O degradation!—is preferred to the human being; where the landlord's hounds hunt the feeble and naked man—no, I speak of the richest parts of England. (11)

84 Ledru-Rollin, *Decline of England*, 27.
85 Freitag, 'Introduction,' 7.
86 Ibid., Bensimon, 'French Exiles and the British,' 91.

Furthermore, he reveals the devastating effects of England's international invest-ment: 'England is dependent upon the foreigner for one quarter of her food annually; through free-trade in corn, although a necessary measure, her landlords are ruined, her farmers are ruined, and the labourers are compelled to seek in crime the satisfaction of their wants' (238). Therefore while Ledru-Rollin has been accused of criticising Britain, this perspective is dependent on which imag-ined British community is being given the voice for all. His critique resonates with that of British thinkers on political economy, such as John Stuart Mill, but because he is foreign within the British context, the legitimacy of his vision is considered suspect. Even so, he captures the distinct hunger of Britain within his appraisal. One could easily hear Dickens's Nancy saying, alongside Ledru-Rollin's interviewee, 'Nobody knows the temptations that beset us poor girls, when in want of food' (166–67).

'Native unsettledness':[87] Itinerancy and travelling performers

Ledru-Rollin's empathy with the British poor can be identified within their mutual marginality as mobile people, disconnected from their community. In establish-ing the long history of Western mobility, Cresswell argues that 'to be mobile was to exist on the margins,' and goes on to give a distinctively pre-modern list of marginal travellers: '[w]andering minstrels, troubadours, crusaders, pilgrims, and some peripatetic monks existed, for periods of time, outside the obligations of place and roots.'[88] He also suggests that '[m]obile people are never simply *people*—they are dancers and pedestrians, drivers and athletes, refugees and citi-zens, tourists or businesspeople, men and women.'[89] These lists and categories, even to the gendering of travellers, speak to the need to categorise mobile people who do not identify clearly with a particular community. Indeed, within such groups of mobile people, there exists a need to create their own sense of com-munity through subculture as they become, in a way, domestic foreigners—not belonging, proscribed from their places of origin. Self-definition is further nec-essary in that, as Fumerton points out, from the time of the 1572 Vagrancy Act there existed a complex relationship between vagrancy and poor itinerant work-ers, with the Act attempting to draw for the first time a clear distinction between the 'professional beggar' and the blameless unemployed.[90] Yet within the need to legitimate their position, the major problem for itinerant workers was that they depended on unknown community spaces to earn a living, having found that their own communities could not provide work for them. Even though they held to the valorous desire to earn their living rather than depend on parish welfare, the need to move meant that they accessed resources from elsewhere. They remained ostra-cised in many cases because, as A.L. Beier observes, '[t]heir chief and abiding

87 Fumerton, *Unsettled*, 12.
88 Cresswell, *On the Move*, 11.
89 Ibid., 4.
90 Fumerton, *Unsettled*, xi.

sin was that they preyed on the settled population to make a living,'[91] potentially taking work that would have otherwise been available to the locals. While it was possible to rationalise this ostracism when the travelling workers were from another country, including (and perhaps especially) Ireland, it is more difficult to create exclusionary social narratives within the nation. However, this is achieved through the narrowing ideas of 'domestic' and 'foreign' as discussed in Chapter 2. The itinerant worker is a foreigner, with little or no investment of social capital within the local community.

Both Martineau and Gaskell provide narrative examples of the itinerant worker, characters who, no longer able to work in their community, become travelling performers. Yet rather than focusing on their removal from the community, both representations reveal a kind of entrepreneurial spirit, an optimistic view of itinerancy within a devastating economic situation, and in both cases, centre on Manchester. In stark contrast to the starving local community, Martineau's and Gaskell's itinerant workers are presented as healthy and prosperous. In *A Manchester Strike* (1832), Bray and his daughter, Hannah, provide a foil to William Allen and his daughter, Martha. Martha, at the age of eight, is near crippled from working in a factory, while her father, William, because he is a worker held in high esteem by both his fellow employees and the masters, is compelled, against his better judgement, to become a union leader in a strike. After the strike is unsuccessful, William remains in the community, but is unable to find real work: he is ostracised as a union leader, and must live in reduced circumstances in a desperate attempt to provide for his family, even though he did not want to lead the union in the first place. Bray is the victim of a previous strike, but rather than trying to stay in the community, he had decided to become a travelling performer with his daughter. While this move is seen as morally dubious by the community he left, the physical health of both father and daughter challenges criticism of the decision to be mobile. In response to such criticism, Bray says:

> 'You had rather see her covered with white cotton flakes than with yellow ribands; but remember it is no fault of mine that she is not still a piecer in yonder factory. . . . Look how strong and plump she is! so much for living in the open air, instead of being mewed up in an oven. Now, don't take off the hat on purpose to shake your head. What can a man do . . . what can a proscribed man do but get his living, so as not to have to ask for work?'[92]

Bray's defence is that he had no choice but to leave the community; however, from his marginal position, he is able to choose the extent to which he engages with the current strike. Therefore his exile provides him some level of agency, at the sacrifice of fully legitimate communal belonging.

---

91 Beier, '"Takin' It to the Streets,"' 97.
92 Harriet Martineau, 'A Manchester Strike,' in *Illustrations of Political Economy*, ed. Logan, 139–216, 147.

It is the contrast between Hannah and Martha, though, that creates the most emotive response. Hannah spurs Martha's imagination and hope with her talk of good food:

> 'You should have meat for dinner every day as I have,' said Hannah, 'and then you would grow fat like me. Father gets such good dinners for us to what we used to have. He says 'tis that, and being in the air so much that prevents my being sickly, as I used to be. I don't think I could do the work that I used to do with all that noise, and the smell of oil and the heat.' (150–51)

Again physical strength is attributed to meat, as well as spirit and determination, and Martha is thus inspired: '[she] flushed with flattery and with the grand idea of earning a great many silver sixpences every day if her father would let her make music in the streets instead of going to the factory' (152). Hannah's musical ability enables her to exchange the factory noise for music, providing her an ironic form of civility—in spite of her nomadic lifestyle, she earns a living by exchanging cultural capital instead of physical labour. Although she is still a child having to earn a living rather than playing with her friends, she at least has a concept of play, unlike her counterparts in the factories.

Gaskell's Margaret Jennings in *Mary Barton* also becomes a travelling performer, but her decision is based on her increasing blindness that excludes her from conventional female work within the locality of Manchester. Importantly, her increasing blindness is attributed to the poverty in which she must live.[93] However, as in the case of Hannah Bray, the venture into singing brings health to Margaret's body. Initially Margaret is described as 'a sallow, unhealthy, sweet-looking young woman, with a careworn look' (32); but once she is singing, there is a sense of comparative luxury in her position compared to that of Mary. Mary longs to be able to sing like Margaret, but Margaret says, 'Many's the time when I could see, that I longed for your beauty, Mary! We're like childer, ever wanting what we han not got. But now I must say just one more word. Remember, if you're sore pressed for money, we shall take it very unkind if you donnot let us know' (168). It is from a position of luxury—of having an excess—that Margaret is able to philosophise over desire and unfulfilled longing, but Mary is consumed by her hunger for more: for food; for stability; and most importantly for a way to move out of her desperate situation. The removal from her community that Margaret experiences because of her mobility is reflected in her blindness. Yet from Mary's perspective, distance and sensory disconnection seems a small sacrifice to make for the sake of not being in want.

Domestic spaces and property

The combination of communal disconnection through mobility and physical hunger focalises the importance of property and access to familiar food within the social context. The desire for property is an extension of this dual hunger.

93 Gaskell, *Mary Barton*, 136.

Property is also a symbol of respectability, a means to groundedness, while the absence of it, like the absence of the means to acquire recognisable food, creates a distrust similar to mobility itself. In writing of contemporary Travellers in Europe and Great Britain, Jim McLaughlin states:

> The modern racialisation of Travellers as 'inferior people' has its roots in nineteenth-century theoretical defences of bourgeois property rights which legitimised the domination of nomadic societies by white 'settlers'. This theoretical discourse also justified the marginalisation of nomadic groups within Europe on the grounds that, as propertyless people, they had no right to be included within the political or moral structures of metropolitan society.[94]

This context is crucial in understanding the way in which food and furniture are necessary to creating the sense of home, or a home space, more so than the physical structures in which the transient population reside. They represent in a diasporic setting 'the hunger of desire for what one cannot have, and particularly the hunger for status, place, and solidity.'[95] Conversely, John Plotz observes the advantages of a portable culture in 'protecting or producing a sense of group cohesion,' through the capacity it creates for 'fluid cultural forms' and adapting 'with chameleonic ease to every new setting, and to purely immobile bits of local life.'[96] In some respects, the acquiring of portable property rather than land creates the ability to survive and adapt, as well as to adopt cultural practices eclectically. It also buys into the increasingly middle-class economic behaviour of investing in stocks and shares rather than in land. However, there is still a need to form a sense of communal identity within that adaptation. For those who rent on short-term leases, whether in lodging houses or in private dwellings, the ability to make that space their own by transporting furniture and being able to partake in familiar foods is critical. In many cases, the crowdedness of the rented home space increases in correlation with the desperation for a sense of home, while the smell of food creates a nostalgic longing for stability and communal rootedness. Putting down roots becomes no longer about an attachment to place, but the arrangement of easily transported familiar objects. The domestic space becomes a paradoxical assimilation of settlement and mobility, as there is, in their desire to remain, a constant sense that they may have to move on.

Shore argues that the decline in apprenticeship reorganised the general household composition in nineteenth-century Britain, which contributed significantly to perspectives connecting youth to delinquency. She attributes the social disconnect to children living with their parents longer, or living in lodgings, rather than

---

94 Jim MacLaughlin, 'The Evolution of Anti-Traveller Racism in Ireland,' *Race & Class*, 37.3 (1996): 47–63, 47.

95 Gwen Hyman, *Making a Man: Gentlemanly Appetites in the Nineteenth-Century British Novel* (Athens: Ohio University Press, 2009), 109.

96 Plotz, *Portable Property*, 19.

having live-in apprenticeships; yet she fails to explain how this change in living arrangements leads to apparent delinquency.[97] Although I am hesitant to attribute delinquency to a politically conservative view of family breakdown, it is possible to see that without having a sense of investment or accountability in the home environment, there is less moral inclination to value that space and then, by extension, the surrounding community. Also, there is perhaps a more provocative cause to be found in Fumerton's observation that apprentice-like situations created 'highly problematic "nowhere" positions—simultaneously high and low—which could destabilize a sense of a secure place.'[98] Taking this suggestion alongside Shore's account of living in lodgings, there is a potential for social unrest through this destabilisation of social identity, working together with a lessening sense of social accountability and the rise of self-interest over communal good within that more isolated space. This perspective does not account for Shore's argument regarding children living longer with their parents, though, particularly given the tradition within the gentry and middle classes of children staying in the family home until marriage. The narratives I address here, however, show a deep hunger to establish a sense of home within the rented or transient space, through attachment to portable property and access to regional foods from home—or foods that are at least reminiscent of that from the place of origin. Amy B. Trubek points out that the nostalgic association 'between taste and place . . . extends beyond a taste memory for certain foods and drinks of a region, but also for a certain way of life,'[99] braiding together the physical and social hungers bestowed through desires for particular tastes. The nostalgia inherent in these desires predicates that the hunger cannot be satisfied: one is *not* rooted in the space, nor is the food being eaten in the place it signifies; but the taste of the remembered home provides some sense of belonging, even if it remains diasporic. Indeed, as David E. Sutton poignantly observes, 'the hunger is in the memory, not in the biscuit, berries and cream.'[100] Because the hunger cannot be filled, there remains a compulsion to fill the space to excess in an impossible attempt to sate it.

Mayhew's descriptions of the home spaces of Irish migrants in London give a sense of performing hunger—perhaps, then, performing Irish cultural heritage— thus creating a spectacle for his middle-class readers in a way that simultaneously helps them to enter into that starved space. His narrative has almost an air of the *tableaux vivant*, as he takes his reader through the streets of London, observing Irish domestic spaces as captured living images, framed by the doorways of their homes: '[a]s the doors to the houses were nearly all of them kept open, I could, even whilst walking along, gain some notion of the furniture of the homes.'[101] Mayhew's construction evokes two key aspects—first, the voyeuristic tourism of

97 Shore, *Artful Dodgers*, 18.
98 Fumerton, *Unsettled*, 15.
99 Amy B. Trubek, 'Place Matters,' in *Taste Culture Reader*, ed. Korsmeyer, 260–71, 268.
100 Sutton, 'Synesthesia, Memory, and the Taste of Home,' 310.
101 Mayhew, *London Labour and the London Poor*, vol. 1, 110.

the slums that was so popular in the mid-century, as explicated by Seth Koven, and second, the spectacle of the sensation theatre. The doorways frame the stage, and the furniture is the set design. In both constructions there is a sense of perfor-mance, which crucially enables the English-reading public to distance themselves from the Irish figures with which they are presented: they are performers to be gazed upon, perhaps with the thrill of terror gained by a gothic novel or play. They do not seem quite real, just as the *tableaux vivants* were real actors, but because they were not physically moving, the audience could believe that they were objects. But then Mayhew goes a step further and enters the homes, becom-ing a part of the production—a move that reflects Britain's desire to assume distance from Ireland, while remaining inevitability tied politically, socially, and culturally. By presenting the Irish as performing hunger—becoming hunger artists—Mayhew endows them with the solidarity of identity and political pur-pose that motivates crowds to protest and move. It cannot be ignored that the starving Irish are in the centre of the nation, and therefore of the Empire, because their hunger at home has been denied. Within this context of performance, Mayhew refuses to mitigate Britain's involvement and investment in Ireland, and, more importantly, refuses to allow Britain to be blind to their presence. In this way, he creates a provocative image of colonial interpenetration, with the Irish having invaded London, but then he, as a Londoner representing the Empire, subsequently invading the Irish domestic space.

Like Mayhew, Dickens ventures into the domestic spaces of the Irish in London, although Litvack pertinently observes that '[f]rom the way he recounts the inci-dent, it seems that Dickens never doubted his prerogative to break in and wake up the trampers as they took their poor rest: clearly he uses the presence of the police to justify this intrusive surveillance.'[102] Dickens certainly takes the idea of colonial power further, crowding the Irish and dehumanising them in one sweep: 'Ten, twenty, thirty—who can count them! Men, women, children, for the most part naked, heaped upon the floor like maggots in a cheese!'[103] Not only are Dickens's Irish migrants denied the civilisation of clothing, they are compared with maggots— the reference to food choices and practices also being called into question. While Dickens's portrayal of the Irish is often difficult to pin down, the way he describes the migrants in London very clearly marks them as the uncivilised Other invading the civilised Britain. Writing in the same year as Dickens, Mayhew's ambivalence toward the Irish presence in London is similarly evident in his first mention of entering the Irish space, although he is more elusive than Dickens in the way he juxtaposes expectation and observation. 'In all the houses that I entered,' Mayhew writes, 'were traces of household care and neatness that I had little expected to have seen' (1: 110). Later he goes on:

> [t]he better class of Irish lodging-houses almost startle one by the comfort and cleanliness of the rooms; for after the descriptions you hear of the state

102 Litvack, 'Dickens, Ireland and the Irish,' 51.
103 [Charles Dickens], 'On Duty with Inspector Field,' *Household Words*, 3 (14 June 1851): 265–70, 266.

in which the deck passengers are landed from the Irish boats, their clothes stained with the manure of the pigs, and drenched with the spray, you somehow expect to find all the accommodations disgusting and unwholesome. But one in particular, that I visited, had the floor clean, and sprinkled with red sand, while the windows were sound, bright, and transparent. (1: 111)

While it does seem that in this spacious image Mayhew is trying to overturn some of the prejudices against the Irish, his surprise is telling, giving the sense that he has stumbled across something rare. However, there is an implicit reminder that this is a lodging house, not a privately owned home. The house is an English structure, into which the Irish have just moved. He says, '[i]n one corner of the principal apartment there stood two or three boxes still corded up, and with bundles strung to the sides, and against the wall was hung a bunch of blue cloaks, such as the Irishwomen wear' (1: 111), which serves as a reminder that they have just arrived, and therefore have not had time to settle: they have not had time to corrupt or pollute the clean English space.

In contrast, he goes on to describe a more settled Irish establishment:

[i]n one of the worst class of lodging-houses I found ten human beings living together in a small room. The apartment was entirely devoid of all furniture, excepting an old mattress rolled up against the wall, and a dirty piece of cloth hung across one corner, to screen the women while dressing. . . . All these people seemed to be utterly devoid of energy, and the men moved about so lazily that I couldn't help asking some of them if they had tried to obtain work. Every one turned to a good-looking young fellow lolling against the wall, as if they expected him to answer for them. . . . The chosen spokesperson then told me, 'They paid half-a-crown a week for the room, and that was as much as they could earrun, and it was starruve they should if the neighbours didn't hilp them a bit.' I asked them if they were better off over here than in Ireland, but could get no direct answer, for my question only gave rise to a political discussion. 'There's plenty of food over here,' said the spokesman, addressing his companions as much as myself, 'plenty of 'taties—plenty of mate—plenty of porruk.' 'But where the use,' observed my guide, 'if there's no money to buy 'em wid?' to which my audience muttered, 'Thrue for you again, Norah'; and so it went on, each one pleading poverty in most eloquent style. (1: 111–12)

What dominates this description is that the hope of food—the presence of food in England, even if it is not currently accessible—creates a hope of finding a home. Unlike in Ireland, where they have been reduced to famine, there is the possibility that their hunger will be sated in England, and therefore their humanity restored. The food mentioned is associated with home—potatoes and pork. While Mayhew's account seems stereotypical in this case, the relationship between these particular tastes and the Irish home is important to his narrative. Potatoes were central to the Irish economy, while it was standard to have pigs in rural communities because they are easy to raise, they can eat scraps, and pork is one of the easiest meats to preserve. However, these images also buy into English prejudices toward Irish literal tastes and their cultural tastes. Although pigs were practical livestock to have, they were also associated with filth, hence the earlier reference made to the pigs on the boats. In terms of potatoes, De Nie points out that the English associated Irish laziness with their penchant for potatoes because, similar to pigs, potatoes were easy crops to grow.[104] However, the famine had devastated this apparently easy source of food and income. As these Irish figures in Mayhew's account associate these foods with home, a double sense of loss is found in that they have lost their nation as much as they have lost physical sustenance. Mayhew passes quite quickly over the exceptional cases of Irish cleanliness and spaciousness to hover over these kinds of representations that confirm popular fears. They are overcrowded, dependent on assistance from their neighbours—which is more likely to mean fellow Irishmen, but could suggest they will end up on public benefits—and continue to increase in numbers due to the vague belief that there is at least food present in Britain, even if they cannot afford to buy it. Their listlessness creates another aspect of terror, giving them an aura of the consuming undead. The lack of furniture in this setting increases the sense of absence, the insatiable vacuum of their existence and inability to acquire capital; and the details of the rent they pool together undergirds their inability to make this space home.

In another Irish tableau, Mayhew begins by describing yet another house, in which there is a family of five persons—half of the previous account—who have twice as much space, living in two rooms on the ground floor. Consistent with the connection between spaciousness and cleanliness, the boards are here 'strewn with red sand,' and there is room for (and assumably capital to afford) furniture: in the *front* room there are three beds, not just a rolled-up mattress (1: 110). But even in this more palatable situation, Mayhew refuses to allow a reduction in fear. He takes his narrative beyond the veneer of the front room, with its door open to the public:

> In a dark room, at the back, lived the family itself. It was fitted up as a parlour, and crowded to excess with chairs and tables. . . . The fire, although it was midday, and a warm autumn morning, served as much for light as for heat, and round it crouched the mother, children, and visitors, bending over the flame as if in the severest winter time. (1: 110)

Mayhew then travels upstairs to 'a man and woman lately arrived in England. The woman sat huddled up in a corner smoking, with the husband standing over her in, what appeared at first, a menacing attitude; I was informed, however, that they were only planning for the future.' Within another room in the same apartment is an old woman, whose nose is described as 'the nostrils entering her face like bullet holes' (1: 110). Mayhew's narrative is overcrowded with dark and violent images, or the threat of violence, wrapped up in the overcrowded domestic spaces of the Irish. David Lloyd observes the mid-century belief that

---

104 De Nie, 'Famine, Irish Identity, and the British Press,' 29.

'[t]he proper and hygienic reformation of Irish spaces is the necessary counterpart to their economic advance,'[105] yet it seems in Mayhew's account that the only way to create this kind of reformation is to remove the Irish from the British domestic space. Yet even then, the transient Irish presence leaves a mark. In the account of the couple with the menacing husband, the room is 'perfectly empty of furniture,' presumably because they are planning on moving on, yet 'the once white-washed walls were black, excepting the little square patches which showed where the pictures of the former tenants had hung' (1: 110). And so in the end, the Irish inhabit British home structures. These spaces are either crowded by the Irish people, or crowded by Irish furniture—their cultural baggage. Yet even more terrifying is the idea that even if the Irish migrants move on, the domestic space remains haunted by their presence. David Lloyd suggests that '[w]hat complicates this haunting . . . is that the specter that returns is not simply that of the myriad unburied dead of the Famine, but the haunting resonance of the victim's dehumanization this side of death, the dehumanization that made their extirpation thinkable and admissible.'[106] As much as the British public may have sought to avoid or dismiss the overwhelming horror of the Great Famine, Mayhew's representation of Irish domesticity within London establishes the domestic space as a site of haunting trauma and poverty. Rather than distancing the English-reading public from Ireland, the tragedy is embedded, with immediacy, urgency, and permanence, firmly within Britain's boundaries.

The desperate and excessive display of transportable capital in Mayhew's final tableau resonates with the description of home spaces in *Mary Barton*, and Gaskell's work has a similar effect of emotively bringing middle-class readers into an alternative domestic space. Indeed, Jenny Uglow asserts that '*Mary Barton* touched and shocked its middle-class readers to an unprecedented extent because it showed how the poor suffered not in the mill or the factory but in their homes, with their wives and children, as the settled rhythms of their lives were shaken and destroyed.'[107] Similarly, Jill Matus writes:

> The several descriptions of homes and dwellings in *Mary Barton* offer spatial representations of their inhabitants. Alice Wilson's humble scrubbed and spotless cellar with its drying herbs shows her straitened circumstances but reassures us of her simple purity, orderliness, and old country ways. Tea at the working-class but respectable home of the Bartons in the opening scenes emphasizes domestic comfort and adequacy, which later contrasts with what the home becomes after John Barton's wife and son die and his fortunes decline. The physical squalor of the Davenports' fetid and rank cellar bespeaks their helpless indigence and suffering.[108]

105 Lloyd, 'Indigent Sublime,' 171.
106 Ibid., 156.
107 Jenny Uglow, *Elizabeth Gaskell: A Habit of Stories* (London and Boston: Faber and Faber, 1993), 194.
108 Jill Matus, '*Mary Barton* and *North and South*,' in *The Cambridge Companion to Elizabeth Gaskell*, ed. Jill Matus (Cambridge: Cambridge University Press, 2007), 27–45, 32.

Hungers, both physical and social, are written in the home space, from the indigent, hopeless starvation of the Davenports, to the Bartons' social hunger that degenerates into the physical. Importantly, the fact that Alice knows she can depend on her neighbours for cups implies that she can also depend on them for food if necessary: she is connected to the community in a way that provides hope, and as a result, her condition seems less dire. Alternatively, John Barton does not know the Davenports; and so although he does try to help them, their disconnection from the community reinforces that their hunger is without hope.

In the Bartons' home, there is a similar sense of the space, albeit 'tolerably large,' being crammed with furniture to make the rented space their own. Also the tone of display is similar to Mayhew's in that there is a sense of the narrator entering the scene with the reader through the second-person narration:

> On the right of the door, as you entered, was a longish window, with a broad ledge. On each side of this, hung blue-and-white check curtains, which were now drawn, to shut in the friends met to enjoy themselves. Two geraniums, unpruned and leafy, which stood by the sill, formed a further defence from out-door pryers. In the corner between the window and the fire-side was a cupboard, apparently full of plates and dishes, cups and saucers, and some more non-descript articles, for which one would have fancied their possessors could find no use. . . . However, it was evident Mrs Barton was proud of her crockery and glass, for she left her cupboard open, with a glance around of satisfaction and pleasure. . . . The place seemed almost crammed with furniture (sure sign of good times among the mills). (13)

Mrs Barton's pride and the emphasis on privacy and exclusivity in the space, speaks of middle-class ambition, a preoccupation that speaks to her social hunger; she is concerned with 'all due form' of the bourgeoisie in her presentation, rather than displaying the 'free-and-easy working-class meal.'[109] However, so many elements of the description of the Barton's house are inconsistent—for instance, the seeming overflow of crockery in the cupboard does not correlate with the fact that they do not have enough cups, so that Alice Wilson needs to bring her own to join the party. The space *seems* crammed with furniture—there is a desire to display abundance and excess of capital—but this opulence has little real depth. The feeling of claustrophobia in this scene is exacerbated by the impression that the capital that the Bartons access within the space is transient. Indeed, when the mills are not doing well, there is little capital to be had. The home space of the Bartons is transformed at the end of the novel, so that Mr Carson reflects that while he had been 'accustomed to poverty' in his youth, 'it was honest, decent poverty; not the grinding squalid misery he had remarked in every part of John Barton's house' (436). This is a very different picture from the opening scenes of the novel. The transformation of

---

109 Pierre Bourdieu, 'Taste of Luxury, Taste of Necessity,' in *Taste Culture Reader*, ed. Korsmeyer, 72–78, 77.

the house from clutter to barrenness shows that the more John Barton disconnects from his community and his identity, and the more starved he becomes physically, socially, and morally, the more desolate becomes his home space.

In comparison, Alice Wilson's tiny home space displays ingenuity in scarcity: '[h]er little bit of crockery-ware was ranged on the mantelpiece, where also stood her candlestick and box of matches' (15). When Alice has guests, she has no qualms about borrowing a cup, and the narrator tells us 'of odd saucers she had plenty, serving as plates when occasion required' (30). Her items of furniture also double up in utility, and over all, her domestic presence throughout the novel, for all its simplicity and lack of excess, seems much more stable. As a girl, Alice had left her home region in search of employment, so she is comparable to an extent with the Irish migrants in Mayhew's account and the European exiles, but she has managed to find a community and has become established there through her ability to adapt. In this way she achieves more in terms of belonging than the itinerant worker. One of the key differences for Alice is that on occasion she is able to access tastes from home. Through her nostalgic connection to home through food—and serving Mary and Margaret food from her childhood while she narrates her story of migration—Alice is able to create a stable home identity in her rented space, with her borrowed crockery.

Alice's clap-bread is her connection to home—her place of origin—even though she never had the capacity to return there. Uglow draws out the importance of bread as a symbol of life within the text:

> Bread, for example, is more than a staple for life: the new loaf Mary buys for the Bartons' party embodies their temporary prosperity and hope; Alice's fragile clap-bread, which breaks in her hands, is her offering to Mary and Margaret of 'the bread of her childhood,' her memories and faith; Mrs Carson's casually ordered roll stands in stark contrast to the single crust Wilson and Barton give to the starving Davenport children (the crumbs which Lazarus craved from the rich man's table).[110]

Alice's clap-bread is fragile, just like her failing eyesight and hearing, yet it remains a powerful medium of transmitting cultural heritage, as she uses it to teach the young girls about her history. The narrative asks, 'Can you fancy the delight with which she watched her piled-up clap-bread disappear before the hungry girls, and listened to the praises of her home-remembered dainty?' before Alice goes on to recount: 'My mother used to send me some clap-bread by any north-country person—bless her! She knew how good such things taste when far away from home' (32–33). Alice's fondness for the clap-bread of her youth parallels the desire, albeit stereotyped, for potatoes and pork expressed by Mayhew's Irish. The nostalgia for home is wrapped up in home tastes, and in both texts national identity is wrapped up in food, as well as—particularly in *Mary Barton*—in what the food is eaten

110 Uglow, *Elizabeth Gaskell*, 200–01.

with, the cutlery and crockery. For migrants, or even for those who risk having to relocate within a region, home cannot be depended on as a physical structure; and as these texts show, more often than not, using furniture and transportable capital as a means to try to ground a sense of home often creates instead an uncomfortable claustrophobia that actually works to reinforce transience. Instead, a stronger sense of home is found ironically in a hunger for the places that have been left behind, a home that cannot quite be reached, but through the transportation of and access to food from home, that home moves close enough to taste it.

Alongside the desire to import familiar food from home—whether from another region or from another nation—lies the reality of the need of Britain to import food because it is not producing enough in itself to be self-sufficient. In 'The Great Exhibition and the Little One' (1851), Richard Horne and Charles Dickens express concerns regarding food production and rapid population growth in Malthusian terms, but celebrate industry as the solution. Horne and Dickens simultaneously promote industry and reinforce ideas of community as they position industrialisation not just as 'mere "civilisation",,' but as the factor that will bring the nation together in a cohesive 'human family.'[111] The imagined community becomes, in this sense, a global one, in which the 'law of human progress' calls upon the generosity of human sympathy. Civilisation means that 'revolutionary excitement has in a great measure subsided into an industrial excitement,'[112] and an image emerges of international interdependence. This vision, however, still positions Britain problematically at the helm of civilisation; for the narrative rewrites Britain's scarcity to celebrate that through the civilising effects of industrialisation, Britain can distance itself from those lower agricultural processes that require one to get one's hands dirty—those tasks are left to the less developed (less civilised) nations and colonies of the world. In England the 'machinery and workshops' become the 'means of obtaining corn. . . . Our machinery and engines are our ploughs,'[113] and the British mainland can scour the globe to create a variety of taste possibilities. While this power relationship deserves greater attention, the salient point I seek to draw out here is the way in which divisions of labour and civilisation in this sense lends itself to choice—of capital and of tastes—in a way that relates to imagined communities. Certain forms of labour and of capital, like particular tastes in food, become associated with particular imagined communities—namely, the cleaner one can keep one's hands, and the more one can use intellectual labour rather than the literal sweat of the brow to gain capital, the more civilised one becomes. Within the industrialised world, there is a growing impetus to choose and redefine how one associates within the community through the acquirement of cultural capital, but also, crucially, through the cultivation of sensory and aesthetic tastes.

111 [Richard Horne and Charles Dickens], 'The Great Exhibition and the Little One,' *Household Words*, 3.67 (5 July 1851): 356–60, 356.
112 Ibid., 356–57.
113 Ibid., 357.

4   Educating transgressive tastes

'When I am king, they shall not have bread and shelter only, but also teachings out of books, for a full belly is little worth where the mind is starved.'

(Mark Twain, *The Prince and the Pauper* (1881), 22)

'Natural taste' is evidently an oxymoron: since what is considered tasteful at any particular historical moment is always a cultural construct, anyone who has taste has already been cultivated.

(Marjorie Garson, *Moral Taste* (2007), 9)

Mark Twain's iconic Prince Edward can be read as generous and forward-thinking, seeking to better the conditions of his future subjects. Indeed, he provides his looka-like, Tom Canty, with 'a repast . . . such as Tom had never encountered before except in books,'[1] giving an impression of luxurious generosity. However, when the Prince determines to provide both bread and books, his mission is not tied to the altruistic improvement of his subjects' condition; rather it is to teach them to respect the cultural and social hierarchy as a means to diffuse violence. Being mistaken for the Pauper, he has just been physically attacked by the boys at Christ's Hospital, a charitable house where he (or his father) is already providing them with bread (albeit a sparse provision in comparison to the bounty laid before Tom). His desire to educate them comes from wanting to teach them to be grateful and to placate them: 'for learning softeneth the heart and breedeth gentleness and charity.'[2]

There is a long history of the link between food, education (both formal and informal), and social conditioning, which has been drawn out effectively through the cultural turn in historical studies. Indeed, Garson's recognition of the historical and cultural construct of taste, which aligns with David Hume's eighteenth-century perspective on taste aesthetics, notes that taste, whether sensory or metaphorical, cannot exist without a cultural point of reference. Mark M. Smith has argued that 'taste and gustation' have, throughout history, 'helped arrange social authority,'[3]

---

1 Mark Twain, *The Prince and the Pauper* (1881; London: Penguin, 1997), 16.
2 Ibid., 22.
3 Smith, *Sensory History*, 76.

while Jack Goody refers to the 'culinary differentiation of culture' as a means to reinforce class status.[4] Hunger intervenes in this understanding of taste, acting as a radical dimension within the social organisation, while satiety becomes a form of social conservatism. To an extent, taste depends on access to food; however, the knowledge that other tastes exist widens the space of desire: it increases the capacity for hunger, as well as the capacity for consumption. While to consume when one is not hungry is the structure of excess, a small taste of a particular food can create a craving for more. This kind of hunger can be manipulated, either by being trained into one, or out of one, but, like other forms of hunger, it remains potentially chaotic. In this chapter, hunger and taste, both metaphorical and literal, merge even further to reveal the manner in which they combine as a social force, on the one hand to control social identity of the self or others, but on the other, to challenge the boundaries of relatively newly established social norms within the mid-nineteenth-century context. What to eat, how to eat, and when to eat become at once deeply personal and political, conventions that act as social markers within a cultural milieu that aimed to separate itself from the all-too-recent (and still present for some) Hungry Forties.

Twain's Prince Edward's desire to diffuse the violence of the impoverished classes of London through education, although written in America in the 1880s, resonates powerfully with the way in which Britain essentially diffused the threat of Chartism and revolution through the establishment of ragged schools, among other 'charitable' institutions, as well as the merging of Chartism's working-class impetus with middle-class trade agendas. The appropriation of middle-class social and formal education arguably redirected revolution to reform. To a degree, economic recovery resulting from good harvests played a large part in the progression from riots to strikes to organised political protest.[5] However, equally significant is the way in which Chartist literature began to appropriate 'middle-class tastes and levels of education,' establishing a 'political alliance between the middle and labouring classes.'[6] The social hunger to be heard is evident in the 'turn to the popular,' as Chartism attempted to compete with the 'commercial popular press'; and although this endeavour ultimately failed, it clearly marked a desire to appropriate the cultural forms and materials of the middle classes through literature and education to achieve Chartism's ends.[7]

It is not the object of this chapter to give a history of Chartist education as such, but rather to use it by way of introduction to the impact of cultural and literal tastes alongside degrees of hunger in defining and cultivating individuals and communities toward the middle of the century. D.G. Wright, for instance, argues not so much in terms of the literary and cultural production of Chartists

---

4   Goody, 'The High and the Low,' 58.
5   See Royle and Walvin, *English Radicals and Reformers 1760–1848*, 109; 124.
6   Sally Ledger, 'Chartist Aesthetics in the Mid-Nineteenth Century: Ernest Jones, a Novelist of the People,' *Nineteenth-Century Literature*, 57.1 (2002): 31–63, 33.
7   Ibid., 32.

as contributing to their diffusion, but attributes it to 'the inherent stability of the British state,' although that in itself works seasonally, 'and the skill of governments in applying a subtle blend of concession and coercion.'[8] The relationship of the working classes, as manifested through the Chartist movement, has a complexity beyond the scope of this study, engaging the effective strategic management of social hunger by the British government, the influence of middle-class economic agendas, the vast array of ambitions and aspirations rising within the labouring classes, and also the competing social narratives from within the labouring classes that sought to maintain the familiar. However, the complexity of these relationships informs the way I perceive the literary representations of hunger, taste, and social position. The fused rhetoric of education, hunger, and taste in Dickens, Brontë, Eliot, and Martineau reveals the tensions between aesthetics and politics, and the way education seeks to tame and control—to moderate or regulate—social position, while ironically providing the dangerous and chaotic possibility for excess.

With its emphasis on tempering physical and social appetites, moderation in itself can take on a perverted kind of excessive behaviour through hoarding and through privileging the range of tastes over a moderate quantity of food: a moderate amount from a wide choice, like a smorgasbord, can lead to deceptive gustatory excess as well as wasted leftovers. While Howes and Lalonde discuss the way in which middle-class taste moves toward an 'emphasis . . . on quality rather than quantity, or delicacy rather than gluttony,'[9] moderateness is disturbingly displayed through the food left on the plate: the eater visibly performs the middle-class ideology of self-control, seemingly avoiding 'both the decadence of the aristocracy' and 'the "violence" of the working class'[10] in terms of what they take into their body, but remains blind to the decadent implications of waste. In this sense, the *luxury* of moderation takes on critical meaning, and the relationship of individual characters to food comes to represent their interaction with and place in their community, in a spectrum from those who are either disgusted by or envious of choice, to those who glut themselves. Importantly, this social identification is often both controlled from within and manipulated from without through the medium of hunger, revealing the complex construction of taste and the roles that education and social ambition play in mediating it.

Educating the palate

Let these children be taken at an early age, and put into a Ragged School. They will there receive elementary instruction in the various branches of secular knowledge, and the great truths of religion will be impressed upon

---

8 Wright, *Popular Radicalism*, 22.
9 Howes and Lalonde, 'History of Sensibilities,' 127.
10 Marjorie Garson, *Moral Taste: Aesthetics, Subjectivities, and Social Power in the Nineteenth-Century Novel* (Toronto: University of Toronto Press, 2007), 8.

their understandings and their hearts. Let this education be adapted to their capabilities, and suitable to the position in life they may be expected to occupy. When their educational course is ended, let employment be obtained for them, that, by honest labour, they may be able to earn their bread. *Having once tasted the sweets of industry and the happiness of an honest life, very few of them will ever feel a desire to depart from it*; for there is nothing intrinsically pleasant in a life of vice that should lead them for its own sake to desire or prefer it.[11]

The frequently used metaphor of education as nourishment throughout the *Ragged School Union Magazine* is particularly telling in terms of determining cultural consumption and deciding what is appropriate for maintaining social stability. While suggesting that education should be 'adapted to [the] capabilities' of the students, in this instance referring specifically to children in prisons, or due to be deported, the role of education in socially conditioning individuals to be satisfied with their lot in life comes to the fore, rather than promoting social advancement. Formal education can be used to train tastes—to educate the palate—in ways that lead to social pacification. The type of education received is not just through books, but the socialisation achieved through the institution, by which means the student seeks acceptance within the community: conforming to the cultural expectations inherent in the institution is 'what makes you acceptable in your society at the end of the socialisation process known as education.'[12]

The provision of food within the school context complicates and aids the socialisation process, with school meals defining the level to which the student can aspire. Physical nourishment, foundational in sustaining life, fused with intellectual provision, is a potent mechanism for social differentiation. Margaret Visser notes that even in twentieth-century Britain, 'boarding schools for boys seldom provided their pupils with milk, fruit, or salads, largely because they were considered unnecessary luxuries, feeble and female foods which were unlikely to help in turning out real men.'[13] Even more telling, in the late 1880s, the Victorian poet and novelist Jean Ingelow wrote of schoolteachers prescriptively training children's tastes:

But taste, though an untrustworthy, is a very obedient sense; we are easily, as it is called, *set against things*. What has been called 'nasty' and 'horrid' by a mother or teacher will soon be really disliked by a child, and if carefully drawn and coloured pictures of these plants and some others were shown to children in infant schools, and they were told stories of how these berries were so horrid that even the hungry birds could not eat them, and how they made poor little children very ill and burned their mouths, they would soon dislike them.

11 'The Political Economy of Ragged Schools,' *Ragged School Union Magazine*, 9 (June 1857): 101–04, 102–03. Emphasis added.
12 Susan Bassnett and André Lefevere, *Constructing Cultures: Essays on Literary Translation* (Clevedon: Multilingual Matters, 1998), 42.
13 Margaret Visser, *Much Depends on Dinner* (Toronto: McClelland & Stewart, 1986), 18.

'Don't they look nasty and slippery!' was said by a lady to some children of the berries on twigs of *mezereum*. 'And they feel soft,' she went on; 'how disgusting!' *Slippery* is not a very expressive or disgusting epithet, but the children looked at the berries with strong disfavour, and not one of them would put out a finger to touch them and verify her words.[14]

The idea of distaste exceeding hunger in Ingelow's anecdote reveals the social conditioning accessed through the medium of taste. Metaphorically, it does not matter how hungry (or ambitious) one is, one should not transgress the safe confines of the social position one has been trained within; the risk aversion defined through taste conditions the mind as much as the tongue and the belly.

Ingelow does facilitate hunger in her vision, though, when she goes on to describe the way hunger can pervert 'wholesome' tastes:

Children, as a rule, like milk, sweet fruits, and farinaceous food, while highly flavoured dishes and the fat of meat disgust them.

It is only when half starved that children like fat, as may easily be seen in places where dinners are given to the poor. A fat joint growing cold in the dish, and a quantity of dripping encrusting the gravy, will be very attractive to them; they will, if allowed, dip bits of bread into the greasy stuff and eat them with avidity.[15]

Ingelow's determinist view of hunger and taste here becomes couched in scientific terms, as she goes on to say that a 'medical friend' informed her that the children's 'natural distaste' for fat will return once they are no longer hungry;[16] however, this perspective does not acknowledge the types of food available to the poor—and that they are therefore able to become accustomed to types of food that the well-to-do might find distasteful—and perhaps unintentionally provides a justification for institutions to maintain the poor diets of children in workhouses and schools. In terms of cultural signalling, ways of eating are also flagged, with the act of dipping bread in gravy associated with poverty. To do so is to lower one's social estimation; so the manners of eating come into play as well, influenced by perceived middle-class mores. Social position is delineated by the extent to which individuals have agency regarding what they consume; and so what becomes most evident is that those who have the authority to control what is eaten, how, and how much, are able to define, to a large degree, the social position of their charges.

Lowood Institute in *Jane Eyre* (1847) provides an extreme representation of the way food and food deprivation can be used to tame the appetite physically, socially, and intellectually. Mr Brocklehurst, horrified that the girls at Lowood have been given bread and cheese because the porridge had been burnt, declares that the school diet—both intellectual and alimentary—is planned

---

14 Jean Ingelow, 'Taste,' *Good Words*, 29 (December 1888): 413–14, 413. Ingelow's emphasis.
15 Ibid.
16 Ibid.

'not to accustom [the students] to habits of luxury and indulgence, but to render them hardy, patient, self-denying. . . . Oh, madam, when you put bread and cheese, instead of burnt porridge, into these children's mouths, you may indeed feed their vile bodies, but you little think how you starve their immortal souls!'[17]

The relationship between religion, education, and hunger will be explored more fully in the following chapter. Here, however, it is crucial to note the way taste is used to control social positioning within the school context. Brocklehurst continues:

'Should any little accidental disappointment of the appetite occur, such as the spoiling of a meal, the under or over dressing of a dish, the incident ought not to be neutralised by replacing with something more delicate the comfort lost, thus pampering the body and obviating the aim of this institution.' (75)

Lowood inmates are expected not to notice the taste of spoiled or rotten food; instead they are to be tastelessly grateful. Furthermore, they are kept in a state of perpetual hunger through the scarce provision, and therefore thankful for any scrap of food that they are given. Both these factors contribute to the reduction of their social prospects, reducing their human differentiation of taste to a mere animalistic need to fill their bellies. The idea of the girls being reduced to brute animals is extended through the way they eat the distressingly 'scanty supply of food,' as Jane recalls that the 'famished' older girls 'would coax or menace the little ones out of their portion' (71).

In contrast to Jane's boarding-school experience, John Reed provides an example of where the school mission to educate is undermined by indulgence from home, to John's eventual self-destruction. Jane's description of her cousin as 'large and stout . . . with a dingy and unwholesome skin' and 'gorg[ing] himself habitually at table, which made him bilious, and gave him a dim and bleared eye and flabby cheeks' creates an image of alimentary excess that crosses over into his violent excess toward Jane, his mother, and his sisters (12). His removal from school marks a different kind of alimentary social conditioning, caused primarily by his mother to her own detriment:

He ought now to have been at school; but his mamma had taken him home for a month or two, 'on account of his delicate health.' Mr Miles, the master, affirmed that he would do very well if he had fewer cakes and sweetmeats sent him from home; but the mother's heart turned from an opinion so harsh, and inclined rather to the more refined idea that John's sallowness was owing to over-application, and, perhaps, to pining after home. (21)

17 Charlotte Brontë, *Jane Eyre: An Autobiography* (1847; London: Penguin, 2006), 75.

While Mr Miles's suggestion is written in alimentary terms, the underlying meaning is that the indulgence from home, manifested through food, is disruptive to John's intellectual and social development. Mrs Reed's attempts to gain her son's affection through food nourish his abusive, excessive nature throughout the text, teaching him selfishness and excess rather than restraint. Indeed, it is telling that John's abuse of Jane is preceded by him 'thrusting his tongue at [her] as far as he could without damaging the roots,' his abuse tied to the organ used to taste, perhaps suggesting that he would harm himself in order to hurt others—as his later demise reveals—but he would not risk his capacity to eat, or his capacity to enjoy his taste for violence and excess (12).

Mrs Tulliver in Eliot's *The Mill on the Floss* (1860) is a similarly indulgent mother, who also encourages her son's self-interest and self-destruction through the social conditioning available through food, again in ways that contradict the education system. While there is evidently a gender divide, with girls, like Jane Eyre, expected to learn moderation and restraint through the school system, while boys are indulged as a matter of course, it cannot be denied that such indulgence of boys is critiqued through these narratives. It is also important to note that Jane's starved experience of school is much more tied to class, and the type of school she was placed in, than it is to her gender. It is a point of pride to Mrs Tulliver that both Maggie and Tom 'can eat as much victuals as most,'[18] but the difference remains, of course, that Tom is able to go away to school. While Maggie does eventually go to school, it does not satisfy her intellectual hunger, and this lack is written in terms of food: '[e]ven at school she had often wished for books with *more* in them. . . . And now—without the indirect charm of school emulation—Télémache was mere bran; so were the hard dry questions on Christian doctrine: there was no flavour in them, no strength' (298, Eliot's emphasis). School for Maggie, as for the girls at Lowood, is intended to keep her familiar with hunger and minimise her access to taste. While in *Jane Eyre* this is written in terms of literal food, in Eliot's novel it is the centrality of intellectual hunger that predominates Maggie's school experience.

Tom, however, while given access to the intellectual world that Maggie desires, has no taste for it. His classical education is deemed a waste, given that he must go into business and learn again. The waste of his education with Mr Stelling is underwritten by Mrs Tulliver's indulgence:

> 'Howiver, if Tom's to go to a new school, I should like him to go where I can wash him and mend him. . . . And then, when the box is goin' backards and forrards, I could send the lad a cake, or a pork-pie, or an apple; for he can do with an extry bit, bless him, whether they stint him at meals or no.' (12)

Tom's psychological violence toward his family, especially Maggie, through food access is written more subtly than the physical abuse Brontë's John Reed

18 George Eliot, *The Mill on the Floss* (1860; London: Penguin, 2003), 12.

metes out to his family. It is similarly connected in the narrative, though, with the mother deliberately indulging the son's physical appetite while he is away at school, encouraging the belief in their social entitlement to indulgence. It is when this narrative of entitlement is disrupted that Tom behaves in an emotionally abusive manner, such as when *he* divides the plum puff between him and Maggie, yet Maggie wins the best part instead of him. Maggie, more hungry for her brother's approval than for the pastry, offers her brother the best part, but he refuses it, and then deems her 'greedy' for having accepted it (50). Tom's abuse spoils the taste of the pastry for Maggie, thereby re-establishing his entitlement: 'Not but that the puff was very nice, for Maggie's palate was not at all obtuse, but she would have gone without it many times over, sooner than Tom should call her greedy and be cross with her' (51).

Contributing to the tragedies of Maggie and Tom, along with their cousin Lucy Deane as the three Dodson descendants of their generation, is the entrenchment of their social training, and their inability to exceed it. Their childhood responses to food mark their adult roles in their community. On a visit to their aunt and uncle Pullet, their uncle gives them each a sweetcake, but their aunt 'desired them to abstain from eating it till the tray and the plates came, since with those crisp cakes they would make the floor "all over" crumbs' (99). The varying responses of the three children to having to hold onto the cake—seeing, touching, and smelling without eating—reveals their individual responses to the world:

> Lucy didn't mind that much, for the cake was so pretty, she thought it was rather a pity to eat it, but Tom, watching his opportunity while the elders were talking, hastily stowed it in his mouth at two bites, and chewed it furtively. As for Maggie, becoming fascinated, as usual, by a print of Ulysses and Nausicaa, which uncle Pullet had bought as a 'pretty Scripture thing,' she presently let fall her cake and in an unlucky movement, crushed it beneath her foot. (99)

Lucy maintains her ideal femininity by choosing aesthetic visual distance over taking the cake into her body, while Tom, the mercenary capitalist, takes his opportunity to eat quickly and surreptitiously: aesthetics are of no value to him, only his stomach. Maggie, however, as the third extreme of the triad, hungers for a different kind of aesthetic. Her intellectual hunger overrides the physical, causing her to become unconscious of her food, to her detriment and humiliation. Maggie is like Jane Eyre in that she has a metaphorical hunger that overtakes the physical—Jane's is for human emotional connection, where Maggie's is for intellectual nourishment—but unlike Maggie, Jane is able to negotiate her hunger more effectively, learning not just from books, but also from observing how to play the game: she learns to use the restraint trained into her to overcome and exceed it. Jane learns asceticism from Helen Burns, which tempers her passion and hunger for justice, but she is also significantly aided by the generosity of Miss Temple, who teaches her how to extend her cultural space. Miss Temple's willingness to take responsibility for giving the girls more edible food is mirrored by her capacity to enable her pupils to move a degree beyond their social fate through education. In this way, she instils in Jane the eventual entitlement to social independence.

Exceeding the boundaries of taste

The intellectual and social hungers of Maggie Tulliver and Jane Eyre resonate with that of the eponymous hero of *David Copperfield* (1850). Dickens's narrative, like Brontë's, is unusual in that it gives a first-person voice to the child in a way that consciously shows the social conditioning that shapes their adulthood. Brutalised by his stepfather, David, in a similar situation to Jane, escapes alienation at home to the harsh confines of a boarding school, where the hunger for food and learning merge. Under his stepfather's roof, David is rarely given access to specific tastes, only imaginary ones, both in food and narrative. Recounting Murdstone's regime, David recollects:

> Even when the lessons are done, the worst is yet to happen, in the shape of an appalling sum. This is invented for me, and delivered to me orally by Mr. Murdstone, and begins, 'If I go into a cheesemonger's shop, and buy five thousand double-Gloucester cheeses at fourpence-halfpenny each, present payment'—at which I see Miss Murdstone secretly overjoyed. I pore over these cheeses without any result or enlightenment until dinner-time, when . . . I have a slice of bread to help me out with the cheeses, and am considered in disgrace for the rest of the evening.[19]

The torturous arithmetical imaginary cheese to go with the actual bread is telling in regard to the deprivation of David's situation. Like Jane Eyre's experience at Lowood, bread is the base necessity, but cheese is considered a luxury. David is given the barest necessities, and left to imagine other tastes, but even the imaginary is tainted by his stepfather's cruelty. The lack of taste variation is crucial, for the 'idea of taste . . . presupposes absolute freedom of choice, [and] is so closely associated with the idea of freedom that many people find it hard to grasp the paradoxes of the taste of necessity.'[20] Later, after he has been locked away for having bitten Murdstone for beating him, Jane Murdstone brings David, in silence, a fare of 'bread and meat, and milk' (108). The presence of meat, like in *Oliver Twist*, suggests strength; yet where Oliver is deprived of meat to weaken him, here David is given meat, perhaps because Murdstone considers David weak. Even so, the food is non-descript, not intended to provide for taste; similarly vague, David recalls that in that time of isolation, eating and drinking gave him 'fleeting intervals of something like cheerfulness,' although that feeling disappeared along with the food (110). The denial of choice of taste to David marks his bondage to the Murdstones, and their dehumanising power

19 Charles Dickens, *David Copperfield* (1850; London: Penguin, 1966), 104–05.
20 Bourdieu, 'Taste of Luxury, Taste of Necessity,' 73–74.

over him. However, his capacity for imagination is ironically developed through deprivation, as well as through his access to literary narrative, which feeds him alongside troublesome arithmetic about extraordinary amounts of cheese, the taste of which he is not likely to experience under the Murdstones' roof. This kind of self-education creates an inner capacity or potential to choose, rather than choices being made for David. Like Jane Eyre hiding with books behind the curtain of the window seat, it is David's access to his father's books, all but forgotten in the room adjacent to his, that enables him to escape mentally, emotionally, and to a degree physically from Murdstone's regime, and these narratives also give him access to the intellectual capital of arithmetic later, when at Mr Creakle's school, Steerforth trades assisting David with his 'sums and exercises' for hearing David's storytelling (145).

The relationship between David Copperfield and James Steerforth is complex in regard to David acquiring cultural and social capital. On their first encounter, Steerforth coerces David into allowing him to spend all David's money to buy a feast of almond cakes, biscuits, fruit, and currant wine. Steerforth places the words, and these tastes, in David's mouth—for David is not aware that he desires these items until Steerforth suggests them to him. While Steerforth is clearly in control and presides over the 'royal spread,' distributing the food to the boys—'with perfect fairness' in David's naïve estimation, but clearly taking advantage of the new pupil—it is of benefit to David within the school to have an advocate in Steerforth, the 'one boy in the school on whom [Mr Creakle] never ventured to lay a hand' (139). Yes, David is manipulated and controlled by Steerforth, but at the same time, this connection extends the scope of David's sphere, written through the ways in which Steerforth exposes him to new tastes. Whereas initially David had treasured the paper his mother had wrapped his coins in over the coins themselves, when Peggotty sends David a letter, the focus of the narrative is not on the content of the letter, but on the edible bounty accompanying the missive, which is offered to Steerforth as if to a revered idol: 'Peggotty's promised letter—what a comfortable letter it was!—arrived . . . and with it a cake in a perfect nest of oranges, and two bottles of cowslip wine. This treasure, as in duty bound, I laid at the feet of Steerforth, and begged him to dispense' (145).

While David remains emotionally loyal to Peggotty throughout the novel, this transition marks David's growing awareness of where he can attain social capital, and the vital need he has of such capital to survive in his world—in this case, in the boarding school—even though he remains unconscious of the manipulation, staying fond of, and thankful toward, Steerforth until Steerforth's own destruction and ruin of Em'ly exposes him on moral grounds. Even so, David's offering to Steerforth of Peggotty's bounty provides a compelling insight into their relationship. After David offers him all to distribute among the boys, Steerforth decides magnanimously to keep the cowslip wine under lock and key in order to 'wet [David's] whistle when [he is] story-telling' because he tends to grow hoarse. This is for the benefit of Steerforth's hearing pleasure, not for concern over David. While the wine will be for David alone, Steerforth will maintain complete control over it. Even more intriguing, though, is the power Steerforth has to manipulate the taste of the wine. Elisabeth Rozin and Paul Rozin observe that the 'flavoring of food—that is, the deliberate manipulation of food by adding ingredients that will reliably alter the taste—is a uniquely human behaviour,'[21] and so by manipulating the flavours available to David, Steerforth controls David's social and cultural development—perhaps controlling David's 'rehumanisation' after the Murdstones' brutality. David does not understand the flavours he is given, while Steerforth maintains his authority and shapes David through the perceived attention he shows him. He keeps David hungry—for the wine and the varying tastes produced, but also inevitably for the social connection he provides:

> Accordingly, it was locked up in [Steerforth's] box, and drawn off by himself in a phial, and administered to me through a piece of quill in the cork, when I was supposed to be in want of a restorative. Sometimes, to make it a more sovereign specific, he was so kind as to squeeze orange juice into it, or to stir it up with ginger, or dissolve a peppermint drop in it; and although I cannot assert that the flavour was improved by these experiments, or that it was exactly the compound one would have chosen for a stomachic, the last thing at night and the first thing in the morning, I drank it gratefully and was very sensible of his attention. (145–46)

Steerforth's absolute control of David's access to his own wine, as well as his manipulation of its taste, overturns the idea of taste marking freedom, for although David gains access to new tastes, it is not to new *choices*: he has no choice in the flavours that Steerforth gives him, or when, or how much. Moreover, by meting out small, medicinal doses of taste, Steerforth reinforces both David's social hunger, as well as his desire for more tastes. Therefore while being exposed to new cultural capital, David remains in bondage, perhaps safely so given the harshness of Creakle's institution, but it is not until David has escaped to his aunt, Betsey Trotwood, who asks him what *he* wants, that he can begin to access true choice, freedom, and agency.

Steerforth's regulation of David's wine is comparable to the way in which St John Rivers seeks to control and moderate Jane Eyre's appetite. From the very beginning of their interactions, he reveals an unrelenting desire to moderate and control her food, as well as her moral and intellectual well-being, claiming this authority as his right: first, as her saviour from starvation; then as a parson and her employer; and finally as her cousin and prospective husband. Like Steerforth, St John provides Jane with more tastes than she has previously accessed, especially relative to her starvation on the moors, through food, employment, and education; but importantly, in all these circumstances, he is in control of her access, and the provision he gives is limited in terms of Jane's capacity. When the Rivers family

---

21 Elisabeth Rozin and Paul Rozin, 'Culinary Themes and Variations,' in Korsmeyer, ed., *Taste Culture Reader*, 34–41, 36.

takes Jane in, seemingly as a beggar, while Diana and Mary encourage her to eat, St John orders, 'Not too much at first—restrain her . . . she has had enough,' even though one of his sisters pleads for Jane, 'A little more, St John—look at the avidity in her eyes' (287). While eating too much too quickly after starving would lead to sickness, in this restriction, St John shows his determination to speak *for* Jane's appetite, in a way that continues throughout their relationship. His obsession with Jane's appetite becomes even more evident once Jane emerges from her sickbed, when she and St John are sitting alone in the parlour. He does not acknowledge her presence, continuing, or feigning, to read a book. However, as soon as Diana offers Jane some food, and Jane's 'appetite [is] awakened and keen,' St John closes his book, approaches the table, and fixes his eyes on her. He needlessly observes, 'you are very hungry,' and then justifies his need to moderate her appetite as if for the sake of her health: 'there would have been danger in yielding to the cravings of your appetite at first. Now you may eat, though still not immoderately' (396–97).

Elizabeth Rigby's infamous review of *Jane Eyre* in the *Quarterly Review* objects to the cry of social hunger she perceives throughout the novel, written in revolutionary terms, revealing—to Rigby's horror—the deep dissatisfaction of an unequal society:

> There is throughout a murmuring against the comforts of the rich and against the privations of the poor, which, as far as each individual is concerned, is a murmuring against God's appointment—there is a proud and perpetual assertion of the rights of man, for which we find no authority either in God's word or in God's providence—there is that pervading tone of ungodly discontent which is at once the most prominent and the most subtle evil which the law and the pulpit, which all civilized society in fact has at the present day to contend with. We do not hesitate to say that the tone of mind and thought which has overthrown authority and violated every code human and divine abroad, and fostered Chartism and rebellion at home, is the same which has also written Jane Eyre.[22]

Rigby's social conservatism, mingled with her religious dogma, provides a fascinating context for St John's attempts to moderate Jane. If Jane's independence, and willingness to articulate her hunger—physically, socially, and emotionally—is interpreted through a broader political lens, as Rigby does, then St John's attempts at control, and his ultimate failure to maintain it, speak to a darker social vision of revolution and reform, evoking the violence of reform riots contemporary to the publication of the novel. In this manner, St John's shock at the apparent violence of Jane's words as she refuses to marry him—thereby refusing to relinquish her political, economic, social, and alimentary freedom—is a response to the perceived dangers of social change. With disbelief, St John repeats emphatically,

22 [Elizabeth Rigby], Review of *Vanity Fair* and *Jane Eyre*, in *The Quarterly Review*, 84 (1848): 153–85, 173.

'*I should kill you—I am killing you?*' and condemns Jane as trespassing the bounds of her social sphere:

> 'Your words are such as ought not to be used: violent, unfeminine, and untrue. They betray an unfortunate state of mind: they merit severe reproof: they would seem inexcusable, but that it is the duty of man to forgive his fellow even until seventy-and-seven times.' (459, Brontë's emphasis)

Jane's apparent violence and madness in this way reflect the Conservative response to Chartist ideology, inflected by fears of Continental revolution, as expressed by Rigby. Just as Jane asserts herself toward Rochester to claim social equality, her declaration to St John that she will not marry him redefines her as an uncontrollable figure, potentially dangerous to the social order. St John's fear of Jane's self-assertion, however, is foiled by his sisters' response to Jane's hunger. Diana and Mary provide an alternative political mode for addressing social hunger.

Like St John, Diana also determines when Jane eats, but in a way that seeks to sate her appetite, rather than control her through denial. In the parlour scene where St John ignores Jane, Diana instead brings Jane a small cake, saying, 'Eat that now . . . you must be hungry. Hannah says you have had nothing but some gruel since breakfast' (396). In essence, Diana and Mary recognise Jane's hunger and seek to sate it while extending her tastes; St John, however, recognises Jane's hunger and seeks to harness it and limit her tastes as a means to manipulate and control her. In both strategies, the physical diet flows into the intellectual, undergirded by Jane's recollections of her intellectual endeavours with the family being written in terms of appetite and taste. Once she has recovered to some degree, she recalls that she 'could join with Diana and Mary in all their occupations. . . . There was a reviving pleasure in this intercourse, of a kind now tasted by me for the first time—the pleasure arising from perfect congeniality of tastes, sentiments, and principle' (402). The harmony of flavours suggested in this metaphor speaks to the comfort of familiarity of taste, and enables Jane's palate to be extended through this association. This idea resonates with Megan Ward's observation that 'recognisability' is crucial in heightening the desirability in the 'subjective experience of taste.'[23] Furthermore, Rozin and Rozin speak of the way in which by adding familiar flavours to foods unknown, the newly introduced food can be more readily accepted and adopted into the diet.[24] For Jane Eyre, Diana and Mary's familiarity of taste does this work in terms of intellect:

> They were both more accomplished and better read than I was; but with eagerness I followed in the path of knowledge they had trodden before me. I devoured the books they lent me: then it was full satisfaction to discuss

---

23 Megan Ward, '"A Charm in those Fingers": Patterns, Taste, and the Englishwoman's Domestic Magazine,' *Victorian Periodicals Review*, 41.3 (2008): 248–69, 257.
24 Rozin and Rozin, 'Culinary Themes and Variations,' 36.

with them in the evening what I had perused during the day. Thought fitted thought; opinion met opinion: we coincided, in short, perfectly. (403)

Not only is the narrative written in terms of eating, in that Jane 'devour[s] the books,' but it is also crucial that she finds 'full satisfaction' in terms of her intellectual development. It is not just consuming the material, but discussing with the sisters the way in which she should perceive it—that is, how she should *taste* it—that provides satiety. This factor reinforces Jane's character in that she is a moderate, sometimes self-denying taster: the range of access she has to tastes, and learning how to consume them, is of more significance to her than actual fullness. For this reason, there are benefits to her in learning Hindustani from St John: she has not mastered the German that Diana and Mary have been teaching her, yet she has tasted it; her palate is then further extended into the Asian language, broadening Jane's cultural scope even further while opening up potential (although ultimately unclaimed) opportunities for geographical exploration.

The confinement of St John's austerity, however, prevents the possibility of Jane finding expansion through his path, which, it should be noted, is not particular to Jane, but an integral aspect of St John's own hungry character. In his asceticism, St John reinforces his own starvation so that what looks like moderation is, in fact, a commitment to perpetual, insatiable hunger, even though at least partial satiation is possible. His approach is a perversion of moderation, as he chooses to deny himself tastes out of his sense of morality. He argues that by choosing self-denial, he is actively crafting his 'own fate,' according to the 'measure' that

> 'God has given us; . . . and when our energies seem to demand a sustenance they cannot get—when our will strains after a path we may not follow—we need neither starve from inanition, nor stand still in despair: we have but to seek another nourishment for the mind, as strong as the forbidden food it longed to taste—and perhaps purer; and to hew out for the adventurous food a road as direct and broad as the one Fortune has blocked up against us, if rougher than it.' (416)

In this way, St John reveals that his self-denial is rooted in his fear of his own hunger and its potential chaos. He tries to contain it and attempts to kill off the addiction by denying any taste of its object, although he is not always successful. This failure is seen most clearly in the fifteen minutes he allows to indulge of thoughts of Rosamond Oliver, yet even here he exerts his will over his hunger. This level of self-denial, of unnecessarily denying hunger and taste, is shown to be self-destructive, leading to St John becoming a wandering, socially disconnected missionary, still hungry, although masochistically revelling in that sacrifice. Conversely, Jane, through her willingness to face and articulate her hunger with independence and, unlike St John, to seek ways to satisfy it, is able to find a different kind of mobility: a social mobility grounded through the convention of marriage and motherhood that, while disturbing from a feminist perspective, does satisfy her desire to move from her orphaned, discarded state in childhood to an established member of the wealthy classes. She is, after all, made independently wealthy through her inheritance, although this fortune is then legally absorbed by Rochester.

St John constantly, although inadvertently, provokes Jane's independent spirit by drawing attention to her hungers, whether physical, intellectual, or emotional. Well before her rejection of his marriage proposal, Jane offends St John by promising assertively that she would not be eating long at his expense (397). This declaration recalls the earlier childhood scene where John Reed tells Jane she has 'no business to take our books . . . you have no money . . . you ought to beg, and not to live here with gentlemen's children like us, and eat the same meals we do' (13). John's subsequent use of a book as a physical weapon against Jane makes a powerful statement regarding his abusive, entitled state. But the adult Jane has learned how to acquire tastes without being mastered by the possessor of the food. She allows St John to teach her Hindustani, extending the scope of her tastes, but ultimately he does not master her: she says she will go with him to India as a missionary as his cousin, but not as his wife.

While both St John and Jane operate in terms of hunger, Jane's dextrous navigation of her multiple hungers becomes her advantage as she learns to master them, using them against each other to increase her sphere. Her willingness to face her hunger becomes most marked during her time at Thornfield: '[i]t is in vain to say human beings ought to be satisfied with tranquillity: they must have action; and they will make it if they cannot find it. Millions are condemned to a stiller doom than mine, and millions are in silent revolt against their lot' (129). Jane is like St John, both of them restless from their hunger; yet in this revolutionary image, Jane reveals her capacity to rebel against and overcome her social hunger in a way that St John cannot. This work requires imagination, which ties back into the connection between books and hunger within the educational framework. The imagination itself is marked by hunger, defined by experiencing what is lacking—what is not presently material. In this way, it creates the intellectual capacity to comprehend hunger, and therefore steps toward satiation by contemplating what might fill the emptiness.

The two-edged sword of a taste of freedom

While *Jane Eyre* and *David Copperfield* both present characters who use imagination and fictional narratives to escape the present and to mark a path of social mobility through self-education, Dickens's *Hard Times* (1854) provides a darker vision of contained hunger written through the denial of imaginative or creative education. Dickens's famous sustained critique of both political economy and aesthetic education operates through the language of hunger and taste. The reductive, claustrophobic nature of Gradgrind's educational vision creates in his own children 'a starved imagination,' while the teacher he employs, Mr M'Choakumchild, epitomises the containing, socially conditioning vision of education, by being, with 'some one hundred and forty other schoolmasters . . . lately turned at the same time, in the same factory, on the same principles, like so many pianoforte legs.'[25] For Gradgrind, the role of education is to suppress the masses—the 'bad lot altogether' that encompasses the people of Coketown—and keep them in their defined social sphere (31). Gradgrind and Bounderby both fear and despise the hunger of the people, marking them in terms of their dissatisfaction: 'that they were restless, gentlemen; that they never knew what they wanted; that they lived upon the best, and bought fresh butter; and insisted on Mocha coffee, and rejected all but prime parts of meat, and yet were eternally dissatisfied and unmanageable' (31).

The access to physical taste in this complaint very evidently mirrors the social hunger of the factory workers, who go on to strike. But what is particularly interesting is the way in which Gradgrind takes hold of taste in both its sensory and aesthetic forms in order to work at maintaining his social authority. In his classroom, taste is not imaginative; it must be reduced to a determined fact, even an arithmetical equation. He is introduced as always carrying 'a rule and pair of scales, and the multiplication table always in his pocket . . . ready to weigh and measure any parcel of human nature, and tell you exactly what it comes to. It is a mere question of figures, a case of simple arithmetic' (3). Furthermore, his colleague, in an attempt to confine taste within science, states that what 'is called Taste, is only another name for Fact,' and that students 'must discard the word Fancy altogether' (8–9). Yet throughout the narrative, it is evident that Gradgrind's method is not only self-destructive and destroys his family, but that it has no real power to prevent the hunger of the people from overflowing into uprising.

To a degree, Gradgrind is providing access to cultural and social capital, in that he teaches his students—if they can accept it—the language of political economy and social conservatism that can enable them to progress within the limits that Gradgrind allows—such as Bitzer, who goes from being Gradgrind's prized pupil to working for Bounderby as Mrs Sparsit's light porter, although he does manage a limited degree of subversion by becoming Mrs Sparsit's spy. Gradgrind's manner of educating aesthetic taste buys into the nineteenth-century 'emergent idea of taste as both a social virtue and a trainable sensory experience,'[26] as well as, most importantly, the capacity for cultivating taste as a means of social control. On the one hand, participants experience a kind of self-improvement; and Sissy's decision to go with Gradgrind after her father has deserted her, rather than staying with the carnival people she has grown up with as if they were family, comes from a desire to acquire such capital, knowing that it is what her father wanted for her. But on the other, Gradgrind's direction of such improvement measures gives him control over his pupils beyond the classroom. Like Mr Tulliver with Tom, Sissy's father never had her apprenticed because he wanted her 'to be taught the deuce-and-all of education' (44), culminating on her gaining admission into Gradgrind's school. This aspiration leaves Sissy in a vulnerable social position,

25 Dickens, *Hard Times*, 16, 10.
26 Ward, '"A Charm in those Fingers",' 249.

which Gradgrind is able to manipulate. Gradgrind promises Sissy that she 'will be reclaimed and reformed' by the education he offers her (50); yet the idea of reclaiming means little more than providing his own household with more domestic conveniences. As with Bounderby's porter, Gradgrind's system only permits social improvement to the extent that Gradgrind allows.

Sissy's empathy and imagination, however, do not allow her to fit into Gradgrind's system, marked most clearly in her inability to reduce human nature to numbers. Dickens's satire in this regard is displayed in a conversation between Sissy and Louisa Gradgrind, in which they discuss Sissy's propensity to make 'mistakes' in class:

> 'Miss Louisa, I said I didn't know. I thought I couldn't know whether it was a prosperous nation or not, and whether I was in a thriving state or not, unless I knew who had got the money, and whether any of it was mine. But that had nothing to do with it. It was not in the figures at all. . . . Then Mr M'Choakumchild said he would try me again. And he said, This schoolroom is an immense town, and in it there are a million of inhabitants, and only five-and-twenty are starved to death in the streets, in the course of a year. What is your remark on the proportion? And my remark was—for I couldn't think of a better one—that it must be just as hard upon those who were starved, whether the others were a million, or a million million. And that was wrong, too.' (75)

Sissy's response not only exposes the tensions between statistics and the human face in the economic vision, and emphasises that communities are made up of individuals, it brings to the fore Dickens's satirical response toward aesthetic education, in which any perspective differing from the standard capitalist economic vision is deemed incorrect. To think outside the world of statistics—or 'stutterings,' as Sissy's malapropism unconsciously critiques—is to think outside the bounds of Taste, and therefore Fact. This type of education, rather than providing a means for social mobility and progress, instead seeks to condition the pupils to be content with their hunger, and indeed to redefine it as satiation: one may be starving, but if the statistics say that the nation is prospering, then starving individuals must consider themselves a part of that prosperity regardless of their individual circumstances.

Dickens's disturbance of political economy and aesthetic education through social hunger enters into a similar critique of cultural capital as Harriet Martineau's novella *Ireland* (1832), the ninth volume of her *Illustrations of Political Economy*. Later narratives (post-1850) tend to have a greater emphasis on excess and consumption, therefore with more psychological room for considerations of tastes, whereas Martineau's 1830s tale is more concerned with literal starvation. Yet while Martineau does not write specifically in terms of taste in her educational critique, the idea of aesthetic taste, in correspondence with the way in which communities and individuals respond to familiar and unfamiliar tastes, is a useful metaphor in examining the manner in which she draws out the complexities of, and tensions between, cultural production and cultural heritage in education.

The familiar taste for the Irish Catholics in Martineau's tale is the language of political rebellion, as well as the perceived 'superstitions' of Catholicism and the legends associated with their Celtic cultural heritage. Rozin and Rozin suggest that '[t]raditional flavors may serve the same function as traditional costume or traditional religious practice. They are a means of defining a culture group, of identifying an individual within it, and of separating that group from others,'[27] which highlights the connection between various types of material culture in determining individual and communal identity. The distrust of new flavours, like the resistance to learning new things, is tied to the fear of losing one's identity. Therefore introducing new flavours—new ideologies, or new knowledges—can risk the purity and stability of the cultural heritage, and even more so in a context in which one feels threatened. Resistance, then, to an English-style education is intimately tied to the Irish resistance to English colonisation. The unfamiliar tastes of English Protestant rationalism, and the critical emphasis of the English education system that Mr Rosso seeks to introduce, need to be domesticated by being connected to the familiar—in this case, through Mr Rosso's appointment of a Catholic teacher in the school, as well as his inclusion of Father Glenny's lessons in the curriculum.

The way in which hunger—for Martineau, very literal hunger—interacts with and disrupts the social conditioning intent of this type of education establishes a form of critique that persists throughout nineteenth-century literature. Matthew Potolsky, for instance, argues that Thomas Hardy's presentation of aesthetic education in *Jude the Obscure* (1895) reveals the regime as 'a form of brutal discipline,' rather than an admirable training of 'beauty and morality,' or an ethical conformity to fact.[28] This perspective could as easily be applied to Gradgrind's school. Sissy's inability to become absorbed into Gradgrind's social vision ultimately protects her from the kind of destruction faced by Gradgrind's children. Louisa eventually confesses to Gradgrind: 'With a hunger and thirst upon me, father, which have never been for a moment appeased; with an ardent impulse towards some region where rules, and figures, and definitions were not quite absolute; I have grown up, battling every inch of my way' (289). The devastating side of hungering for and consuming social capital—or at least the wrong *kind* of social capital—through education reveals its chaotic potential within the Coketown community. The social vision presented by Martineau, however, in the midst of famine in the Irish county the Glen of the Echoes, 'of which little is heard . . . except during the periodical returns of famine, when the sole dependence of its miserable population is on public benevolence,'[29] is further darkened by physical starvation. Even though this tale was written in 1832, it reverberates into the middle of the century with the Great Irish Famine, and Martineau

27 Rozin and Rozin, 'Culinary Themes and Variations,' 37.
28 Matthew Potolsky, 'Hardy, Shaftesbury, and Aesthetic Education,' *SEL: Studies in English Literature, 1500–1900*, 46.4 (2006): 863–78, 864.
29 Harriet Martineau, *Ireland. Illustrations of Political Economy*, vol. 9 (London: Charles Fox, 1832), 1.

herself maintained her concern about Ireland. In 1853, Martineau wrote for the *Westminster Review*,

> The world is weary of the subject of Ireland; and, above all the rest, the English reading world is weary of it. . . . The sadness of the subject has of late years increased the weariness. . . . Something ought to be done for Ireland; and, to readers by the fireside, it is too bewildering to say what.[30]

While understanding the moral weariness resulting from the combination of England's own economic difficulties and over-consumption of reading about Ireland, as well as, crucially, the seasonal recurrences of Ireland's famines in spite of any interventions, Martineau continued to canvass for a solution to Ireland's economic problems, promoting education as the primary means of self-advancement and social agency, and therefore economic sustainability, in the face of Britain's mismanagement of Ireland's resources.[31] As *Hard Times* begins with an introduction to Gradgrind's school, the opening pages of Martineau's *Ireland* include an account of Mr Rosso's school. The Anglo-Irish Mr Rosso is a Protestant landowner, who founds a school because he 'wishe[s] his poor neighbours to have such an education as they were willing to receive, though it was mixed with much that appeared to him very baneful superstition,' seeing 'no harm in giving them reading, writing, and arithmetic, in addition to that instruction, of a different kind, which their zealous priest, Father Glenny, took care that they should not be without' (4). Mr Rosso's vision to help his neighbours to progress is hampered, though, by the economic situation of the pupils as well as the educational tastes of the Irish Catholic community. While initially the narrative states that their poverty ironically gives the pupils the leisure to go to school, one of the most promising, Dora Sullivan, must give up school to help pay her father's tenancy agreement, an agreement that would not have taken place if Dora's education, which has taught her to reason, had been respected.

The narrative first hints at the authority of cultural heritage in determining what is valued in education, and therefore what is learned, when it states that one interference Mr Rosso presumes to make is to see 'whether the children could be induced to give attention to something besides arithmetic, which is, almost universally, the favourite accomplishment of the Irish who have had the advantage of any schooling at all' (5). Social stability begins through practical productivity, with an emphasis on economic capital and financial substance, hence arithmetic is crucial in managing production. The next stage of development is that of cultural capital, which is disseminated through literacy. Numeracy is positioned as passively practical—it helps to maintain cultural norms. Literacy, however, gives access to ideas and enables the development of critical analysis. It is within this ability that the dominant culture is threatened. The irony is

---

30 Harriet Martineau, 'Conditions and Prospects of Ireland,' *Westminster Review*, 59 (1853): 35–62, 35.
31 Martineau, *Ireland*, ii–iii.

that Martineau's Irish-Catholic working class in general refuses to value this skill, and thus reinforce their subjugation. Therefore while there is potential for 'material improvement' through Mr Rosso's school, the cultural heritage of the scholars impedes their 'real advancement'—their way is 'to be always reading, never learning; to be listening to legends, when they should be gaining knowledge' (6). At this point, Martineau, as the imperialist educator, critiques Rosso's method, perhaps suggesting he should interfere more; but for Martineau the scope of Ireland's social instability goes beyond the Irish schoolroom, education itself encompassing more than formal learning to include the lessons learned through social inequalities, injustices, and the mismanagement of property by absentee landlords.

While Mr Rosso's motive could be condemned as an insidious form of colonisation, manipulating his pupils into a social position or vision oppositional to their heritage, the need to adapt is made clear throughout the text. The characters who seek to maintain a pure 'Irishness' (a term problematic in itself) become desolate, while those who look to enterprise and physical mobility are more able to succeed. This contrast is drawn out both in terms of the physical diet and the metaphorical one, and the Irish obsession with potatoes and pigs is a common trope throughout nineteenth-century literature that critiques the Irish inability to diversify and adapt.[32] The resistance to adaptation is understandable, in the same light as discussed in Chapter 2 in regard to the narrowing perception of foreignness: the desire to hold onto cultural heritage as a means to identity is powerful; however, in Martineau's narrative, this desire is ultimately destructive, creating a cultural famine as powerful as the physical famine that blights the land. Writing of a twenty-first-century potato-centric community, M.J. Weismantel emphasises the need of communities to adapt flavours in order to survive in a dynamic, global community. Zumbahua in Ecuador suffers a similar fate to nineteenth-century Ireland, unable to grow potatoes because of

> decreasing soil quality due to erosion. . . . The lack of potatoes is keenly felt; families who can afford to buy them do so, using funds they would have used to buy fruits from the lowlands or maize from the valley lands, foods increasingly defined as exotic or luxury foods.[33]

This economic situation resonates with that of the Sullivans in Martineau's tale, whose land has similarly decreased in quality, although from being overworked rather than through erosion. In the case of the Sullivans, the overuse of the land means that the quality of crops is affected: 'but when the soil became exhausted, he could raise only an inferior kind [of potato], which is far more fit for cattle

---

32 This perspective is quite different from Mayhew's some twenty years later, when the Irish ability *to* adapt becomes a locus of terror; however, this difference can also be accounted for in that Martineau is writing of those who remain within Ireland's shores, while Mayhew's focus is the more intrepid London migrants.

33 M.J. Weismantel, 'Tasty Meals and Bitter Gifts,' in *Taste Culture Reader*, ed. Korsmeyer, 87–99, 89.

than for men, and on which he and his family could not have subsisted, if it were not for the milk with which they varied their meals.'[34] What is evident in both Weismantel's account and Martineau's narrative is that this kind of devastation affects both the income of the families—because they are sellers of the produce— but also their own diets, because they eat from the land.

Weismantel refers to consumption being driven by 'changes in the economy as a whole and especially . . . changes in the realm of production, as an overde- termined cycle of ecological, economic, and social decline continuously weakens the subsistence economy.'[35] But even more crucially, she observes: '[c]onsump- tion is driven not only by material constraints, or what is possible, but also by the immaterial, culturally shaped definition of what is desirable.'[36] Cultural heritage, in its immaterial form, is inherently tied to the extent to which individuals and communities are willing to taste new flavours. The connection between the mate- rial and the immaterial, the sensory and the aesthetic, is fundamental to the effect of formal education on Martineau's Irish pupils.

Mr Rosso's ecumenical approach to education 'astonish[es]' both his Catholic neighbours and his Protestant visitors (4). While reading, writing, and arithmetic are, to an extent, set up in opposition to Catholic religious instruction— rationalism as opposed to superstition—Mr Rosso espouses religious tolerance. Even when invited to speak to the children in his capacity as benefactor, 'he always took great care to do so as to convey to them some useful information, or moral impression, which Protestant and Catholic would equally allow to be good' (5). In terms of the taste of cultural material, Mr Rosso looks for flavours that are familiar to both, in order to find common ground. It could be argued that from his position, Mr Rosso has the luxury to defer his social and cultural power in this regard: as the wealthy landowner, he is in an unquestionable position of authority over his poor tenants. However, the narrative makes a point of the fact that his pupils are not just the children of Mr Rosso's tenants, but all the families in the region. Ironically, his Protestant friends 'might . . . have forgiven him, if he had had the good of a tenantry of his own in view, but . . . began to doubt the goodness of his religion, morals, and politics, when they considered that he had no tenantry but a farmer's family or two, who did not need his assistance' (4–5). In this way, Martineau challenges the self-interest consuming English economic social thought, with the Protestants going to accuse Mr Rosso of 'gratuitously offering support to the most damnable faith in religion, and the most iniquitous creed in politics' (5).

Mr Rosso does not gain economically through the establishment of the school, although he may gain social capital within the community through his approach. Father Glenny, however, as the neighbourhood's priest and confessor, holds more cultural power over this group. That Mr Rosso actively promotes the priest's

---

34 Martineau, *Ireland*, 14.
35 Weismantel, 'Tasty Meals and Bitter Gifts,' 89.
36 Ibid.

authority, as well as that of the unnamed Catholic schoolteacher, is significant. Rather than promoting Protestantism through the English curriculum, he allows the teacher and priest educational ownership. This ownership then extends to the authority, privilege, and internalisation of an English-style education within a securely Catholic context. Cultural hybridity is made possible through the blending of flavours to incorporate the unfamiliar. The potential, then, for gaining cultural privilege is there, although the tolerance of hybridity is undergirded by the initial conviction that Protestant rationalism and critical thought will eventually overcome Catholic superstition, which could come from the cultural complacency belonging to a group assured of its superiority. This perspective of cultural complacency could be articulated in terms of the wealthy Protestants not being hungry—their social satiation and lack of need encourages their social unconcern. Martineau's text importantly reveals the dangerous potential of such luxurious conviction, with both the physical and social hunger of the poor remaining unseen by those who do not experience it for themselves, the content blinded by their (albeit transient) stability.

Martineau's presentation of political economy idealises class interdependence, while unapologetically portraying the reality of community breakdown. In *Ireland*, Dora Sullivan, as a literate, working-class Irish-Catholic woman, focalises the tensions between the Protestant landowners and the impoverished Catholic community. Her hybridity comes from having tasted another culture, but her tragedy comes, arguably, from the way she restricts herself—albeit from necessity—to earlier, familiar tastes. She gives up her education and embraces her working-class position, yet this is due to necessity. She does not have the freedom of her future husband, Dan, who is able to transgress Ireland's shores to seek his fortune. Therefore Dora must forget her social hunger for the sake of the more immediate physical hunger of her family. The narrative first introduces Dora as 'one of the most promising of the troop' in Mr Rosso's school, and this promise is derived in that not only is Dora literate, she thinks critically and rationally (7). Evidently she has not been intellectually damaged by the Catholicism of her education; however, in spite of her knowledge and understanding, her voice is not heard because of her age and gender. Yet what is most disturbing in the text, and cannot be ignored, is that it is *because* of her education—her literacy—that Dora is *able* to commit a crime punishable by death. Dora has a voice because she can write, but because she is not listened to, her voice can be manoeuvred to further the political agendas of others. Her literacy skills first make her a pawn for her father's mismanagement, and then for her husband's crime, before Dora's self-determined action of perjury to protect her husband becomes her undoing. Throughout these moments, Dora's entanglement within conflicting moral and economic values complicates the validity and accountability of her actions.

There are three key moments in the novella when Dora is asked to write. First, her father asks her to sign on his behalf a promissory note to pay the rent due from not just his own lease, but that of his two partners. When she questions the content of the agreement, stating, 'I'm not clear of the meaning of it all, but I'm thinking it is much to pay, and more than we have to pay with,' her father clasps onto her claim of not understanding: 'Be easy, Miss Dora, since it comes out of your own mouth that the meaning is not clear. Only sign, my jewel; that's what is still to be done' (10–11). The painful irony of Mr Sullivan 'laugh[ing] at the easiness of putting a man off with a scrap of paper instead of the rent' is followed close upon by Dora having to leave behind schooling in order to scrape together earnings to pay for the agreement. Not only is she not listened to, her own social progress suffers as a result. She must sacrifice cultural capital for the sake of her family's material needs. But a greater injustice arises when Dan, having banded with the rebel whiteboys, uses Dora's education to implicate her by coercing her, as the literate one, to pen a threat to one of their opponents. Dan initially interprets Dora's lack of protest as her giving in to 'the weakness of being flattered'; however, the narrative explicitly states that her 'passiveness arose from a sense of the uselessness of opposition' (78). It could be argued that Dora's acquiescence to her husband's request makes her accountable, but the fact that she even has to make that decision reveals the moral crisis of education and cultural heritage throughout the text as Dora seeks to protect her family, even though doing so requires a criminal act.

The third time that Dora is asked to write is the most destructive. While it is a moment in which she asserts her agency independently, it comes from a place where she has given up on social progress: apart from her physical hunger, her social hunger has reached a point of hopelessness. Her political stance is defensive, and she effectively becomes a figure of sacrifice. She speaks against social injustice, but without any hope that the circumstances will change. Dora is interrogated by officers in regard to her now renegade husband's whereabouts. When she says she does not know where he is, the officer asks her to sign a note in declaration of this statement. Dora is now no longer the pupil of promise, but 'simple Dora,' in a scene powerfully reminiscent of the early scene with her father's promissory note: 'delighted with so easy a way of escape, and suspecting no artifice, [Dora] wrote the required promise in the officer's pocket-book' (86). The officer, however, is able to use this note to prove the identity of the handwriting in the earlier threatening letter sent to Major Greaves. Dora is arrested and charged, and within this state of individual hopelessness, she becomes the social prophet, speaking for the stricken Irish:

> 'But when you have driven us from our homes, and taken from us all the bread but that which comes by crime . . . then you expect us of a sudden to fear an oath, and to point out the one hiding-place, and to deliver them up to be hanged in the midst of a gaping crowd. This is the way you make it a crime to love one another as God made our hearts to love. . . . This is what you call the course of justice. It is such a crooked course, that you will surely lose yourselves in it one day.' (87)

The connection between starvation and crime is crucial, but so is Dora's ability, from her condition as a poor Irishwoman, to articulate this protest.

While reviews of Martineau's tales often criticised the way in which she puts unbelievable speeches in the mouths of her characters, in this instance, Dora's ability to express her community's physical and social hunger can be attributed to her access to education. The true hybrid education in Martineau's *Ireland* is not the fusion of Catholicism and Protestantism, but the fusion of intellectual education and the social education wrought through dire poverty and injustice. As Dora is being led away to be transported on a convict ship, members of her community who are in the courtroom discuss her acts, one vocally blaming her education for her crime—'If she had never been taught to write . . . this murtherous letter could never have been brought against her'—while another points out that she would still have been guilty of perjury (125). The way in which these crimes are brought together shows the extent of Dora's education, and Dora is given voice, in spite of being a prisoner, to express to the courtroom the true source of her education:

> 'Is there no language to threaten in,' asked Dora, speaking rapidly as she passed, 'but that which is spelled in letters? Overthrow every school in the country, empty all your ink into the sea, make a great fire of all your paper, and you will still find threats inscribed wherever there is oppression. . . . The school in which my husband and I learned rebellion was the bleak rock, where famine came to be our teacher.' (125–26)

For Dora, the cultural capital gained through formal education is not powerful enough to overcome the social and physical hunger inflicted upon her and her family. While she had acquired taste through her learning, the threat of physical hunger forces her to turn her back on this acquisition. As a result, the small education that she gains seems to become her downfall, although her social education would still have led to her conviction for perjury.

Cultural capital, and therefore social progress, is a luxury Dora cannot afford; yet given the possibilities for advancement within the colonies, Martineau perhaps offers Dora some hope in that she is being transported rather than hanged. Her volume following *Ireland*, *Homes Abroad* (1832), details the social advancement of a family who moves to the colony of Van Diemen's Land, some as convicts and some as indentured servants.[37] Although such hope is not expressed in the narrative of *Ireland*, the text itself enters into a literary context in which such avenues are commonly appropriated, and would continue to do so throughout the nineteenth century. Where social stability is not considered possible at home, the potential to find it elsewhere becomes attractive. In terms of hunger, such possibilities can restore hope of satiation, enabling the possibility to progress after all. What becomes crucial is the ability to manage one's own hunger—maintaining a

---

37 I have written elsewhere on the way in which Martineau envisages the colonies as a means to acquire social, cultural, and economic capital unavailable at home. See 'Retracing the Domestic Space: English National Identity in Harriet Martineau's *Homes Abroad*,' in *Domestic Fiction in Colonial Australia and New Zealand*, ed. Tamara Wagner (London: Pickering & Chatto, 2014), 21–36.

certain level of desire, but not losing oneself through losing hope that fulfilment is possible. Social agency comes through being able to moderate the self, and one's relationship to physical and social hunger, rather than having moderation imposed. In this sense, moderating hunger enters into a similar Romantic aesthetic as the later Chartist discourses. The 'democratizing tendencies' revealed through Chartism's move toward the 'individual and his rights'[38] can be read back through texts such as Martineau's *Ireland* toward the French Revolution; yet in this tracing through historical traumas that are both political and environmental, with seasonal implications as well as economic ones, while it is not possible to remove hunger—there are always seasons of floods, drought, and war—liberty lies in being able to manoeuvre oneself within that space in order to find some relief. The potential for geographical and ideological mobility is inherently tied to the ability to moderate one's own physical and social hunger, yet this potential is often a luxury. Meanwhile, the inability to be moderate, or to move, remains destructive, with individuals responding to hunger with extreme measures, from the self-denying waste of hoarding to reckless abandon in squandering the little they possess.

Self-moderating hunger

> 'We can never give up longing and wishing while we are thoroughly alive. There are certain things we feel to be beautiful and good, and we *must* hunger after them. How can we ever be satisfied without them until our feelings are deadened?'[39]

Philip Wakem's passionate hunger is quite unlike Tom Tulliver's 'very strong appetite for pleasure' (321). Whereas Tom has the luxury to forego his appetite for 'treats and benefits' to fulfil his other desire—his 'practical shrewdness' leading him toward 'abstinence and self-denial' in order to gain greater capital and therefore pleasure (321)—Philip's hunger is of a sickening variety, leading him to reflect on the 'things that other men have, and that will always be denied [to him];' and so he tells Maggie, 'My life will have nothing great or beautiful in it—I would rather not have lived' (314). The difference between the two young men is that whereas Tom can choose deferral, 'determin[ing] to achieve these things sooner or later' (321), Philip cannot be content watching others participate fully in the world, knowing that he will never be able to do so himself.

While memories of famine reinforce that hunger is inevitable, the individual response to hunger becomes crucial to whether progress is possible. Returning to the 1860s, anxieties around hunger become less about physical necessity and more about desire. Within the range of social hungers presented in *The Mill on the Floss*, however, Eliot suggests that hunger either maintains the status quo, or brings

---

38 Ledger, 'Chartist Aesthetics,' 36; 32.
39 Eliot, *Mill on the Floss*, 314. Eliot's emphasis.

devastation. Even for the characters who seem to have control over their hunger, such as the Gleggs, moderation is only made possible through exerting one form of hunger over another. Mrs Glegg's hoarding of silk gowns that have acquired mould, and her austerity in eating gruel, is merely a subtler manifestation of the excess displayed by Maggie, who in childhood sacrifices food because her emotional hunger overwhelms her, and in adulthood sacrifices emotional pleasure for what she perceives to be the moral right. Deanna Kreisel even goes so far as to refer to Mrs Glegg as possessing an 'unruly body: one that takes pleasure in "secreting" in inappropriate places, one that demands an erotic "pleasure of property" akin to gastronomic delectation.'[40] While Kreisel's assessment is a stretch in regard to Mrs Glegg in terms of the female body, her observation regarding Maggie in terms of moral economy is apt: 'she wants too much . . . she "hoards" and "saves," she defers gratification, too well . . . her unruly sexuality is inextricably tied up with her perverse economics,' and, most crucially, 'her elimination is less about punishing female desire than about imagining a release of stored economic potential, a circulating "flood" of released value.'[41] Indeed, it is not Maggie's lack of restraint, but rather her unwillingness to transgress moral boundaries, that ultimately leads to her downfall.

Kathleen Blake similarly draws upon the way in which Eliot's narrative describes Maggie 'as if her life were a stored-up force that was being spent in this hour, unneeded for any future' as she rows her boat, struggling to get it in the current of the Floss.[42] Eliot is constantly questioning '[w]hat sort of economic exchange might be productive of ethical human relations,'[43] addressing the challenge between the growing momentum of capitalist individualism and the passionate desire to belong to and be accepted by a community. Although writing about *Middlemarch*, Gordon Bigelow captures Eliot's socio-economic understanding when he suggests:

> no matter how much the world is subject to the private distortions of its individual residents, those residents craft their opinions and their desires in complex interplay with others. They do not regard the objects of the world . . . in direct encounters, but rather in scenes that are mentally populated by families and lovers and rivals. They evaluate resources not in isolation but from within a highly magnetized social field.[44]

Thus in every encounter with capital in *The Mill on the Floss*, especially in regard to food and hunger, the relationship to social belonging, position, and responsibility

40 Deanna Kreisel, 'Superfluity and Suction: The Problem with Saving in *The Mill on the Floss*,' *NOVEL: A Forum on Fiction*, 35.1 (2001): 69–103, 69.
41 Ibid., 71.
42 Eliot, *Mill on the Floss*, 539.
43 Blumberg, 'Beyond the Cash Nexus,' 61.
44 Gordon Bigelow, 'The Cost of Everything in *Middlemarch*,' in *Economic Women*, ed. Dalley and Rappoport, 97–109, 108.

is inextricably entwined. Within this appraisal, though, economic restraint does not equal moral (or ethical) restraint. Blake sees Maggie's life as a wasted energy along the lines of political economy's conception of 'capital as saved up or stored energy, a force of human labor,' but in the case of Maggie it is not 'expended to sustain, augment, and reap a benefit to present labor.'[45] In this way Maggie embodies a critique of the extremes of political economy in Eliot's vision, one that positions restraint not as moderation, but as waste. Maggie becomes, then, an obvious example of the dangers of hoarding, revealing the meaninglessness of hoarded capital once the hoarder is dead. However, Eliot's critique goes even further, for even in the characters whose demise is not as explicit as that of Maggie or Tom Tulliver, the excess and addiction of hoarding, stemming from the fearful memory of famine, displays emptiness.

The moderation displayed by Mr and Mrs Glegg, especially in regard to Mrs Glegg's aversion to speculation, provides a provocative example of wasted capital and wasted, ungenerous lives, in which such waste is disguised as a virtue. The pain of self-sacrifice internalises a form of morality, regardless of the external consequences, embodying another dangerous form of individualistic excess. As Blake argues, 'to save is to give up, to go without. As such it involves pain, the pain of foregone pleasures of consumption,' which seems to express a kind of virtuous self-denial; however, the effect, on the contrary, is that 'the pain of privation is not to be justified in itself but only as it serves ultimate gain in a theory that, above all, *validates* self-interest, value-in-use, utility, meaning pleasure.'[46] Ironically, by marking capital as worth deferring, the individual desire for that capital is reaffirmed, and the denial of enjoyment becomes a signifier of worth. In this way, characters like Maggie (in the extreme), but also Tom and the Gleggs, buy into Malthus's ideal of 'moral restraint,'[47] while challenging the understanding of Adam Smith's view that every man is 'rich or poor according to his ability to enjoy the necessaries, conveniences, and amusements of life.'[48] Crucially, Tom and the Gleggs do have the *ability* to enjoy such objects; yet their choosing not to indulge those tastes comes from a fear of returning to scarcity that leads them to value accumulation over use.

Unlike Philip, Tom has two hungers to choose between, and therefore more space in which to moderate his hunger, even though it is still limited. Blake observes that 'Tom, as a capitalist, has a strong appetite for pleasure and looks forward to living well someday but meanwhile faces privation and exercises abstinence and self-denial to save.'[49] Significantly, Tom's capacity to make this sacrifice comes not independently, but through the enforcement of his social hunger: he seeks to restore his father's reputation and pay his father's debt,

---

45 Kathleen Blake, 'Between Economies in *The Mill on the Floss*: Loans Versus Gifts, or, Auditing Mr. Tulliver's Accounts,' *Victorian Literature and Culture*, 33.1 (2005): 219–37, 231.

46 Ibid., 220. Emphasis added.

47 Qtd in Blake, 'Between Economies,' 220.

48 Blake, 'Between Economies,' 220.

49 Ibid., 224.

and even more importantly, to wreak revenge on Mr Wakem, through his son, for ruining his father. Tom's single-minded social hunger consumes him just as destructively as physical hunger, ultimately leading to his death. Even if he is granted a final reconciliation with Maggie, this connection between the siblings is essentially emptied of worth because their deaths, albeit in each other's arms, prevent any possibility of real restoration within the family and community. Their deaths, then, draw into question the value of such reconciliations alongside the meaninglessness of the initial fissure. To some extent, though, Mrs Glegg's situation is even more tragic in its relentless consistency: while the Gleggs do not fail economically in the text, neither do they progress, in spite of their mutual austerity, apart from in a minimal way when Mr Glegg enters into speculation (to a smaller degree than he would wish, for Mrs Glegg prevents him) with Bob Jakin.

Indeed, as Blake observes, Mrs Glegg's propensity to hoard, 'sequester[ing] valuable silk gowns in the clothes-chest from which they emerge later, in order of antiquity, to be worn spotted with mold,' not only reveals a lack of progress, but works against the 'capitalist practice . . . [of] accumulation' because what she stores actually 'loses value over time rather than increasing it by going forth to be consumed by laborers who create new goods by productive labor.'[50] Mrs Glegg would, however, see herself as the epitome of economic rightness, much as Mr Glegg considers her 'household ways a model for her sex.'[51] Kreisel suggests alternatively that Mrs Glegg, like her sisters, displays competing capitalist narratives:

> On the one hand, the Dodsons demonstrate a great faith in the benefits of accumulation and an unquestioning belief in capitalism's infinite growth, which we see in their veneration of 'capital,' interest, and profits, as well as in their professed faith in the continuing and limitless prosperity of the new industrial economy. On the other hand, their habits and predilections demonstrate the deep suspicion of credit and memoranda of debt—and the concomitant obsession with gold and hoarding—that I have argued is the effect of the contradiction between competing narratives of capitalism.[52]

The tenuous line between accumulation and hoarding that can be drawn from this assessment recalls the fear of loss, and eventually means that the capital not used will go to waste. While Kreisel is more forgiving of the Dodsons' accumulation, the self-destruction written in the valorised mouldy dresses cannot be ignored. Eliot critiques the capitalist vision of accumulation as wasteful greed, with the accumulated capital not even being tasted by the hoarders themselves.

Self-destructive austerity perversely juxtaposed with hoarded capital becomes even more evident through the manner in which the Dodsons eat together, and the

50 Ibid.
51 Eliot, *Mill on the Floss*, 130.
52 Kreisel, 'Superfluity and Suction,' 85.

demands they make on each other through meals. While female Dodsons 'always ate dry bread with [their] tea and declined any sort of preserves' when in 'strange houses,' even within the family they isolate and hierarchise each other through modes of eating.[53] Their resistance to unfamiliar tastes reflects their suspicion for learning new things. Alain Corbin writes of the importance of regulating and training tastes, and the acculturation of food, observing that 'the number of meals and their distribution throughout the day varied according to place, tradition, occupation, season, social status and position,' suggesting that the 'hour of the meal, like diet and table manners . . . became one of the cultural cleavages whose sharper definition constituted a major historical fact of the early nineteenth century.'[54] With the meal positioned so centrally, it is unsurprising that Mrs Glegg is first introduced in the novel seeking to assert her authority in the family by criticising what she sees as her sister's lack of regimented timing at dinner: 'Yes, yes, I know how it is wi' husbands—they're for putting everything off—they'll put dinner off till after tea, if they've got wives as are weak enough to give in to such work' (60). This statement asserts Mrs Glegg's belief in her power to restrain her own husband, as she intimately connects economic extravagance with keeping to a tight meal schedule. Her obsession with timing and austerity continues as she goes on to harangue Mrs Tulliver over the content of the meal:

> 'And I hope you've not gone and got a great dinner for us—going to expense for your sisters as 'ud sooner eat a crust o' dry bread nor help ruin you with extravagance. . . . A boiled joint, as you could make broth of for the kitchen . . . and a plain pudding with a spoonful o' sugar and no spice, 'ud be far more becoming.' (60)

The way in which Mrs Glegg seeks to limit the tastes that the Tullivers are allowed to consume or provide for their guests is not far removed from her expectations of her own restraint; however, the situation becomes complicated by potential self-interest as it is revealed that Mrs Glegg has given Mr Tulliver a loan of £500 at 5 per cent interest, and so any perceived extravagance on the part of the Tullivers could have implications for Mrs Glegg's own accumulation of capital. The meal in question ends in a quarrel with Mr Tulliver accusing Mrs Glegg that the only thing she is 'over-ready at giving' is advice, with Mrs Glegg responding that she's been 'over-ready at lending,' and that she may 'repent o' lending money to kin' (78).

While Mrs Glegg prides herself on her economising, her austerity is a masochistic form of martyrdom. Her glorying in self-destruction is most clearly shown in her self-starvation—she does not deprive herself of food entirely, but just of pleasurable tastes. This type of self-denial is particularly acute because it highlights

---

53 Eliot, *Mill on the Floss*, 48.
54 Alain Corbin, *Time, Desire and Horror: Towards a History of the Senses*, trans. Jean Birrell (1991; Cambridge: Polity Press, 1995), 1–2.

that she *could* consume what is pleasurable if she chose. On the morning after her disagreement with Mr Tulliver, cross with her husband for not defending her to her brother-in-law, Mrs Glegg joins Mr Glegg at their breakfast table in a 'cloud of severity.' Mr Glegg's more passive, habitual economy contrasts with his wife's active self-spite: 'Mr Glegg . . . sat down to his milk-porridge, which was his old frugal habit to stem his morning hunger with, prudently resolved to leave the first remark to Mrs Glegg' (131). Mr Glegg's moderation infuriates his wife further: 'she made her tea weaker than usual this morning and declined butter. It was a hard case that a vigorous mood for quarrelling, so highly capable of using any opportunity[,] should not meet with a single remark from Mr Glegg on which to exercise itself' (131–32). However, still not receiving the mollification she desires, Mrs Glegg seeks to punish her husband by punishing herself: 'Sally . . . light a fire upstairs, and put the blinds down. Mr Glegg, you'll please to order what you'd like for dinner. I shall have gruel' (134). Mrs Glegg closes herself off from companions in darkness, and denies herself nourishment, in a masochism reminiscent of Dickens's Scrooge. Her excess of austerity is highlighted in that Mr Glegg can actually order what he would like; yet in his moderation, he remains unmoved by his wife's actions, and Mrs Glegg's efforts, like her linens and satin gowns, likewise go to waste.

Eliot's *Mill on the Floss* can be read as a study of transgressive hungers, and the tragedies that occur come from characters failing to be moderate—not so much from decadence, but from excessive restraint. *Felix Holt* similarly addresses excess of restraint, but also an excess of tastes—and in both novels, Eliot displays her suspicion of a political economy that is driven by capitalist ideology, wherein taste and luxury are explored in terms of excess. The returning landowner in *Felix Holt*, Harold Transome, is repeatedly described in terms of his fat hands. In his first conversation with his mother he asks, 'How is it that I have the trick of getting fat?' as he 'lift[s] his arm and spread[s] out his plump hand.' His parents, however, are described in wasted terms, his thin mother's drawn appearance and 'anxious and eager face' expressing her social hunger, while Harold remembers his father as being 'as thin as a herring' (17). Both fatness and thinness are indicative of waste and desire, and are revealed to be entrenched within the unequal wealth and political distribution within the community of Trelby. The 'fat livings' of the landowners and the 'aristocratic clergy' are juxtaposed with the 'land . . . blackened with coal-pits, the rattle of handlooms to be heard in hamlets and villages' (6). Eliot's political novel opens with a nostalgic image of abundance, yet this vision is haunted by 'a Birmingham unrepresented in Parliament' (3), thereby connecting closely from the beginning of her narrative social and physical hungers and tastes, critiquing the waste accumulated in such struggles.

In Dallas's review of Eliot, the 'panting after some high ideal of what ought to be' in *Felix Holt* can be read on an individual level as much as it expresses the broader political agendas of Radicalism and Liberalism at play in the novel, and in doing so, the dichotomy of those 'seeking honestly for the general good' and 'others selfishly grasping at power and pelf' is broken down and complicated by individual agendas.[55] Harold Transome has his excesses of tastes, shown in his being 'ill-satisfied as to his palate, trying red pepper to everything, then asking if there were any relishing sauces in the house,' then 'falling back from his plate in despair' in his first meal at home (32). His response to British food epitomises the response of one who has been allowed to taste beyond their original cultural space, but then must return to the limitations imposed. Harold's transgressive tastes, explored abroad, must be trained and tamed anew. Having returned home, seemingly as a prosperous heir, he encounters a new hunger: a desire to return to the exotic sensory and cultural flavours of the East. This hunger is exacerbated by the restriction to the familiar tastes of home, which now seem bland, a response that can be understood in terms of Pierre Bourdieu's 'generalized Engels' law' in which 'what is rare and constitutes an inaccessible luxury or an absurd fantasy for those at an earlier or lower level becomes banal and common.'[56] It is ironic that although Harold's return to England, and therefore English food, is due to his becoming heir to the Transome estate, yet for him the restriction of taste becomes a kind of impoverishment as he hungers for the freedoms he has known. He quickly discovers that he does not have the social room to move that he expected, from his desire to run for Parliament and having to *kau tau*, ironically, to Matthew Jermyn, to his failure to gain Esther's affections. His seeming economic advancement compromises the cultural and social space he had previously been allowed.

Felix, for all his moral austerity, is revealed to be no more virtuous than Harold. Felix's cultural movement occurs in a different direction, however: having been encouraged by his parents to receive an education that would enable him to exceed his working-class boundaries, he rejects this opportunity, justifying his actions in terms of political morality. This determination could be innocuous if he did not also seek to impose his politics and morality forcibly on the community around him. Both Felix and Harold are examples of destructive responses to being exposed to cultural capital and cultural tastes outside their origins, and both risk social punishment as a result: 'Harold, like Felix Holt, must give up his substantial bodily presence. . . . This proud, stout, florid man, tanned by eastern suns, presumably coddled in exotic culinary as well as sexual pleasures . . . must learn to turn pale and go without dinner.'[57] Yet while Harold's arrogant rejection of his home culture is punished through him losing his right to his property and his family, Felix's drive to control his community through political and moral currency remains disturbingly unaccounted for: his use of excessive physical strength, unmitigated by the inebriation of his followers, results in the death of a police officer, yet Felix remains unscathed and even rewarded, in that Esther gives up her property and marries him, after speaking in his defence in court.

Felix, Esther, and Harold are shown to be liminal figures in terms of class, a situation that is further complicated by their access to cultural material outside their

55 [Dallas], Review of *Felix Holt*, 6.
56 Pierre Bourdieu, qtd in Ward, '"A Charm in those Fingers",' 254.
57 Carlisle, 'Smell of Class,' 14.

original social position. In this way, they each, in Bourdieu's terms, 'manifest [the] discrepancy between ambition and possibilities' that result in the opposition between cultural 'practices designated by their rarity as distinguished' and those 'identified as vulgar because they are both easy and common.' Bourdieu suggests that the 'intermediate position' is 'perceived as pretentious';[58] and it is clear that this pretention, which can evoke a lack of empathy, is key to understanding these characters. Pretention or ambition is not merely about positioning oneself higher than the community believes they should, but positioning oneself outside those cultural expectations, relocating oneself in relation to the community structure. Importantly, pretention marks a hunger for something outside what the community offers, suggesting the lack within. The relocations of Felix, Harold, and Esther throughout the novel are unsettling to the community: Felix's rejection of his father's trade and the education it bought challenges the integrity of his family heritage and the dissenting religion to which they belong; Harold's rejection of Englishness leads to him being excluded by discovering his illegitimacy; while Esther experiences a double relocation, learning that she is by birth a member of the class she desires, but then rejecting that class by marrying Felix. It is crucial, however, that while Esther gives up her economic rights, she is still legitimately entitled to the cultural capital she has gained while believing herself to be illegitimate and a member of the working classes.

To an extent, the marriage of Felix and Esther marks an armistice between the working and landowning classes, which, while being a common trope of many nineteenth-century romances, is particularly significant in relation to cultural and social hunger, as well as the possibility for social progress. It also reflects the merging of the working and middle classes that led to the diffusion of Chartism. In spite of Felix's adherence to a life of poverty, he very quickly envisages the uses he will make of Esther's wealth: 'Why, I shall be able to set up a great library, and lend the books to be dog's-eared and marked with bread-crumbs.'[59] Janice Carlisle argues that this move is the narrator's 'final attempt to establish for Felix working-class credentials that are rightfully not his,' but that it fails because it marks 'his adoption of middle-class security' and 'an embrace of an incongruously material discursivity.' Therefore, Carlisle suggests, 'the ploy does not succeed.'[60] I would reinterpret this passage, however, in light of the fact that Felix was born into the working class, but was moved upward through his father's work to exceed those boundaries. Instead, it is crucial that Felix and Esther remain liminal, providing a means of advancement for the working classes. The connection between dog-eared books (therefore often-read) and bread crumbs, suggests the possibility of increasing the scope of tastes as well as improving provisions for the poor. While Carlisle suggests that Felix's provision of books, albeit free, is not that far removed from his father selling drugs, what is important is that

58 Bourdieu, 'Taste of Luxury, Taste of Necessity,' 72.
59 Eliot, *Felix Holt*, 474.
60 Carlisle, 'Smell of Class,' 13.

both distribute material to the working classes for their health, either physical or moral. It is perhaps a dark reading to suggest that Felix's lending of books would be as materially useless as the drugs his father sold; yet perhaps the fact that they are lent for free, rather than sold, offers the possibility of social advancement untainted by self-interested capitalist gain.

Rebecca Stern has suggested that the Victorian economy relied 'heavily on the properties of education, social connections, and self-presentation,'[61] which are 'tied to personal identity, deeply equating personal credit with self-worth.'[62] The development of this kind of capital is inherently tied to the cultivation and moderation of taste: '[e]ven the field of primary tastes is organized according to the fundamental opposition, with the antithesis between quantity and quality, belly and palate, matter and manners, substance and form.'[63] Felix and Esther's library could potentially provide this cultural capital, with the possibility of it leading to economic capital. Yet for such progress to be made possible, a balance must be maintained between hunger and taste; and it is also evident that, as it is Felix's library, he will be able to control the cultural capital to which his community is exposed. He becomes the educator, paternalistically holding authority over the tastes of others. Felix's valorisation of the working-class existence throughout the novel is made clear, and so it seems likely that he would seek to reinforce this ethos through the books he lends, rather than promoting any kind of middle-class advancement. His social power in this regard resonates with that of Twain's Prince Edward, as Felix projects his tastes upon the community. The problem remains, then, in seeking to negotiate boundaries of taste, of how to determine what is necessary and what must be relinquished, and being able to taste without giving in to hungry excess; but even more significant is the question of agency in determining access to taste.

61 Rebecca Stern, *Home Economics: Domestic Fraud in Victorian England* (Columbus: Ohio State University Press, 2008), 8.
62 Leann Hunter, 'Communities Built from Ruins: Social Economics in Victorian Novels of Bankruptcy,' *Women's Studies Quarterly*, 39 (2011): 137–52, 141.
63 Bourdieu, 'Taste of Luxury, Taste of Necessity,' 73.

5   Social communion

And Maggie had forgotten even her hunger at that moment in the desire to conciliate gypsy opinion.

(George Eliot, *The Mill on the Floss* (1860), 116)

Kant's communal table is the material embodiment of shared ideals; the sense of security and equality in this environment encourages the exercise of collective judgement.

(Corinna Wagner, *Pathological Bodies* (2013), 185)

Maggie Tulliver's fantasy of running away to join the gypsies, to become their Queen and teach them wonderful things, begins to fall apart first when her nose encounters the 'odorous steam' coming from the gypsies' kettle, and her eyes are disconcerted by the absence of teacups.[1] She resists her own disconcertion by telling one of the gypsies that she wants to wear a 'red handkerchief, like yours' rather than a bonnet, but finds herself craving familiarity even more: 'I *want my tea so*' (116–17, Eliot's emphasis). Like her brother, Tom, Maggie is a character of conflicting physical and social hungers, but whereas Tom's dominant hunger is for vengeance and material advancement, Maggie's is for communal belonging: she wants to be a part of a community that values her intellectual abilities, which are linked to her greatest hunger—and thus she would be set apart within the community. In this way, Maggie embodies the nineteenth-century ideal of democratic citizenship, associated with theorists such as John Stuart Mill, Matthew Arnold, and Friedrich Schiller, which sought to 'envision a model of political society that respects the rational autonomy of individuals' while also 'address[ing] the intersubjective dimension of membership and participation in collective life.'[2] Maggie is torn between her hunger to belong and her hunger to excel, and both are brought into focus by her physical hunger. Her desire for tea, as an exhausted, hungry child, causes her 'in spite of herself' to have

---

1 Eliot, *Mill on the Floss*, 115–16.
2 Bentley, 'Democratic Citizenship in *Felix Holt*,' 271.

'a sudden drop from patronising instruction to simple peevishness' as she has been informing the gypsies of Christopher Columbus and Geography,[3] but even more significant in this moment is Maggie's sense of social dislocation. As much as she had desired to teach the gypsies, she finds that she longs to be somewhere where she does not have to explain herself, where she does not need to explain her hungers, and where she can have a tea that she recognises. The gypsies' tastes do not resonate with hers: they give her bacon, which she does not like; they have no tea, nor butter, nor, in the absence of butter, the treacle for which Maggie asks. The gypsies' poor 'suppl[y of] groceries' marks a 'rapid modification' in Maggie's idea of what gypsies were: '[f]rom having considered them very respectful companions, amenable to instruction, she had begun to think that they meant perhaps to kill her as soon as it was dark, and cut up her body for gradual cooking' (120).

While Maggie's prejudices are developed through a disparity of tastes, in spite of the attempted kindness of some of the gypsies to give her food that she would like, the importance of familiarity in taste emphasises the significant connection between eating and community. In *Pathological Bodies*, Corinna Wagner observes that 'while our food choices may seem an expression of individuality, they are largely determined by the human history that precedes us,' and goes on to discuss the ways in which Kant's *Anthropology from a Pragmatic Point of View* (1798) addresses the sociability of eating.[4] From his Enlightenment perspective, Kant sees the appeal of the shared meal as 'sensibility and understanding unit[ing] in one enjoyment,' with the food itself becoming secondary, the 'vehicle for supporting company' and 'reciprocal and common conversation.'[5] Yet on the other side of this idea of reciprocity and commonality lie the divisions created by not sharing food, or through attempting to share food that others find unpalatable. It also remains that *individuals* eat, even if they are eating in the same space, from the same table: they cannot swallow the same morsels of food. In this context, the deeply personal and intimate act of eating and tasting is rewritten as a social performance, and what becomes even more critical is who is permitted to eat with whom, and who is excluded from the table. Food centres social stability, with communal eating creating a sense of belonging, and shared tastes merging between the sensory and the ideological. Such belonging can be, in turn, disrupted by geographical mobility, or reinforced by the forging of mobile groups, moving with a common purpose. In Maggie's encounter with the gypsies, a mobile group to which she does not belong, their lack of shared tastes not only creates division, but creates suspicion and the possibility of violence, manifested in terms of taste, as Maggie fears that she will be on the gypsies' menu. At the same time, social mobility manifests through meals, with the occurrence of cross-class eating

3 Eliot, *Mill on the Floss*, 117.
4 Corinna Wagner, *Pathological Bodies: Medicine and Political Culture* (Berkeley: University of California Press, 2013), 184.
5 Immanuel Kant, *Anthropology from a Pragmatic Point of View* (1798; Cambridge: Cambridge University Press, 2006), 139.

presenting possibilities of social progress. The hunger for social status or social significance can be read through a desire for commonly shared food, or even for that food to be arranged in a particular way. Organising tastes organises society.

When Philip Wakem coerces Maggie into meeting him regularly in secret, he uses the language of extreme hunger—a rhetoric she is particularly prone to empathise with and be swayed by, given her own myriad of hungers. Kathleen Blake draws out the language of Maggie's 'hungry nature' and 'illimitable wants,' that she 'wants too much,'[6] arguing for Maggie's excessive, transgressive hunger in economic terms. Even her self-sacrifice, Blake argues, is written in terms of excess, as she prefers St Thomas à Kempis's *The Imitation of Christ* over the popular, and significantly more moderate, advice book *The Economy of Human Life*.[7] Yet while I agree with Blake's argument of excess, what I want to focus on in this chapter are the multiple intersections of hunger within particular characters that pull against each other—sometimes to create moderation, as discussed in the previous chapter in regard to Tom Tulliver, but at other times these tensions become self-destructive, and can also make characters vulnerable to external abuse. Rather than a hierarchy of needs, what comes into play is a dialogic engagement between types of hunger, with the level of necessity evolving and changing depending on the particular social or communal circumstances of the characters.

With the emphasis on ideas of social communion, there is a deliberate gesture toward a kind of spirituality, albeit secularised, in the construction of community. The role of community in sating its members both physically and socially is evident, with hunger, taste, and community creating a nexus toward a means of individual agency within the communal context. Yet such connections can be fraught with abuse as well as providing stability. Focusing particularly on the works of Eliot, Gaskell, and Brontë, I examine the ways in which social agency is achieved through the self-moderation of food and shared meals, but also the ways in which such agency is denied or abused from without, specifically by human intervention, although larger institutions such as church and government provide a broader context. The necessity of agency that I suggest in this respect resonates with J.S. Mill's claim in *On Liberty* (1859) that

> [a] person whose desires and impulses are his own—are the expression of his own nature, as it has been developed and modified by his own culture—is said to have a character. One whose desires and impulses are not his own, has no character, no more than a steam-engine has a character.[8]

It is useful to read Mill's 'desires and impulses' in terms of hungers, in the way that they represent the multiplicity of hunger; furthermore, he makes clear that

---

6 Blake, 'Between Economies,' 226.

7 Ibid., 227.

8 J.S. Mill, *On Liberty* (1859), in *On Liberty and Other Essays* (Oxford: Oxford University Press, 1991), 67.

these hungers are arrived at through culture, yet autonomy within that defined space is necessary in claiming humanity, rather than being a machine. Mill's perspective reveals the perpetuating challenge of individuality within a community, and raises the question as to the extent that one's desires can indeed *be* one's own. It is possible to see the excesses of hunger as attempts to find that sense of ownership denied within the confines of community, while the self-regulation of hunger, whether that be to sate or deny it, can be seen as an external obligation, for instance when one feels compelled to share food—to not consume it all oneself—against the individual will.

Self-starvation, as one form of excess or extreme, can become an internalisation of institutional abuse, a form of self-exclusion, often written in terms of moral choice. At the same time, however, the idea of communion and eating together conjures ideas of the Eucharist as an equaliser, creating likeness and association between characters. In *Mary Barton*, tea drinking is ritualised as a form of Holy Communion, bringing people together and calming tempers, while in *Jane Eyre*, Jane's bread and coffee being taken from her at Lowood School is an ironic form of an individual being denied communion, but her willingness to sacrifice her access to the figurative sacrament is motivated by her hunger for community and belonging.[9] Korsmeyer's *Taste Culture Reader* explores the concept of 'foods as spiritual nourishment' across a range of cultural and religious traditions,[10] and while D.T. Suzuki's chapter in Korsmeyer's collection specifically examines tea drinking in Japanese culture, the spiritual importance of eating and drinking, and perhaps tea drinking in particular, resonates powerfully within the British tea-drinking context.[11] The connection of social and spiritual hunger with specific tastes and food consolidates the connection between literal and metaphorical renditions of hunger, and ideas of community and belonging. In this way, the individual's relationship to their community is written through their ability to contend with and operate within their own range of hungers.

A little solace from Sabbath to Sabbath: self-starvation and institutionalised abuse

Gwen Hyman reveals the tension between institutional and individual power through the definition found by eating in a way that extends the individual versus the community dilemma. 'Aliment is an unavoidable locus of power and danger,'

---

9 It is important to note that *Mary Barton*'s context is that of a secularised industrial community, while *Jane Eyre* is more concerned with the communities formed around religious institutions. The contrast between the spiritual and industrial community is brought into close focus in Gaskell's *North and South*, when Margaret is confused regarding the extent of Thornton's moral responsibility toward his workers.

10 Carolyn Korsmeyer, Preface to Part IV, 'Body and Soul,' in Korsmeyer, ed., *Taste Culture Reader*, 145–46, 145.

11 See D.T. Suzuki, 'Zen and the Art of Tea,' in Korsmeyer, ed., *Taste Culture Reader*, 166–74.

she argues: 'it is the means by which the individual writes and rewrites him- or herself, the marker by which societies define themselves.'[12] Hyman's recognition of danger is particularly important in light of Edmund Burke's belief, according to Marjorie Garson, in the reliability of 'natural' feelings being divested through and 'embodied in institutions,' seeing 'the great landowner, whose taste has been cultivated within a privileged environment, as the one most likely to judge and act rightly on social issues.'[13] Such perspectives led to the debates on democratic citizenship in the nineteenth century, raising 'questions of personal sovereignty and social relations,'[14] and defying the doctrine that political voice and social agency were predicated on owning land. Both Hyman's and Garson's critiques reveal the potential for the institutionalised abuse of individuals through taste, an idea that is further punctuated by Wagner's observation that '[e]xotic tastes lead to inhumane acts and greedy politics, at home and abroad.'[15] Mrs Transome's social hunger in *Felix Holt* is compared with 'a black poisonous plant feeding in the sunlight,' and Eliot's narration goes on to speak of this as an insatiable hunger, in which 'men and women who have the softest beds and the most delicate eating, who have a very large share of that sky and earth which some are born to have no more of than the fraction to be got in a crowded entry, yet grow haggard, fevered, and restless.'[16] Mrs Transome's hunger depicts the Malthusian capitalist need for new hungers to be continually created, in which the result is a kind of starvation in spite of luxury.[17] The hunger becomes self-consuming: '[s]o her life had gone on till more than a year ago, when that desire which had been so hungry while she was a blooming young mother, was at last fulfilled—at last, when her hair was grey, and her face looked bitter, restless, and unenjoying, like her life.'[18]

Mrs Transome's social hunger is significant, not just in its individual insatiability and lack of satisfaction, but also in that she exerts her will over others—namely the estate's servants and tenants, but also the wider Trelby community—in order to create hunger in them, in an attempt to sate her own needs. Eliot writes in imperial terms of Mrs Transome's 'high-born imperious air,' which 'would have fitted an empress in her own right, who had to rule in spite of faction, to dare the violation of treaties and dread retributive invasions, to grasp after new territories' (28);

12 Hyman, *Making a Man*, 2.
13 Garson, *Moral Taste*, 9.
14 Bentley, 'Democratic Citizenship in *Felix Holt*,' 272.
15 Wagner, *Pathological Bodies*, 222.
16 Eliot, *Felix Holt*, 23.
17 In *Principles of Political Economy*, Malthus wrote: 'No country with a very confined market, internal as well as external, has ever been able to accumulate a large capital, because such a market prevents the formation of those wants and tastes.' While there remain debates in regard to Malthus's changing views on determining value, in this context I am reading him in terms of the capitalist need to increase the variety of tastes in order to maintain growth in consumption. See *Principles of Political Economy*, ed. John Pullen (1820; Cambridge: Cambridge University Press, 1989), 448.
18 Eliot, *Felix Holt*, 25.

and out of this unsatisfiable imperial desire, juxtaposed with how little social power she actually wields, Mrs Transome is seen to 'sweeten' her days by attempting to create her own small empire in Trelby:

> [u]nder protracted ill every living creature will find something that makes a comparative ease, and even when life seems woven of pain, will convert the fainter pang into a desire. Mrs Transome, whose imperious will had availed little to ward off the great evils of her life, found the opiate for her discontent in the exertion of her will about smaller things. She was not cruel, and could not enjoy thoroughly what she called the old woman's pleasure of torment-ing; but she liked every little sign of power her lot had left her. (30)

Eliot seems to express some sympathy for Mrs Transome's hunger through map-ping its development through her flawed education. However, she also emphasises the futility and pettiness of Mrs Transome's focus on the courtesy shown to her by the labourers and her ability to deliver orders in such a manner that '[i]f she had only been more haggard and less majestic, those who had glimpses of her outward life might have said she was a tyrannical, griping harridan, with a tongue like a razor' (30). Her bitterness makes her an unpalatable character, one who becomes increasingly insipid and skeletal throughout the text. In this way, it is possible to see her effective disappearance as both a result of her own hunger, and a punish-ment for the hunger she imposes on others. Her desire effectively to adopt Esther almost provides her with a means to escape hunger, but Esther recognises the danger of allowing herself to dwell in such a position. After all, this is a means of gaining some kind of power again, over Esther, when the rightful authority in Trelby Manor is actually Esther's. Mrs Transome's thinness is the counter of her son's fatness, both suggesting a kind of excess, but for Mrs Transome it is an excess of austerity and her focus on exerting her social will that is bodily expressed. Ultimately, Mrs Transome is unable to navigate a path toward satisfac-tion because of her obsession with a social power she can never gain.

The recognition of multiple hungers can be a means to renegotiate social position. Michael Vander Weele suggests that in *Jane Eyre*, 'one of the lessons Jane learns is that self-assertion always has a social as well as a psychological force. The dominant society cannot be dismissed exactly, but alternative socie-ties, or communities within a society, can be sought and . . . sometimes found.'[19] Mrs Transome's failing is that she is never able to find an alternative commu-nity, or rather that she is unable to imagine a different community, apart from the paradoxical one she desires but can never enter. Jane Eyre, however, is able to use her range of social and physical hungers to negotiate and assert herself within varying social frameworks, sometimes in self-destructive ways, but ulti-mately toward finding herself within a palatable social and economic position.

---

19 Michael Vander Weele, '*Jane Eyre* and the Tradition of Self-Assertion; or, Brontë's Socialization of Schiller's "Play Aesthetic",' *Renascence*, 57.1 (2004): 5–28, 6.

As such, it is not necessary for her to exert an abusive will over others, but rather she is able to overcome that which has been exerted over her. As Vander Weele suggests, 'Jane must find a different tradition and a different society to live by. She must construct a different memory and learn a new anticipation.'[20] 'Anticipation,' in this sense, can be read as hunger; and it is through creating new hungers and negotiating between them that Jane is able to acquire independence. Anna Krugovoy Silver's reading of the 'slender body' as 'a sign not simply of the pure body, but of the *regulated* body'[21] is particularly significant in this understanding of Jane Eyre's self-moderation, in stark contrast to figures like Maggie Tulliver, who resonate more with Susan Bordo's 'anxiety about internal processes out of control—uncontained desire, unrestrained hunger, uncontrolled impulse.'[22] Not only does Jane move between a variety of economic situations, on a spectrum from abject poverty begging on the moors, to marrying a wealthy man, to being independently wealthy in her own right, she moves between a range of social spaces and communities that work to reinforce her economic position. In each case, the role of hunger is at the fore, with Jane's control of her appetite—or aspiration—driving the narrative.

Eating or not eating, and social inclusion or exclusion, are inherently linked in *Jane Eyre*. Helena Michie observes that *Jane Eyre* is a 'novel obsessed with feeding and starvation,'[23] and this literal statement of physical hunger can be easily extrapolated to encompass Jane's social and spiritual hungers. The connection in Brontë's novel between religion and starvation has been addressed by critics such as Maria Lamonaca and Kathleen Williams Renk, who both compare Jane with the medieval starving saints—women who fasted to draw closer to God, or, it could be argued, to evoke some sense of spiritual and social agency: there was a sense of independence from male priests in their relationship to God.[24] Rather than emphasising an ideological connection between fasting and agency, though, in this respect I see self-starvation as evidence of internalising institutionalised abuse. Williams Renk mentions that the fasting women would often be denied the Eucharist by priests, who thought the women were 'too exuberant'—the denial of the Eucharist was a means to seek to regain control over them.[25] What is crucial in this observation is that the women are being punished for their physical starvation by excommunication: they are being cut off spiritually by not being able to commune with God, and socially by being excluded from the community of

20 Ibid., 7.
21 Anna Krugovoy Silver, *Victorian Literature and the Anorexic Body* (Cambridge: Cambridge University Press, 2002), 10.
22 Susan Bordo, *Unbearable Weight: Feminism, Western Culture, and the Body* (Berkeley: University of California Press, 1993), 189.
23 Helena Michie, *The Flesh Made Word: Female Figures and Women's Bodies* (Oxford: Oxford University Press, 1987), 23.
24 See Maria Lamonaca, 'Jane's Crown of Thorns: Feminism and Christianity in *Jane Eyre*,' *Studies in the Novel*, 34.3 (2002): 245–63, and Kathleen Williams Renk, 'Jane Eyre as Hunger Artist,' *Women's Writing*, 15.1 (2008): 1–12.
25 Williams Renk, 'Jane Eyre as Hunger Artist,' 6.

worshippers who *can* partake in the bread and cup. Because of their desire for an independent connection to God, rather than through the community, they are denied access to that community.

In becoming a nun, Eliza Reed is comparable to Jane, and perhaps suggests an alternative path that Jane could take. Indeed, Eliza's decision to join a convent is very similar to the choice Jane almost makes in going to India as a missionary with St John, although the difference lies in that while Jane would have been seeking to do something useful for others—yet another life of service—Eliza is merely seeking to order her own isolated life. In this way, Eliza is very much like Dickens's Scrooge, which is evident from the novel's earliest accounts of her character. Eliza is an economic child: she has her own poultry, and sells the eggs to the housekeeper, and sells roots and seedlings to the gardener (who are under strict instructions from Mrs Reed to buy everything Eliza wished to sell). But Eliza displays an extreme that is similar to her brother: whereas he hoards fat on his body, Eliza hoards the money she earns,

> first secret[ing] it in odd corners, wrapped in a rag or an old curl-paper; but some of these hoards having been discovered by the house-maid, Eliza, fearful of one day losing her valued treasure, consented to intrust it to her mother, at a usurious rate of interest—fifty or sixty per cent.—which interest she exacted every quarter, keeping her accounts in a little book with anxious accuracy.[26]

Jane respects her cousin's independence; yet Brontë shows, much as Eliot does in *The Mill on the Floss*, that the hoarding of capital for the sake of having more, rather than expending it, is a waste of energy. Unlike the Gleggs, however, there is no sense that Eliza is harbouring memories of scarcity to justify her hoarding. Rather, she is more like a childhood version of Mrs Transome, seeing the accumulation of capital as a means to exert social power—over the housekeeper, the gardener, and her own mother. In adulthood, after the death of her brother and with her mother's death imminent, Eliza also seeks to exert her will over her sister, Georgiana, whom she has already prevented from making a good marriage match. She berates her sister, '[h]ave you no sense to devise a system which will make you independent of all efforts, and all will, but your own?' and goes on to tell her,

> 'After my mother's death, I wash my hands of you: from the day her coffin is carried to the vault in Gateshead Church, you and I will be as separate as if we had never known each other . . . if the whole human race, ourselves excepted, were swept away, and we two stood alone on the earth, I would leave you in the old world, and betake myself to the new.' (271–72)

Brontë's irony in Eliza joining a religious order is a part of her critique of religious institutions and establishments. Economically, Eliza is like Scrooge, and she

---

26 Brontë, *Jane Eyre*, 36.

relishes her social hunger. She is also like Brocklehurst at Lowood, and also, perhaps even more poignantly, St John. Like St John, Eliza chooses self-exile, and respects Jane to a degree because she believes that Jane is of the same mind. However, as much as Jane leans more toward Eliza's asceticism than Georgiana's excess and laziness, she refuses to choose a life solely devoted to religious service, as displayed by either the cousin she grew up with, or the one she discovered later. Spiritually, as socially, Jane seeks to remain independent, and potentially sees the paradox of dependence in Eliza's choice in joining a convent: Eliza is self-isolating, but she is also joining an order where instead of her being able to devise her own hourly schedule, as she has done since childhood, the schedule will be determined for her. In spite of her worship of ascetic independence, Eliza joins a community, but her motivation remains one of economic and social control: having endowed her fortune upon the convent she enters as a novitiate, she ends up becoming the convent's Superior.

Elizabeth Rigby took offence at Jane Eyre's spiritual and social independence, showing a distaste for the orphaned child who 'continues to enlist our sympathies for a time with her little pinched fingers, cropped hair and empty stomach.'[27] Rigby's own sympathy is lost in what she sees as Jane's 'ungrateful[ness],' arguing—rather unpleasantly—that it 'pleased God to make her an orphan, friendless, and penniless,' but what is pertinent in Rigby's reading is that she suggests that Jane 'thanks nobody, and least of all Him, for the food and raiment, the friends, companions, and instructors of her helpless youth—for the care and education vouchsafed to her till she was capable in mind as fitted in years to provide for herself.'[28] While Rigby focuses on Jane's pride and apparent ingratitude, her reading also raises the question as to what happened to Jane's friends from school. Although Helen Burns died, there are other girls that Jane mentions associating with, as well as the friendship she developed with Miss Temple, particularly after Jane becomes a teacher at Lowood, although this period, notably one not of physical starvation, is glossed over. It would seem that Jane deliberately cuts herself off from these human connections, deeming herself friendless, or perhaps not trusting in those friendships because of the abuse she had suffered at the hands of her relatives as a child. Jane's determination not to be indebted to anyone stands in contrast to Eliot's heroines, who, Leeann Hunter argues, 'perform best when they feel indebted to other people, especially their family.'[29] However, while Hunter is speaking specifically of Maggie Tulliver, who does find an element of independence by default through her father's ruin, her determined indebtedness is ultimately destructive, while in Brontë's text, Jane's independence does eventually allow for *equality* in connection. Rather than seeing Jane as a kind of social Scrooge, it is more useful to see in her a lack of trust in unequal human connections, which motivates her toward her adamant social and

27 [Rigby], Rev. of *Vanity Fair* and *Jane Eyre*, 163.
28 Ibid., 173.
29 Leeann Hunter, 'Communities Built from Ruins,' 140.

economic independence—an independence that is indicative of Jane being able to regulate her own hungers in a way that Maggie never learns. It is not until after she becomes financially independent in her own right, and also able to bestow wealth on her newfound cousins, that Jane truly begins to trust in the human relationships she has formed. Even in her engagement to Rochester, she maintains a distrust in their connection, the outcome of that betrothal merely proving Jane's case for independence. Only once she is no longer dependent on other characters for satiety is Jane able to enter into an equal communion with them.

Continual allusions to the communion cup and bread, and the mortification of the flesh, reinforce in *Jane Eyre* the connections between spiritual, social, and physical hunger. Vander Weele notes, specifically referring to the meal that Jane and Helen share with Miss Temple after Brocklehurst has humiliated Jane, that the 'formality of the language of invitation and approach, and the deliberateness ascribed to the sharing of food, recall the language of the Bible and of church order.'[30] Sharing food in the novel, like the Eucharistic meal, alludes to connection: giving food to someone who is starving can be motivated either by sympathy, or from a desire to connect with them. Crucially, however, the one who has control over the distribution of food, like the priest, has the power to control the one who is starving. Throughout the novel, this power is abused; however, as Jane learns the language of starvation, she internalises its methods in order to find her own agency and, importantly, she does not fear hunger. Jane's self-denial and self-starvation are inherently linked to her desire to dissociate herself from situations or aspects of society, whether it be her threat to starve herself to death as a ten-year-old child to separate herself from the cruelty of her relatives, or her refusal to eat with Rochester until after they are married.

Conversely, Jane shows a notable determination *to* eat once she is with the Rivers family (although she does not know at this stage her relationship to them), although St John constantly seeks to moderate her appetite. Starvation is institutionalised and internalised in *Jane Eyre* as a means to assert social power—either over other characters by starving them physically, emotionally, and spiritually, or through self-starvation. Ironically, starvation simultaneously becomes the cause and effect of separation, but also the perceived means to social identity and belonging for the abused subject. Within this context, Vander Weele's assessment of community in the novel takes an even darker hue, for he argues that Jane Eyre 'finds an alternative society within society where she can be taught and nurtured, and where she in turn can teach and nurture others. Perhaps the truth of Brontë's novel is that there is no self-assertion outside of community.'[31] If what Jane learns is the language of hunger and starvation, and that is the lesson she teaches, questions must be raised for the future of Adèle Varens, who, as an orphan like Jane, is sent away to boarding school—presumably not of the variety of Lowood, but still a removal from the family home, and therefore from the community.

---

30 Vander Weele, '*Jane Eyre* and the Tradition of Self-Assertion,' 19.
31 Ibid., 22.

From the perspective of mid-twentieth-century psychiatry and psychotherapy, F.S. Perls writes of the inevitable ties between hunger, aggression, and the survival instinct in a way that resonates with Jane Eyre's navigation of her physical and social hungers. Hunger is divisive, compelling the individual subject to sacrifice others in order to save the self, and this is evident in Jane's resistance to maintaining familial and relational ties. The potential destructiveness of this impetus, however, is constantly brought into tension with the fact that '[n]o organism is self-sufficient. It requires the world for the gratification of its needs . . . there is always an inter-dependency of the organism and its environment.'[32] Perls's argument evokes not just Darwinian theories of evolution, and later discourses of social evolution, but the early theories of political economy that reified meritocracy and class interdependence. While interdependence is necessary, what is evident in Brontë's text, as in many others, is that the system of interdependence fails, due, usually, to self-interest or human error. Outside the myth of a self-moderating social or economic market, Jane Eyre must fend for herself; and if she must starve, it will be by her own hand, rather than that of another.

At Lowood School, where starvation is institutionalised as a perverted form of religious discipline, physical and social starvation are combined. Jane's refusal of the path of religious asceticism as a means to community is marked, however, from the first meal in which she partakes—or, more accurately, does *not* partake in—at Lowood. The first meal she is offered consists of oatcake and a communal cup of water, thus mirroring the Eucharist, although this water does not turn into wine. Jane recalls that she was unable to eat this first meal out of excitement and exhaustion, although later she learns to eat what she can with the other students, as there is so little ever offered. The degrees of social separation experienced by the girls at the school are striking, and are highlighted by this communal cup. They are cut off from the wider society, with little mention of going beyond the school grounds except to go to church twice on Sundays, and many of them do not go home for holidays. Furthermore, they are separated from each other within the school, an internal separation instigated through the creed of starvation. Mr Brocklehurst's control is exerted through the scant provision of food, and because of their perpetual hunger, the girls' focus is almost constantly on their stomachs. The days are marked out by meals, and Jane acknowledges the abuse of the bigger girls who would 'coax or menace' the smaller girls out of their insufficient meals in an attempt to sate their own hunger.[33] The narrative does not say, nor could it be expected to say, given the first-person narration, if Jane herself, as she grew into the school and its systems, learned herself to coax or menace the students younger than herself as a means to survival. Instead, Jane goes on to relate that she would often share—as if willingly—her morsel of

---

32 Friedrich Salomon Perls, *Ego, Hunger and Aggression: The Gestalt Therapy of Sensory Awakening through Spontaneous Personal Encounter, Fantasy and Contemplation* (New York: Vintage, 1947), 38.
33 Brontë, *Jane Eyre*, 71.

bread and mug of coffee with three other girls, swallowing what was left 'with an accompaniment of secret tears' (71). The trauma of deprivation, as well as the absence of community—no one protects the younger girls from this abuse, even in the unsatisfactory way that Steerforth protects David Copperfield—constructs within Jane a distaste for dependency. The fierce independence that she develops, though, works to separate her further from community connections.

Jane's independence is consolidated at Lowood, but it has its beginnings in the physical and psychological abuse she suffers at the hands of the Reeds. While physically attacking Jane, John Reed tells her she ought to be begging, not eating the same meals as her cousins, thereby denying her an equal status (13). After Jane's imprisonment in the Red Room, she is indeed forbidden to eat with the family any longer, yet this exclusion is a relief to her—by being excluded in this sense, she becomes ignored rather than harassed. This perspective reveals the beginnings of a destructive pattern of exclusion for Jane, though, who is 'habitually obedient to John,' in spite of his cruel treatment (12). In the early scene of John's torture, explored in my previous chapter, abuse and eating are explicitly combined. Jane's habitual obedience evidences her acceptance of John's bullying on her small, delicate frame. In contrast, the bully's appearance is bloated, one of excess, and even while fearing his blows, Jane muses over the way John 'gorged himself habitually at table.' The paralleled repetition of habit here reinforces Jane's internalisation of the abusive power dynamic between the cousins. John's overindulgence with food is equated with his torture of Jane, with Jane's body becoming not just the object of John's abuse, but flesh for him to consume: 'every nerve I had feared him, and every *morsel* on my bones shrank when he came near' (12, emphasis added). John Reed's behaviour adds to Jane's self-denying pattern through creating a disgust with excess. This disgust is reinforced through Lowood, and psychologically entwines with Jane's independence.

In my previous chapter, I drew attention to the likeness between John Reed and St John Rivers in terms of their desire to control Jane. Even though the adult Jane who encounters St John has learned to moderate her hungers and social agency, she still responds to a degree with the lessons learned in childhood. Both cousins emphasise the link between excess, deprivation, and abuse, although it is important to note that while John Reed is described as ugly and St John as beautiful, they are equally abusive toward Jane. St John is deceptively attractive—he saves Jane from physical starvation, but subsequently seeks to control her appetite, as well as deprive her emotionally and spiritually. Jane's habitual obedience toward John Reed had been both self-preserving and self-denying, and it is crucial to note that a similar kind of habitual obedience comes into play in her dealings with St John Rivers. While moderating Jane's physical and intellectual appetite, St John also seeks to impose his moral diet upon her. Once Jane learns of her fortune and wishes to transform her cousins' home and make it her own, like the priests of the starving saints, St John fears that Jane's delight in domesticity is too exuberant, and warns her that he is going to watch her 'closely and anxiously,' telling her to 'try to restrain the disproportionate fervour with which you throw yourself into commonplace home pleasures' (451). St John could be justified in his concern, given that this home that

Jane is determined to make *hers* actually belongs to him and his sisters—although Jane has wealth, and is now known to be their cousin, the home does not belong to her. In this way, there is potential for Jane to abuse the social power that she has gained, especially through the gift of £5,000 she gives to each of her cousins, even though she says it is because it is a fair division. By sharing her wealth with them, she gains some control over them. Yet having found the true satiation that she has desired all along—a family, a home, and financial independence—Jane is able to assert her social independence again: 'I feel I have adequate cause to be happy, and I *will* be happy' (451, Brontë's emphasis).

In seeking to curtail Jane's satiation, the substance that St John most tries to deny her is the possibility of sexual and romantic love, instead seeking to manipulate her into a life of religious servitude. He tries to shape her, telling her she was built not for love but for labour, and seeks to bind her to a marriage of loveless duty (464). As a cousin and a potential lover he is able to gain some power over Jane, for he is a part of her fulfilled desire for family—she does not want to be separated from the family she has found. However, she begins to recognise, in the almost vampiric imagery of St John's 'bloodless lip,' that his religious and moral asceticism would both consume and destroy her (476). Hearing Rochester's voice, the voice that had promised fulfilment, in a seemingly ironic moment of divine intervention, Jane finds the strength to assert herself against St John. However, this move toward obliging her sexual hunger would not have been possible if not for Jane's financial independence, which gives her the means to provide for her own physical—and perhaps spiritual—appetite. While St John sought to control and deprive, Jane offers him measured freedom through her gift of wealth, which he understandably rejects, not wanting to be obliged to Jane any more than she wishes to be obliged to him. St John chooses social hunger as his means to independence. Importantly for Jane, however, she is able to find agency in her wealth because she can relieve her own hunger, which opens up a new possibility for her: an independence predicated on the hope of fulfilment rather than starvation.

The doctrine that Jane discovers at Thornfield, and returns to in the end, is one of solace. At Lowood the girls had looked forward to the Sabbath, not for spiritual edification or the invigorating long walk to the church in the snow, but for the 'little solace [that] came at tea-time, in the shape of a double ration of bread—a whole, instead of a half, slice—with the delicious addition of a thin scrape of butter' (72). At Thornfield there is, notably, no mention of church attendance until the day Jane and Rochester intend to marry; yet there is a sense that every day is the Sabbath for Jane. For the first time she has enough: of food, so that Mrs Fairfax even comments on how well she looks after she has been at Thornfield for some time; and of society, through Mrs Fairfax's kindness, Adèle's adoration, and through finding her equal and companion in Mr Rochester. Jane remembers: '[s]o happy, so gratified did I become with this new interest added to life, that I ceased to pine after kindred: my thin-crescent destiny seemed to enlarge; the blanks of existence were filled up; my bodily health improved; I gathered flesh and strength' (171–72).

The absence of starvation at Thornfield is linked to true communion, and Rochester frequently positions himself as Jane's saviour. Even after his betrayal has become known, he feeds her bread and wine, and refers to her as his lamb (345). While St John saves Jane from physical starvation but then seeks to deprive her of spiritual, social, and sexual fulfilment, Rochester's hubristic goal is to save Jane completely, even from herself. From their earliest encounters, he recognises the way she has embraced her captivity to narratives of starvation, and desires to set her free:

> 'The Lowood constraint still clings to you somewhat; controlling your fea-
> tures, muffling your voice, and restricting your limbs; and you fear in the
> presence of a man and a brother—or father, or master, or what you will—to
> smile too gaily, speak too freely, or move too quickly: but, in time, I think
> you will learn to be natural with me, as I find it impossible to be conventional
> with you; and then your looks and movements will have more vivacity and
> variety than they dare offer now. I see at intervals the glance of a curious sort
> of bird through the close-set bars of a cage: a vivid, restless, resolute captive
> is there; were it but free, it would soar cloud-high.' (160)

Rochester fails in that he believes he can be man, brother, father, and master to Jane, and yet still have her claim equality with him. However, he is trying to recognise the way Jane situates herself in order to commune with her. He also rec-ognises that while the prisoner is restless in her imprisonment, she is also resolute: the fierce independence that Jane has learned, tied to self-denial, is critical to her remaining imprisoned in her emotional and social cage. Continually Rochester seeks to claim more equality with Jane, wanting her to dine with him. Even while they are engaged, Jane refuses: she will not eat with him as his equal until after they are married. On the night before their wedding, in a scene that has resonances with the biblical Last Supper, it is notable that Jane's heightened emotional state prevents her physically from being able to eat. Neither can she eat breakfast the next day, and upon leaving Rochester completely, she enters days of physical starvation that reflect her emotionally bereft state, mirroring Christ's forty days of fasting in the wilderness. Rochester, in seeking to be Jane's Christ-figure, has become her Judas, and Jane must be her own suffering saviour. As Jane wan-ders through the wild moors, her isolation from the world is made apparent. The wilderness is personified—nature sustains her through the night—but the people she encounters, of whom she asks for food or work, are strangely alien to her, as though she were another species. As a beggar, she is now, ironically, in the posi-tion to which John Reed had wanted to condemn her.

Jane's return to Rochester can only occur when she has realised, through their telepathic communion, that they are entitled to be joined as equals. Although at this point Jane does not know of Bertha's death, she does know that her tie to Rochester is so strong that she must find him, and find out what has become of him, regardless of the result. Her hunger for that nexus of fulfilment that she found at Thornfield outweighs the life of service that St John offers. Yet it is also her financial and social independence that allows her to seek Rochester out. Throughout her time at Thornfield, even after they were engaged, Jane had maintained Rochester as her master. This social disparity was most profoundly established through Rochester's guests, the Eshtons and Ingrams. When he is disguised as a gypsy, Rochester recognises Jane's separation:

> 'I wonder what thoughts are busy in your heart during all the hours you sit in yonder room with the fine people flitting before you like shapes in a magic lantern: just as little sympathetic communion passing between you and them as if they were really mere shadows of human forms, and not the actual substance.' (229)

Significantly, Rochester is putting the onus on Jane: she is refusing to recognise the humanity of the guests, and therefore her human equality to them; Jane is the one setting herself apart. On Rochester summoning her, she separates herself in the window seat, as she had done as a child at Gateshead. Yet in denying her equality with the Eshtons and Ingrams, she is keeping herself away from Rochester as well. Until she claims her equality to him, they cannot enter into true communion. When Rochester summons Jane as his wife in the garden, Jane's claim of equality is made transient because she must still operate in terms of subservience. Furthermore, throughout their engagement, Jane's means to assert herself is inevitably tied to her self-denial—refusing to allow Rochester to adorn her with jewels and clothes, or refusing his caresses and embrace. Still unable to see herself as Rochester's equal, Jane anticipates that something will keep them from being joined together. It is only after Rochester has called out to her psychically, from Ferndean, a very different place from Thornfield, and once Jane is financially independent and able to be responsible for her own hungers, that she is able to accept a position of equality with Rochester. Jane eats her first meal with Rochester after she finds him at Ferndean, demanding food because she is hungry.

When Jane left Rochester, she 'abhorred' herself: 'I had no solace from self-approbation: none even from self-respect. I had injured—wounded—left my master. I was hateful in my own eyes' (370). Rochester later tells her that at that time he had felt 'desolate and abandoned . . . my soul athirst and forbidden to drink—my heart famished and never to be fed' (501). Jane's determined separation is written in terms of starvation for them both. Yet as her independence turns from self-denial to fulfilment, and is enabled through wealth and provision, she realises (again, notably before she knows that Bertha is dead), '[w]ho would be hurt by my once more tasting the life his glance can give me?' (488). There is a self-interest in this determination that tempers Rochester's later fear that Jane is sacrificing for him, again denying herself. But Jane rewrites the doctrine of self-sacrifice: 'What do I sacrifice?' she asks, 'Famine for food, expectation for content. To be privileged to put my arms around what I value—to press my lips to what I love—to repose on what I trust: is that to make a sacrifice? If so, then certainly I delight in sacrifice' (513). Ultimately Jane rejects the institutions of church and society that would condemn her to physical, social, and spiritual starvation. Instead, her necessity of hunger is relieved, allowing her to enter into her desired satiety of familial communion.

Self-interested hunger in the community

Jane Eyre's question, however, of 'who would be hurt' by her self-interest haunts Brontë's narrative, and bleeds into the other key narratives I address. Maggie Tulliver desperately attempts to save everyone from pain by not going through with her elopement out of her moral consciousness, but Eliot's narrative instead suggests that to have gone through with the elopement would have eventually been less devastating to all involved. Furthermore, Gaskell's *Mary Barton* has a similar potential for devastation through Mary's infatuation with Harry Carson, and Jem Wilson's love for Mary. Narratives of self-denial for the sake of others and self-denial for self-gain proliferate and mingle, with unadulterated motives being rare. While Eliot's Felix Holt, for example, 'will have nothing to do with such eating and drinking' that would associate him with the tradesmen in pubs and the electioneers seemingly out of his moral consciousness,[34] his self-denial, like that of Tom Tulliver, is for a perceived greater political and social gain, even though he misreads his target. Refusing to eat with particular individuals or groups differentiates characters who want to resist their cultural positioning. While Korsmeyer argues that 'the very *flavor* of foods possesses meaning, and in certain cases those flavors are so fundamental to diet and patterns of culture that their meanings are recognized by widely disparate societies,'[35] it stands to reason that to resist flavours is to resist their cultural meanings, just as Maggie resists the flavour of the gypsies' bacon; and indeed, such resistance is necessary to redefine community: '[t]he need for community and the recognition of internal resources for change—both these findings complicate our usual notion that self-assertion stands in natural opposition to tradition.'[36] The shared experience of resistance or complicity with flavour builds into the construction of social identity, and like Jane Eyre, Mary Barton seeks to negotiate between her physical and social hungers to find social and economic independence. For Mary, however, there is more urgency for such independence in the wake of the dire poverty of her world; and paradoxically, independence seems less possible for the same reason. Jane Eyre has cultural capital to which a Mary Barton does not have access, and so Mary's means of independence are more limited.

In the lack of class crossovers in terms of shared food in *Mary Barton*, it is crucial to note that there is no food shared between Mary Barton and Harry Carson, although he is generous in his gifts of flowers. Also, at Miss Simmonds's, the girls have to work for her for two years before they earn the right to share in her edible bounty. This in-class sharing of food resonates with the view expressed most often by John Barton, but also explicitly Gaskell herself in her preface, that only the poor ever truly help the poor because the rich are too ignorant or

---

34 Carlisle, 'Smell of Class,' 11.
35 Carolyn Korsmeyer, Preface to Part III, 'Eloquent Flavours,' in Korsmeyer (ed.), *Taste Culture Reader*, 103–04, 103.
36 Vander Weele, '*Jane Eyre* and the Tradition of Self-Assertion,' 23.

too uncaring to help. To the rich, the poor are 'unrecognisable,' to borrow from Judith Butler's social theory. Yet while the working classes are not in a position to eat their way up the social ladder, what they *can* do is refuse to eat with their own class as a potential means to rise. This occurs, perhaps, in John Barton's refusal to be helped financially by the Union, saying that others need it more than he does. This might be true; however, he himself is starving, and his denial of his situation seems to be at once noble and destructive—especially considering the end to which it leads.

The position of Mary within her hungry world, especially in terms of her relationships with Harry and Jem, is marked by her desire not so much for wealth, but for economic stability. In the preface, Gaskell writes of the working classes resenting the 'even tenor,' the stability of the lives of the rich,[37] which is the luxury of moderation. It is evident that Mary sees the acquisition of luxuries through marriage to someone wealthy as her means to economic stability. Furthermore, even in Mary's childhood innocence, there are traces of the ambitions and desires planted by the absent Aunt Esther, the streetwalking alcoholic who hungrily haunts the text with her failed dreams of social advancement. Esther's hunger for cultural capital is her destruction. Barton expresses regret for her beauty as leading to her fallenness: '[n]ot but what beauty is a sad snare. Here was Esther so puffed up, that there was no holding her in.'[38] Yet in blaming her beauty, Barton is blind to the way Esther's social and physical hunger mirrors his own, and Barton's excess of hunger, written through his opium abuse, is as uncontrollable as Esther's alcohol addiction. The risk that Barton does see, however, is in the influence Esther has over the young Mary, with Esther having appeared to display the economic and social position to which her niece aspires. Barton gives an account of his anger at hearing Esther telling his daughter that she would send for her one day and turn her into a lady; yet his moral anger is not due to Esther's sexual fallenness or her addiction, but to his belief that the life of a 'lady' is idle, and that there is more honour in earning bread by the 'sweat of the brow.' His criticism goes on to critique the wealthy in biblical echoes, as though they are not the disciples of Christ. It is crucial in this moment that while Barton buys into the religious implications of political economy that to sweat in labour is biblically right, he also turns that perspective onto the idleness of the rich. His concern for Mary, though, is that her aunt has put impossible ideas into her head—that she has been given a hunger and aspiration that cannot be fulfilled: 'will a rich lady come and take her to her own home if need be, till she can look round, and see what best to do? No, I tell you, it's the poor, and the poor only, as does such things for the poor' (7–8).

Barton resents his sister-in-law's financial independence, seeing it as the means for her to leave his home, and to live a dissipated life—something that he associates with factory work in general. He tells George Wilson, 'That's the

37 Gaskell, Preface to *Mary Barton*, xxxv.
38 Gaskell, *Mary Barton*, 6.

worst of factory work for girls. They can earn so much when work is plenty, that they can maintain themselves any how. My Mary shall never work in a factory, that I'm determined on' (6). In spite of Barton's fears for Mary's aspirations, he is not without his own ambitions for her. His prejudice against factory work also reveals his middle-class ambitions, similar to his wife's, in that they both seek the social capital of respectability. His involvement as a Chartist in the early stages of the novel is when times are good, and so 'all these feelings were theoretical, not practical,' and so he could afford to aspire for more: at this point, he is not starving (26). In times of plenty, the revolutionary spirit lies dormant. At the same time, though, Mary, who 'took her own way, growing more spirited every day, and growing in her beauty,' in order to avoid the derisive position of idleness 'must do something' (25–26). She remains within the bounds of her father's aspiration, accepting that factory work is 'out of the question,' but she also exerts her own ambition: 'there were two things open—going out to service, and the dressmaking business; and against the first of these, Mary set herself with all the force of her strong will' (26). For Mary, the importance of independence and industry are tied to her desire for economic stability, and as the narrative develops, it is evident that she becomes that stability in the household, even as her father disintegrates.

Mary's independence is centred on social hunger and ambition. By refusing to go into service, she is avoiding, as her father sees it, 'a species of slavery; a pampering of artificial wants on the one side, a giving-up of every right of leisure by day and quiet rest by night on the other' (26). Barton does not buy into Adam Smith's ideal in *Theory of Moral Sentiments* (1759) of the luxurious indulgences of the wealthy creating work opportunities for the poor because it means a loss of physical liberty, a kind of social capital more difficult to define within a word of materiality and productive labour. For Mary's part, she does not want to sacrifice the liberty that she has had in her father's house since her mother's death in order 'to submit to rules as to hours and associates, to regulate her dress by a mistress's ideas of propriety, to lose the dear feminine privileges of gossiping with a merry neighbour, and working night and day to help one who is sorrowful' (26). Importantly, Mary's liberty is not just for herself, but to have the freedom to help others—something that is evident in her father as well—and her liberty of time and dress is not something that can be quantified.

However, Mary's social hunger is fed by her knowledge of her own beauty. She is not content to remain within the bounds of her father's class and expectations, partly because of her aunt's example, but also because she understands the aesthetic power of beauty: beauty, unlike time or dress, is a type of capital that has currency:

> with this consciousness she had early determined that her beauty should make her a lady; the rank she coveted the more for her father's abuse; the rank to which she firmly believed her lost Aunt Esther had arrived. Now, while a servant must often drudge and be dirty, must be known as her servant by all who visited at her master's house, a dressmaker's apprentice must

(or so Mary thought) be always dressed with a certain regard to appearance; must never soil her hands, and need never redden or dirty her face with hard labour. (27)

In 'The Politics of Dirt in *Mary Barton* and *Ruth*,' Natalka Freeland powerfully examines the way in which Gaskell reveals the 'incongruity of applying a middle-class model of domesticity to the real conditions of the urban poor,' connecting ideas of filth and waste to starvation and addiction, but also questioning the level of filth one can bear.[39] Freeland draws on the readings of dirt and cleanliness in regard to the Condition of England Question, and the ways in which cleanliness is connected to social progress, most specifically moving from a working-class context into the middle classes. Mary's unwillingness to sully her hands is an obvious example of her ambition; however, her social hunger forces a complication in her cleanliness, in that she is effectively willing to prostitute herself, as her Aunt Esther did, in order to gain a higher social position. She seeks to legitimate that position, though, through marriage to Harry Carson.

Mary finds her own position at Miss Simmonds's, and is swayed by the 'respectable little street,' the fact that the workwomen were called by Miss Simmonds 'her young ladies,' and that after two years of working without remuneration, she would be able to 'dine and have tea' with Miss Simmonds and be 'paid quarterly because [it was] so much more genteel than by week.'[40] While Mary could be read as calculating, she also shows a forward-thinking potential in terms of business. She would learn a business that she could turn to in her own name after some time, and she is prepared to go without pay for two years in order to learn it well, in a respectable establishment. Gaskell is careful not to make Mary seem cold in her approach: Mary is aware, for instance, of Jem Wilson's affection for her, but she is practical, and knows that it would not bode well to encourage him. She does not want to 'go meddling wi' him,' and is troubled in her conscience in terms of how she deals with him, given his father's friendship with hers. It is evident that Mary has affection for Jem, although she does not admit it, in that she does admit to herself that 'unless I'm always watching myself, I'm speaking to him in a loving voice' (90). Yet rather than condemning Mary, Gaskell reveals a world in which love is a luxury that the poor cannot afford. When Mary dreams, she dreams not of either Jem or Harry, but of being able to drive out in a carriage with her father, providing for him a 'grand house, where her father should have newspapers, and pamphlets, and pipes, and meat dinners, every day,—and all day long if he liked.' As the narration states, 'Yes! Mary was ambitious, and did not favour Mr Carson the less because he was rich and a gentleman' (91), but Gaskell carefully constructs Mary's hunger for social and cultural capital in a direction away from self-interest, and reminds the reader, through the mention of meat dinners for her

39 Natalka Freeland, 'The Politics of Dirt in *Mary Barton* and *Ruth*,' *SEL: Studies in English Literature, 1500–1900*, 42.4 (2002): 799–818, 802.
40 Gaskell, *Mary Barton*, 28.

father, that this desire comes from the very real poverty that Mary experiences in such close proximity to the attractive luxury of the Carsons, who can have their factory burn down and not only not be adversely affected by the disaster because of their insurance policy, but actually be rewarded in that precious commodity of time while the factory is being rebuilt. She also does not understand the lack of independence she would have in the middle-class world, perhaps always tainted by her roots, as the wife of Harry Carson, but even more importantly, she does not realise the practical unlikelihood of Harry Carson actually marrying her. Mary's youth and inexperience are constantly emphasised, punctuated by: '[s]uch were the castles in the air, the Alnaschar-visions in which Mary indulged, and which she was doomed in after days to expiate with many tears' (92).

Jem Wilson is problematic in terms of Mary sating her hunger, however. Even from childhood, he seems to stand in the way of Mary's quest for economic and social stability and independence. In the early scene where the Bartons spontaneously invite the Wilsons to share tea, Mary is both emancipated and bound: she is given the responsibility of going to the market to purchase food for the tea, but at the same time she finds that unless she asks Alice Wilson to bring her own teacup and saucer, Mary would have to share her cup with Jem. Mary maintains her independence, 'secretly determin[ing] to take care that Alice brought her teacup and saucer, if the alternative was to be her sharing any thing with Jem' (15). Given that preceding this exchange Mary had repaid Jem's request for a kiss 'for old acquaintance sake' with a slap on the face (10), the necessity of separation between them is even more evident. Mary needs to assert her independence. She relishes the idea of running to the market to spend money on the food they would share, and exercises her bestowed responsibility with alacrity:

> Mary ran off like a hare to fulfil what, to a girl of thirteen, fond of power, was the more interesting part of her errand—the money-spending part. And well and ably did she perform her business, returning home with a little bottle of rum, and the eggs in one hand, while her other was filled with some excellent red-and-white, smoke-flavoured, Cumberland ham, wrapped up in paper. (16)

Not only is Mary able to spend money, she is able to make choices of the best quality, and is able independently to bring the items home. Importantly, with Alice bringing her teacup, Mary is able to avoid the embarrassing occasion of having to share Jem's cup.

This suggestion of sharing a cup with Jem has a number of connotations, one perhaps being an underlying embarrassment on the part of Mr and Mrs Barton over not having enough cups to serve their guests adequately. But an even more evocative image is that of the Eucharistic communion cup, not just of the regular communion, but in the wedding service, when one cup is not shared between all congregation members, but specifically between the couple being married. Both families—at least, both fathers—seek to create a union between Jem and Mary. While the union does eventually take place, at this early point Mary adamantly resists the idea of being joined to Jem in any way. To share food is one thing, but to share the implement of partaking is a much more intimate act. Her refusal can seem innocent because it is coming from a child; and yet it is evident that she is no longer seen as a child in the village, regardless of how her father sees her, given that she was teased for having a 'sweetheart' when Jem asked to kiss her. Jem clearly sees her as a young woman rather than a child, not just from his request of a kiss, but the look he steals 'to see how Mary took the idea' of him being her sweetheart. Mary's consequent 'air of a young fury' is not just the humiliation of a child, but the awareness of a young woman entering a marriageable age, who is also increasingly becoming conscious of her social hungers—although at this stage she is perhaps not fully aware as to why she is so adamantly against sharing a cup with Jem (12).

The more mature Mary, to whom Jem proposes marriage, is very conscious, though, of why she must refuse him. In his proposal, he says, 'we shall never be rich folk, I dare say; but if a loving heart and a strong right arm can shield you from sorrow, or from want, mine shall do it' (150). But by this point in the novel, it has become painfully evident that a loving heart and a strong right arm are *no* shield from sorrow or want; riches are the only way to find this kind of protection in Mary's mind—although of course riches can also be tenuous, the wealthy seem to have the resources to survive economic downturns, unlike the poor who starve. Mary regrets her decision immediately, based on the realisation that she does love Jem, and this revelation opens up the more romantic plot in the novel; however, it is crucial that although Mary realises that she loves Jem earlier, their union does not take place until Jem is in an economic position to provide the stability that Mary has desired. Her self-interest—or, arguably, self-preservation—consistently depends on this kind of stability throughout the novel. Jem begins to show promise in terms Mary can accept through his work as an engineer, but they do not marry until they are to go to Canada. Their effective transportation is political, and as much about the community they are separated from as it is about their own aspirations for social and cultural capital. In this ending there is still an absence that resonates with hunger, an uncertainty that true satisfaction has been found in their relationship, especially given their distance from home, friends, and family. And yet in that separation and new hunger, Jem and Mary perhaps find the necessary yet bearable hunger to engage in progress.

Relating through taste

One of the notable aspects of *Mary Barton* is that tea drinking becomes a kind of secularised holy communion. It takes on a spiritual as well as social dynamic, with characters entering into communion with each other through this ritual. When Jem's mother is incensed against Mary over refusing her son's proposal, it is through sharing tea that tempers are calmed and conversation is possible. The convention of offering tea to someone entering one's home is commonplace, yet speaks not just of hospitality and providing comfort, but of an invitation to share in community. Sharing food in the novel, like the Eucharistic meal, alludes to connection—a desire to belong—and so having food *to* share provides a currency for social capital as well as a means to sate physical hunger. When Mary Barton gives the Italian waif some bread, he immediately shares it with a rat he has taken as a pet, in a way that resonates with the old man rescued from the Bastille in Martineau's *French Wines*, who befriended rats in his cell and insists on continuing to feed them from his share, even after he has been freed. There is a darker reading in terms of establishing a community and associating with those with whom one eats—in this case dehumanising the poor by having them associate with animals—but at the same time, the need to feed others can be seen as an attempt—sometimes desperate—to maintain one's humanity, as when John Barton pawns his property to buy food for the Davenports.

When cross-class eating is involved, another aspect that comes into play is the willingness of the parties to partake in the same tastes. This idea relates not just to the types and varieties of food available, but also to the quality of the fare. It is at this point that luxury and necessity intersect and complicate each other, revealing the extent to which dominant economic figures are willing to relinquish their power for the sake of equity. Jack Goody has argued that '[l]uxury is a focus for discontent, particularly in regimes where the ideology . . . is egalitarian, where the premise of inequality . . . is challenged by other assumptions about the distribution of resources,'[41] and within this perspective it is evident that taste—and the willingness to share or forego taste—is implicit in visions of social and economic collaboration.

This idea is explored explicitly in *North and South*, through the dining-hall scheme developed by Nicholas Higgins and John Thornton; yet conversely, to refuse to eat with someone speaks of rejection, disconnection, and even disowning, such as in *Mary Barton* when Mary is distressed because her father refuses to eat the food she provides for him. There is the distress at seeing him starve unnecessarily, but also at the loss of communion as he distances himself through not eating. *North and South* is recognised as more optimistic than *Mary Barton* in terms of class relations, and a part of this optimism manifests, I would argue, from the capacity for cross-class eating: the capacity to share tastes, and for characters to relate to each other through those tastes. Class tensions are also marked through discomfort about tastes, such as Margaret's offence at the variety of tastes on offer at the Thorntons' dinner party, or Nicholas and Bessie's pride regarding the idea of Margaret bringing them a basket. Furthermore, Margaret's need to organise fruit on a plate speaks of her desire to control her social situation, so that while Garson asks how 'such apparently trivial aesthetic gestures as arranging fruit on a plate . . . come to function as an expression of what Bourdieu would call "charismatic" moral distinction,'[42] it becomes evident that the ability to control taste, if not in terms of flavour, at least in terms of context, enables Margaret to feel a cultural independence and familiarity with home—even if that home is her idealistic

41 Goody, 'The High and the Low,' 68.
42 Garson, *Moral Taste*, 5.

version of Helstone. Being able to access taste and arrange how it is displayed and consumed is evidence of social and cultural capital.

When Thornton brings Mrs Hale the gift of fruit the day after Margaret has rejected his marriage proposal, Margaret is convinced of her invisibility. However, the way in which she goes 'for the plate in silence, and lifted the fruit out tenderly, with the points of her tapered fingers' reveals not just her softening feelings toward Thornton, especially in regard to his kindness to her mother, but also her understanding of the delicacy of their cross-cultural relations, which have been fraught from the start.[43] Given the misunderstandings of the day before, she wishes to handle it with care. The gift of fruit is a means to reconciliation for Thornton, even though he tells himself that he is giving the fruit in spite of Margaret. His capacity for generosity in this case foreshadows his later change in regard to Nicholas Higgins. But at this point, it is crucial to focus on the gift, more than just of healthy food for an invalid, but of nostalgia and a connection to home. Mrs Hale exclaims over how 'delicious' the fruit is, imploring Margaret, 'love, only taste these grapes!' while both Mr and Mrs Hale encourage Margaret to give up her prejudices against Thornton. The connection of this reconciliation through nostalgia to the fruit is made most clear when Mr Hale, who 'had been peeling a peach for his wife . . . cutting off a small piece for himself, said—"If I had any prejudices, the gift of such delicious fruit as this would melt them all away. I have not tasted such fruit—no! not even in Hampshire"' (212).

Thornton's gift is an act of reconciliation on his part toward Margaret, but it also brings about a reconciliation among the Hales. At this moment, husband, wife, and daughter eat the fruit together, and find themselves (although Margaret is reticent) reconciled to each other and to their new life in Milton. The fact that Mr Hale says that such tastes cannot even be found in Hampshire is daring, for he is suggesting that their life in Milton is in some ways better than the one they had had. More broadly, it is possible that Gaskell is displaying optimism in regard to industrial society in terms of having the capacity to produce abundant and—even more significantly—quality food, with Thornton's hothouse fruits surpassing the flavour of the more naturally grown fruit in Helstone. For Mr Hale to articulate his approval, when he had previously been too fearful to even suggest the move to his wife, is a sign of the moral courage that had allowed him to leave the church but had not extended to speak to his wife about it. Mrs Hale's delight in the fresh taste of the fruit is also a sign of hope for her, given that her previous understanding and expectation of the North was of industry, dust, and dirt. As Mr Hale falls into reverie, however, the fruit becomes a gift of an easier past for them, almost like taking them home: 'Do you remember the matted-up currant bushes, Margaret, at the corner of the west-wall in the garden at home?' (212).

The nostalgia of this moment allows the Hales to commune in an imagined past, one that maintains the freshness of flavour, but is not bound by expectations of social propriety. Early in the novel, when Margaret has returned home

---

43 Gaskell, *North and South*, 212.

to Helstone before the move to Milton has been announced, there is another instance of fruit eating, and again connected to a proposal of marriage. In the case of Henry Lennox, however, the proposal comes after the sharing of fruit. It is worth noting that while Thornton gives the gift of fruit after he has been rejected, and does not partake in the fruit himself, Lennox eats the Hales' fruit—having caused some anxiety by his unexpected visit—with Margaret in the intimate setting of the garden, and then proposes. Mr Hale is unperturbed by the unexpected visitor, casually offering 'the hospitable luxury of a freshly-decanted bottle of wine' while lightly chastising Margaret that she 'might have gathered us some pears for our dessert' (28). Mrs Hale is concerned, though, that desserts at the parsonage would not be perceived as 'impromptu and unusual things,' wishing that Mr Hale would have 'looked behind him' and seen 'biscuits and marmalade, and what not, all arranged in formal order on the sideboard' (28). But fresh fruit is a point of difference to Mr Hale, one that consistently makes him reminisce about his youth.

While Mr Hale suggests that Margaret go to pick some of the pears from the garden, specifically the English variety of brown beurrés, which, he claims, 'are worth all foreign fruits and preserves,' it is Lennox who suggests eating in the garden: 'Nothing is as delicious,' Henry says, 'as to set one's teeth into the crisp, juicy fruit, warm and scented by the sun.' The sensory explosion of Henry's description is intended to be seductive; yet he also reveals the dangers of competition: 'The worst is, the wasps are impudent enough to dispute it with one, even at the very crisis and summit of enjoyment' (28–29). If the wasps stand in for Thornton, with Margaret as the fruit, Lennox's loss of pleasure is foreshadowed from this beginning. However, it is also reasonable in the context of the novel's dialogue between North and South to appreciate the industry of the wasp, representing the North, who works for sustenance, over the idle sensory pleasure and indulgence of the South. This moment is evoked later when Thornton says

'I would rather be a man toiling, suffering—nay, failing and successless— here, than lead a dull prosperous life in the old worn grooves of what you call more aristocratic society down in the South, with their slow days of careless ease. One may be clogged with honey and unable to rise and fly.' (82)

The sweet complacency of the South becomes vapid, even for Margaret who idealises it for so long. After her parents' deaths, on her return to London with her aunt, the meals are so insipid that the food itself is not mentioned—as though it is not even there—and the only notice made is of the emptiness of thought:

[t]hese dinners were delightful; but even here Margaret's dissatisfaction found her out. Every talent, every feeling, every acquirement; nay, even every tendency towards virtue, was used up as materials for fireworks; the hidden, sacred fire, exhausted itself in sparkle and crackle. They talked about art in a merely sensuous way, dwelling on outside effects, instead of allowing themselves to learn what it has to teach. They lashed themselves up into an

enthusiasm about high subjects in company, and never thought about them when they were alone; they squandered their capabilities of appreciation into a mere flow of appropriate words. (397)

The description of 'delightful' seems ironic, and almost as if Margaret is trying to convince herself of this idea; however, in spite of the spectacle of the meals, she cannot help but notice the empty indulgence of the lifestyle displayed. This scene contrasts starkly with the Thorntons' dinner party, for all its apparent excess in a time of want, because at least at that dinner table, the people used the space to debate and discuss the crisis of industry at hand: the northern dinner has urgency of purpose; the London dinner has no need to aspire to progress.

The most powerful meal described in *North and South*, though, is that which takes place in the dining hall Thornton builds for his workmen. In a dialogue reminiscent of Harriet Martineau's exchanges on political economy in her *Illustrations*, Thornton recounts to Mr Bell the way in which the dining-hall scheme came about. The passage reveals the developing respect and friendship that Thornton has for Nicholas first, and then by extension his other workmen, and most importantly, this development comes through sharing meals together. Thornton says that the idea came to him upon visiting Higgins in his home, where he

'saw such a miserable black frizzle of a dinner—a greasy cinder of meat, as first set me a-thinking. But it was not till provisions grew so high this winter that I bethought me how, by buying things wholesale, and cooking a good quantity of provisions together, much money might be saved, and much comfort gained.' (352–53)

Although it required a surplus for Thornton's plan to coalesce, it is important that he was moved by taste: he shows that he begins to see Higgins as his equal by realising that Higgins should be entitled to quality-tasting food. But it is also crucial that the plan retains a business focus: Thornton is a capitalist, although he is becoming more altruistic, recognising his individual relationship to the community. He begins the account by referring to Nicholas as a 'strange fellow,' who is then referred to as 'my friend—or my enemy,' showing a developing mark of respect. Higgins gets his name, however, when, having 'found fault with every detail of the plan' so that Thornton gives it up, he returns to Thornton with a new scheme, which is 'so nearly the same as [Thornton's], that [he] might fairly have claimed it' (353). Although this piques Thornton's pride, the reason it gains his respect is that he realises Nicholas's strategy: the men would not agree to a plan devised by a master, but if it comes from the men themselves, they will agree. There seems to be an unspoken agreement in this perspective between Nicholas and Thornton.

Mr Bell's role in this exchange is of a more feudal nature. When Thornton tells him, 'I can assure you, the hot dinners the matron turns out are by no means to be despised,' Mr Bell asks, 'Do you taste each dish as it goes in, in virtue of your office?' (353) The implication of hierarchical separation is made clear through the double meaning of office, both as a space in which Thornton works (and his work-men do not have ready access) and also in terms of his position in the factory. Yet it is also implied in the idea of him having a 'taste' of the food—as if it would be just enough to examine—and control—the sufficiency of quality, before perhaps going home for a more succulent meal. However, what reveals Thornton's respect for Nicholas the most is his reticence to eat with the men, until they have invited him to join them: it is not a matter of keeping himself apart, but of respecting them, their space, and their endeavours in creating the cooperative:

> 'I think they saw how careful I was to leave them free, and not to intrude my own ideas upon them; so, one day, two or three of the men—my friend Higgins among them—asked me if I would not come in and take a snack. It was a very busy day, but I saw that the men would be hurt if, after making the advance, I didn't meet them half-way, so I went in, and I never made a better dinner in my life. I told them (my next neighbours I mean, for I'm no speech-maker) how much I enjoyed it; and for some time, whenever that especial dinner recurred in their dietary, I was sure to be met by these men, with a "Master, there's hot-pot for dinner to-day, win yo' come?" If they had not asked me, I would no more have intruded on them than I'd have gone to the mess at the barracks without invitation.' (353–54)

Crucially, the dining room breaks down the walls that had caused the damag-ing strike in the novel. While Mr Bell seems condescending in his observation, 'I should think you were rather a restraint on your hosts' conversation. They can't abuse the masters while you're there. I suspect they take it out on non-hot-pot days,' what is evident is that Thornton is working hard to gain his workers' respect. He claims that he is finally beginning to know them in a way that Mr Bell, although he himself is from Darkshire, cannot know them, and in this knowing them, through communing with them, he has faith that 'if any of the old disputes came up again, I would certainly speak out my mind next hot-pot day' (354). Recalling Margaret's demand that Thornton go down to speak to the incensed crowd on the day that the Irish were brought in during the strike, it is made evident that such disputes could not be reasoned away at that time because there existed no relationship between manufacturer and workmen. The difference gained through communal eating is that they relate to each other on a human level, bringing a sense of common purpose and vision. In this manner, the cooperative system functions on a foundation of community, not one that idealistically denies conflict, but one that can dialogically approach potential progress.

Conclusion

'Taste them and try'—the risks of tasting in an insatiable market

'I ate and ate my fill,
Yet my mouth waters still'
(Christina Rossetti, *Goblin Market* (1862), ll. 165–66)[1]

Fruit may provoke hunger as supply provokes demand, but, as poor Laura discovers, mere hunger calls forth no fruit.
(Richard Menke, 'The Political Economy of Fruit,' 114)[2]

Richard Menke's reading of Rossetti's *Goblin Market* positions the poem historically within a time when tastes became inaccessible, even to the wealthy, after the promise of an abundant harvest. The seasonal crisis of 1859, when Rossetti penned her poem, brings to the fore the ultimate inability of human society to contain or control the market industry into which it continues to buy. Jean-Baptiste Say's elegant law of equilibrium, in which supply creates demand while demand creates supply, like Adam Smith's invisible hand, is easily challenged in face of the intervention of chaotic human desire and self-interest; yet it is overturned even more peremptorily by the intervention of climatic extremes. As with economic narratives, environmental narratives are created in order to contain the natural world within a humanly constructed rationale. The hunger to understand, to comprehend disaster, is the most succinct expression of the human desire to moderate and control one's individual and communal sphere. Not just to belong to, but to have agency within the community is predicated on the ability to moderate and to *be* moderate. The term 'moderator' designates a particularly powerful role, assigning both the power to decide what moderation is, and to impose that idea on individuals and the community. Having the capacity to moderate oneself, then— to determine that one has had enough for now—epitomises agency; yet the innate

1 All references to Rossetti's *Goblin Market* are from *The Norton Anthology of English Literature: The Victorian Age*, vol. E, ed. Stephen Greenblatt, Catherine Robson, and Carol T. Christ (9th edn; New York and London: W.W. Norton & Company, 2012), 1496–1508.
2 Richard Menke, 'The Political Economy of Fruit,' in *The Culture of Christina Rossetti*, ed. Arseneau, Harrison, and Jansen Kooistra (Athens: Ohio University Press, 1999), 105–36.

insatiability of the human tongue, encouraged and enabled by the Malthusian market vision that perpetually creates new tastes, actively works against the desire for moderation.

Within this paradox of desire, for any kind of equilibrium to be possible there needs to be a renegotiation between social and physical hunger, involving a critique of necessity. The early Spring frosts and snow of 1859 were reported in extreme terms, evoking the language of famine. The *Gardeners' Chronicle and Agricultural Gazette* evoked memories of Ireland's potato blight, with '[e]xpectations of abundant crops are blighted, and now the cry is that the severe frosts of the last two days of March and the greater part of April have destroyed our fruit,'[3] while, as I noted in my Introduction, the *Economist* became increasingly preoccupied with the scarcity in the marketplace. The scarcity of 1859 reveals the dependence of Britain in foreign imports, but it also shows that the nation had become dependent on a variety of tastes—Menke's example of punch, for instance, draws forth the question as to why one would *need* punch to an extent that it would lead to economic panic. The panic arises from tastes becoming hungers, and the convergence of the nebulous double meaning of want: want as need, and want as desire. Punch becomes a necessity, perhaps, in the same way that cellphones, home computers, and reliably fast broadband connections are necessities in the twenty-first century. While technology may not be necessary for physical survival, it is necessary for human connection and social interaction, and therefore social agency. In this way, the space of necessity is expanded to increase the market's scope.

The addictive qualities of, for example, social media, can be related to the media flooding of the fruit in Rossetti's poem. Albert Pionke observes that 'one of the most striking features of "Goblin Market" is the ubiquitousness of the goblins,'[4] yet more specifically, it is their ubiquitous cry of 'Come buy, come buy' that haunts the poem, preceding its action and lingering beyond its conclusion. The addiction begins before either Laura or Lizzie personally encounter the goblin men: they know of the men, know the story of Jeanie's encounter (insert customer testimonial for marketing purposes here), and are already entranced by the call. It is Laura who implores Lizzie to 'Lie close,' for they 'must not look at goblin men, / We must not buy their fruits' (ll. 40, 42–43), revealing the seductive power the goblins' cry already has over them, especially Laura: at the same time that Laura is telling Lizzie that they must *not* look, Laura clearly *is* looking, for Lizzie cries, '"Laura, Laura, / You should not peep at goblin men"' (ll. 48–49). Laura's peeping is as dangerous as intending on having a little taste of something delicious, but quickly finding that little taste has ended in consuming it all. Laura's failing is, in this sense, her inability to moderate her appetite or control her hunger.

---

3 M. Saul, 'Fruit Prospects,' *Gardeners' Chronicle and Agricultural Gazette* (14 May 1859), 424.
4 Albert D. Pionke, 'The Spiritual Economy of *Goblin Market*,' *SEL: Studies in English Literature, 1500–1900*, 52.4 (2012): 897–915, 899.

Yet Laura's relationship to the goblins and their fruit is more complex than lack of agency over her own hunger. Jill Rappoport crucially notes that 'Laura, less wary than her sister, and less wealthy, makes a hasty disclaimer to the goblin vendors.'[5] In this way, having wealth becomes connected to wariness: Lizzie, with her silver penny, has something to lose, while Laura considers herself safe in her poverty. While Laura thinks to protect herself by openly stating that she cannot afford the product, the goblins offer her a 'taste' without asking for payment. It is Laura who suggests the need to enter into a transaction of exchange with the goblins, showing that the sisters have another social need that affects their interaction with the fruit: the 'compulsory capitalism in which the sisters are inscribed'[6] necessitates their participation in capitalist exchange, motivated by the fear of indebtedness, especially indebtedness to strangers. Laura is willing to be indebted to her sister for her recovery, but neither sister can bear the possibility of being in debt to wandering foreign merchants. While Heather McAlpine observes that '[s]eeing, hearing, speaking, and eating are activities fraught with potential danger in Rossetti's poetry and prose,'[7] *Goblin Market* particularly emphasises the perceived dangers of foreignness—the unknown—in times of scarcity, especially if those foreigners are suggesting an ideology in opposition to capitalist self-interest. For this reason, Rossetti's poem provides a useful example of the interactions of economics and mobility, as well as the implications of community and belonging, within the context of hunger. While the sisters' relationship to food is indicative of an addiction to labour, buying into a capitalist suspicion of what has not been processed and cultivated, the threat of the goblins becomes a demonisation of anti-capitalist ideology. Furthermore, reading Laura's and Lizzie's encounters with the goblins from the goblins' perspective, provides a powerful example of social hunger. As Simon Humphries states, '[s]urely we must understand that they fling it back because they are not in the market for money.'[8] I suggest that the goblins potentially represent the dangers of extreme social hunger, where those who are desperate for a community fall into destructive behaviours. In times of scarcity, as seen in Britain during the Hungry Forties, generosity to the foreigner is limited, while the definition of foreignness is extended. Thus Laura's question, '"Who knows upon what soil they fed / Their hungry thirsty roots?"' (ll. 44–45) reaches the salient point: the goblins represent the displaced foreigner, seeking a community to belong to; yet what is even more dangerous than a foreigner is a foreigner who is perceived to be hungry and thirsty when the community itself is in want. Within an ironic narrative of the necessity of hunger, Rossetti evokes the fear of scarcity.

5 Jill Rappoport, 'The Price of Redemption in *Goblin Market*,' *SEL: Studies in English Literature, 1500–1900*, 50.1 (2010): 853–75, 854.
6 Krista Lysack, 'Goblin Markets: Victorian Women Shoppers at Liberty's Oriental Bazaar,' *Nineteenth-Century Contexts: An Interdisciplinary Journal*, 27.2 (2006): 139–65, 141.
7 Heather McAlpine, '"Would Not Open Lip from Lip": Sacred Orality and the Christian Grotesque in Christina Rossetti's "Goblin Market",' *Victorian Review*, 36.1 (2010): 114–28, 114.
8 Simon Humphries, 'The Uncertainty of *Goblin Market*,' *Victorian Poetry*, 45.4 (2007): 391–413, 396.

Perverting nature in the name of labour

Susan Honeyman has observed the complexity of Lizzie and Laura's relationship with food in *Goblin Market*. The sisters 'must be productive'; therefore the food preferred is the cakes they make with 'oxidized (bleached, processed) flour, which is an important contrast to the otherwise natural fruit "to fill your mouth" that unnatural men will tempt them to devour.'[9] While Honeyman suggests that the girls are productive 'in a decorative, not necessarily substantive way,'[10] though, on the contrary, what is made clear is that human production is a requirement for wholesome food in the capitalist vision that Rossetti creates. The sisters 'Fetched in honey, milked the cows,' and 'Kneaded cakes of whitest wheat, / Cakes for dainty mouths to eat, / Next churned butter, whipped up cream' before feeding the poultry and sewing (ll. 203, 205–07, 208). Rather than being insubstantial, Honeyman perhaps arguing this because the activities seem domestic, these activities signify productive labour. The image of farm productivity conveys ideas of self-sufficiency and, most importantly, the sisters' capacity to operate within, albeit small, a capitalist market.

What Honeyman does pertinently observe is the way in which natural fruit—in this sense, unprocessed by human labour—becomes representative of wickedness, which recalls the hothouse fruit Mr Thornton gives to the Hales, and the potential optimism regarding the benefits of industrialisation. The ideology that emerges is that human intervention (easily equated with ideas of civilisation) is necessary to maintain the safety of food. This attitude is ironic, given the unknown dangers of adulterated flour; yet it also has implications for the sisters in that Rossetti suggests that there is danger in acquiring something for which one has not laboured. When Lizzie approaches the goblins, the 'dainty fruit' (l. 257) parallels the earlier reference to the 'dainty mouths' meant for cake. Both are sweet, appealing to 'sweet-tooth Laura' (l. 115), but natural (unprocessed) sugar is distrusted while that which is processed is deemed healthy, and even virtuous. Honeyman draws attention to the sisters being permitted to 'indulg[e]' in 'nonsubstantial sweets,' positioning the poem in relation to sugar addiction and literary examples of children being given 'saccharine sweets' to keep them 'more tameable than eating wild (or hothouse) fruits.'[11] What is crucial, though, is that in *Goblin Market* it is the source of the sugar, and the extent of intervening human labour in acquiring it, that determines if it is a taste that can be indulged. This morality of taste is not determined by what is physiologically good for the body, but by capitalist ideologies of the virtue of labour. For this reason, Lizzie's offering of fruit juice to Laura—juice having a higher percentage of fructose because it lacks the fibre included in fresh fruit, but this juice also containing the sweat of Lizzie's exertion in getting it to her sister—becomes the 'fiery antidote' to Laura's addiction (l. 559). It must be noted,

9 Susan Honeyman, 'Gingerbread Wishes and Candy(land) Dreams: The Lure of Food in Cautionary Tales of Consumption,' *Marvels & Tales*, 21.2 (2007): 195–215, 205.
10 Ibid., 205.
11 Ibid., 206.

though, that Laura 'loathed the feast' (l. 495), as '[s]he gorged on bitterness without a name' (l. 510). While the taste is extremely unpleasant, Laura is taught that sweetness must be merged with labour in order to make it permissible. In this way, Laura's redemption becomes an expression of what Herbert Tucker refers to as a 'commercialized appetite.' Importantly, Tucker makes mention of 'Lizzie's express delivery to expressed fruit,' the idea of expressing fruit inherently referencing the intervention of human labour and production.[12] The commercialisation of appetite in both sisters reveals the way in which they have bought into the myth that human intervention safeguards consumption.

The goblins as anti-capitalist demons

Humphries suggests that 'we understand that the fruits which are brought by the goblins are not inherently evil but are used by the goblins for their dark purposes—dark because it is never explained why the goblins are so insistent that young women should eat their fruit.'[13] This perspective works against consumption theory's tendency to assign agency to the product, returning responsibility for consumption to the consumer. It also brings to the fore ideas of gift theory, and the capitalist suspicion of gifts. From the beginning of the poem, Lizzie and Laura understand that the goblins offer gifts, but they are considered dangerous: 'Their evil gifts would harm us' (l. 66). Within the implications of gift exchange and indebtedness, the question must be asked as to what the goblins get out of their gift, with an undergirding expectation of motives of self-gain. This question is not answered in the poem; but it is also evident that for both sisters they are the ones who suggest payment, not the goblins, trying to control their encounters with the fruit through transaction and exchange.

A part of the danger of the goblins' seemingly freely offered fruit is the fear that if individuals can acquire what they need without labour, they will have no incentive to work, which is a longstanding simple critique of communism. Rappoport argues that

> [a]fter entering [the goblins' market economy], Laura becomes alienated from her work; she labors 'in an absent dream,' 'sick in part,' 'longing for the night' (lines 211, 212, 214). Indeed, the poem gives more space to Laura's changing perspective toward work than it does to her failing body.[14]

In terms of classical economic theory, labour in a communist context has the reward of ownership and belonging within the community, but the ideal does

---

12 Herbert F. Tucker, 'Rossetti's Goblin Marketing: Sweet to Tongue and Sound to Eye,' *Representations*, 82.1 (2003): 117–33, 127.
13 Humphries, 'The Uncertainty of *Goblin Market*,' 396.
14 Rappoport, 'The Price of Redemption,' 855.

not sufficiently account for the drive of self-interest. Why labour when someone else will do it? However, capitalism fails to promote community investment also, unless there is some kind of self-gain involved. The goblins potentially represent an alternative through a gift economy. While Pionke suggests that it is Lizzie who 'effectively reimagin[es] the market, not as an abstracted cash nexus, nor as a system of barter, but as a gift economy,'[15] the goblins are the ones who seek to establish a gift economy, within the context of a community—albeit a community to which they do not belong, which is the rub. The gift economy that Lizzie tries to establish only exists in relation to her sister; it does not extend beyond the immediate family. What becomes most evident through the sisters' rejection of the goblins' gift economy is their rejection of the goblins as a part of their community, which, in turn, highlights the social hunger of the goblins themselves, who would deceive with language of a non-existent market in an attempt to penetrate the community.

Hunger for community

Readings of *Goblin Market* seem to take as given that the goblins are wicked creatures, without noting that the narrative of the poem is told from the sisters' perspective. Yet the fact that they are described as 'wicked, quaint fruit-merchant men' (l. 553) and that their fruits are denied on the basis that 'Men sell not such in any town' (l. 556) equates their wickedness with their strangeness and mobility. The reference to town speaks of an established community, established roots, and so, as with the earlier question of where they have placed their 'hungry thirsty roots,' it is evident that the perception that they are evil is generated by their foreignness. They show marks of civilisation in their baskets, plates, and dishes, but their violent behaviour and use of these objects, as well as their use of Lizzie in particular, reveal their position as Other. In terms of the mysterious motives of the goblins, it is possible to read their market in terms of their social hunger. Not in the market for money, the goblins show a desperate hunger for community and belonging: 'Worn out by [Lizzie's] resistance,' they 'Flung back her penny, kicked their fruit' (ll. 438–39), yet unlike the perversion of the physically starving destroying food, this action shows that the goblins' hunger is not located within their stomachs. When Lizzie goes to them, before there is any discussion of the fruit, the goblins 'Hugged her and kissed her, / Squeezed and caressed her' (ll. 348–49). This encounter suggests intimacy, much more so than in Laura's encounter. What eventuates is that while Lizzie seeks to maintain social distance through commerce, even 'toss[ing] them her penny' (l. 367) rather than handing it to them, the goblins seek communion with Lizzie:

15 Pionke, 'The Spiritual Economy of *Goblin Market*,' 903.

> 'Nay, take a seat with us,
> Honour and eat with us,'
> They answered grinning:
> 'Our feast is but beginning'. (ll. 368–71)

They continue, "'Sit down and feast with us, / Be welcome guest with us, / Cheer you and rest with us'" (ll. 380–82). That the goblins want Lizzie to eat with them shows that they are socially hungry, not physically: they are the ones in possession of food. But Lizzie is determined in her separation: "'Give me back my silver penny / I tossed you for a fee'" (ll. 388–89).

While Lizzie's encounter with the goblins has often been likened to rape, little attention has been given to the viability of the goblins calling her 'proud, / Cross-grained, uncivil' (ll. 394–95). Even within her capitalist economy, Lizzie does not display courtesy of exchange in the way she tosses her coin. By rejecting communion with the wanderers, she causes offence, an offence that is exacerbated in her determination to use money for exchange, immediately creating a class barrier: she is the seemingly wealthy consumer, seeking to have agency over her purchase by taking the fruit home. The goblins are merely wandering tradesmen bearing the goods Lizzie wants. There is no denying the violence of the goblins' response:

> Their tones waxed loud,
> Their looks were evil.
> Lashing their tails
> They trod and hustled her,
> Elbowed and jostled her,
> Clawed with their nails,
> Barking, mewing, hissing, mocking,
> Tore her gown and soiled her stocking,
> Twitched her hair out by the roots,
> Stamped upon her tender feet,
> Held her hands and squeezed their fruits
> Against her mouth to make her eat. (ll. 396–407)

The goblins try to force Lizzie to eat, to accept them within her community, but to no avail. In this way, their violence resonates with the hungry rioters and revolutionaries seeking social legitimacy. The goblins riot because they are excluded, but the extremity of their reaction perpetuates their demonic position. The excess of goblin hunger is more destructive than Laura's, while Laura's hunger can be satiated through the community of her sister.

As a narrative of hunger, Rossetti's *Goblin Market* epitomises the complex relationship between physical and social hunger. As much as Laura's hunger for the goblins' fruit can be read in terms of addiction and excess, and the goblins' violence marks the excesses of unsatisfied social hunger, the attraction between the sisters and the goblins speaks of hunger's persistence. Millman and Kates argue that it is not the experience of hunger itself, though, but '[h]uman responses to hunger or to the fear of hunger' that can 'serve to prevent or reduce its consequences,' in which case it is the way 'people organize themselves in relation to hunger'[16] that determines the hold hunger has within society: is it a moderate hunger, leading to progress and development, sparked by imagination and ambition—as Adam Smith envisaged—or is it a destructive, abject hunger, that destroys the human will? Furthermore, to return to Amartya Sen's entitlement theory, what capacity do individuals have within their community *to* organise their response to hunger? From Dickens's and Martineau's French revolutionaries to Gaskell's Chartists and Eliot's reformers, to the migrants, itinerants, and orphans in Mayhew and Brontë, the figures who are able to harness their hunger, and find ways to adapt their situation to increase their opportunities—that is, who are able to cultivate their tastes appropriately—are the ones who progress, while those who keep looking back, either through nostalgia or fear, tend to end in devastation. But hunger, like the revenant, returns; and in its seasonal reinventions it complicates the way both social progress and social decline are rationalised. Mythical narratives of market economies persist in the human need to have a sense of control; but such control is only available to those with the social and economic luxury of moderation. The shifting ideals of entitlement and progress, read through constructions of hunger and taste, critique economic ideals of civilisation, creating counternarratives of insurrection and unrest. This breakdown reveals the fractured nature of a community, society, or nation built upon the predication of want.

16 Millman and Kates, 'Toward Understanding Hunger,' 3.

Bibliography

Anderson, Benedict. *Imagined Communities: Reflections on the Origin and Spread of Nationalism* (1983; London and New York: Verso, 2006).

Anderson, Patrick. *So Much Wasted: Hunger, Performance, and the Morbidity of Resistance* (Durham and London: Duke University Press, 2010).

Andriopoulos, Stefan. 'The Invisible Hand: Supernatural Agency in Political Economy and the Gothic Novel,' *ELH*, 66.3 (1999): 739–58.

Aristotle. 'Sense and Sensibilia,' in *The Complete Works of Aristotle*, trans. J.I. Beare (1931); revised Oxford translation, 2 vols, ed. Jonathan Barnes (Princeton: Princeton University Press, 1984), vol. 1, 693–713.

Arnold, Matthew. *Culture and Anarchy: An Essay in Political and Social Criticism* (London: Smith, Elder and Co., 1869).

———. 'The Literary Influence of Academies' (1864), in *Lectures and Essays in Criticism*, vol. 3, ed. R.H. Super (Ann Arbor: University of Michigan Press, 1986).

Ashton, Rosemary. *Little Germany: Exile and Asylum in Victorian England* (London: Faber and Faber, 2013).

Auerbach, Nina. 'The Power of Hunger: Demonism and Maggie Tulliver,' *Nineteenth-Century Fiction*, 30.2 (1975): 150–71.

Baines, Dudley. *Migration in a Mature Economy: Emigration and Internal Migration in England and Wales 1861–1900* (Cambridge: Cambridge University Press, 1985).

Bamfield, Joshua. 'Consumer-Owned Community Flour and Bread Societies in the Eighteenth and Nineteenth Centuries,' *Business History*, 40.4 (1998): 16–36.

Bann, Jennifer. 'Ghostly Hands and Ghostly Agency: The Changing Figure of the Nineteenth-Century Specter,' *Victorian Studies*, 51.4 (2009): 663–86.

Barker, Francis, Peter Hulme and Margaret Iverson, eds. *Cannibalism and the Colonial World* (Cambridge: Cambridge University Press, 1998).

Bassnett, Susan and André Lefevere. *Constructing Cultures: Essays on Literary Translation* (Clevedon: Multilingual Matters, 1998).

Baucom, Ian. *Out of Place: Englishness, Empire, and the Locations of Identity* (Princeton: Princeton University Press, 1999).

Beardsley, Monroe C. *The European Philosophers from Descartes to Nietzsche* (New York: Random House, 1960).

Beier, A.L. and Paul Robert Ocobock, eds. *Cast Out: Vagrancy and Homelessness in Global and Historical Perspective* (Athens: Ohio University Press, 2008).

Bentley, Colene. 'Democratic Citizenship in *Felix Holt*,' *Nineteenth-Century Contexts: An Interdisciplinary Journal*, 24.3 (2002): 271–89.

Berol, Laura M. 'The Anglo-Irish Threat in Thackeray's and Trollope's Writings of the 1840s,' *Victorian Literature and Culture*, 32.1 (2004): 103–16.

Bhavsar, Vishal and Dinesh Bhugra. 'Bethlem's Irish: Migration and Distress in Nineteenth-Century London,' *History of Psychiatry*, 20 (2009): 184–98.

Bigelow, Gordon. *Fiction, Famine, and the Rise of Economics in Victorian Britain and Ireland* (Cambridge: Cambridge University Press, 2003).

Birch, Dinah and Mark Llewellyn, eds. *Conflict and Difference in Nineteenth-Century Literature* (Basingstoke: Palgrave Macmillan, 2010).

Blake, Kathleen. 'Between Economies in *The Mill on the Floss*: Loans versus Gifts, or, Auditing Mr. Tulliver's Accounts,' *Victorian Literature and Culture*, 33.1 (2005): 219–37.

Bohstedt, John. 'Gender, Household and Community Politics: Women in English Riots, 1790–1810,' *Past and Present*, 120 (1988): 88–122.

Bordo, Susan. *Unbearable Weight: Feminism, Western Culture, and the Body* (Berkeley: University of California Press, 1993).

Brantlinger, Patrick. 'The Case against Trade Unions in Early Victorian Fiction,' *Victorian Studies*, 13.1 (1969): 37–52.

———. 'The Famine,' *Victorian Literature and Culture*, 32.1 (2004): 193–207.

———. *Rule of Darkness: British Literature and Imperialism 1830–1914* (Ithaca: Cornell University Press, 1988).

Brantlinger, Patrick and Donald Ulin. 'Policing Nomads: Discourse and Social Control in Early Victorian Britain,' *Cultural Critique*, 25 (1993): 33–63.

Brillat-Savarin, Jean Anthelme. 'The World of the Senses and the Nature of Taste,' extracts from *The Physiology of Taste; or Transcendental Gastronomy, Illustrated by Anecdotes of Distinguished Artists and Statesmen of Both Continents* (Philadelphia: Lindsay & Blakiston, 1854), *New England Review*, 30.4 (2010): 181–94.

Brontë, Charlotte. *Jane Eyre: An Autobiography* (1847; London: Penguin, 2006).

———. *Shirley* (1849; London: Penguin, 1974).

Burke, Edmund. 'On Taste,' *A Philosophical Enquiry into the Origin of Our Ideas of the Sublime and the Beautiful* (1757; 5th edn, London: J. Dodsley, 1767), 1–40.

Butwin, Joseph. 'The Pacification of the Crowd: From "Janet's Repentance" to *Felix Holt*,' *Nineteenth-Century Fiction*, 35.3 (1980): 349–71.

Caldwell, Janis McLarren. 'Conflict and Revelation: Literalization in the Novels of Charlotte Brontë,' *Victorian Literature and Culture*, 31.2 (2003): 483–99.

Capuano, Peter J. 'Networked Manufacture in Charlotte Brontë's *Shirley*,' *Victorian Studies*, 55.2 (2013): 231–42.

Carlisle, Janice. *Picturing Reform in Victorian Britain* (Cambridge: Cambridge University Press, 2012).

———. 'The Smell of Class: British Novels of the 1860s,' *Victorian Literature and Culture*, 29.1 (2001): 1–19.

Carlyle, Thomas. *Chartism* (1840; New York: John W. Lovell, 1885).

———. *The French Revolution: A History in Three Parts* (1837; London: Chapman and Hall, 1857).

Caufield, James Walter. *Overcoming Matthew Arnold: Ethics in Culture and Criticism* (Farnham: Ashgate, 2012).

Clemm, Sabine. *Dickens, Journalism, and Nationhood: Mapping the World in* Household Words (New York and London: Routledge, 2009).

Colley, Linda. *Britons: Forging the Nation 1707–1837* (1992; London: Vintage, 1996).

Coogan, Tim Pat. *The Famine Plot: England's Role in Ireland's Greatest Tragedy* (New York: Palgrave Macmillan, 2012).

Cooper, Brian P. *Family Fictions and Family Facts: Harriet Martineau, Adolphe Quetelet, and the Population Question in England, 1798–1859* (London and New York: Routledge, 2007).

Corbin, Alain. *The Foul and the Fragrant: Odor and the French Social Imagination* (Leamington Spa, Hamburg and New York: Berg Publishers, 1986).

———. *Time, Desire and Horror: Towards a History of the Senses*, trans. Jean Birrell (1991; Cambridge: Polity Press, 1995).

Coriale, Danielle. 'Gaskell's Naturalist,' *Nineteenth-Century Literature*, 63.3 (2008): 346–75.

Corporaal, Marguérite. 'From Golden Hills to Sycamore Trees: Pastoral Homelands and Ethnic Identity in Irish Immigrant Fiction, 1860–75,' *Irish Studies Review*, 18.3 (2010): 331–46.

———. 'Memories of the Great Famine and Ethnic Identity in Novels by Victorian Irish Women Writers,' *English Studies*, 90.2 (2009): 142–56.

Courtemanche, Eleanor. *The 'Invisible Hand' and British Fiction, 1818–1860: Adam Smith, Political Economy, and the Genre of Realism* (Basingstoke: Palgrave Macmillan, 2011).

Craciun, Adriana and Kari E. Lokke, eds. *Rebellious Hearts: British Women Writers and the French Revolution* (New York: State University of New York Press, 2001).

Cresswell, Tim. *On the Move: Mobility in the Western World* (New York: Routledge, 2006).

Curran, Declan and Maria Fröling. 'Large-Scale Mortality Shocks and the Great Irish Famine 1845–1852,' *Economic Modelling*, 27 (2010): 1302–14.

Dalley, Lana L. 'The Economics of "A Bit O' Victual," or Malthus and Mothers in *Adam Bede*,' *Victorian Literature and Culture*, 36.2 (2008): 549–67.

Dalley, Lana L. and Jill Rappoport, eds. *Economic Women: Essays on Desire and Dispossession in Nineteenth-Century British Culture* (Columbus: Ohio State University Press, 2013).

Daly, Suzanne and Ross G. Forman. 'Introduction: Cooking Culture: Situating Food and Drink in the Nineteenth Century,' *Victorian Literature and Culture*, 36.2 (2008): 363–73.

Dames, Nicholas. *Amnesiac Selves: Nostalgia, Forgetting, and British Fiction, 1810–1870* (Oxford: Oxford University Press, 2001).

Darwin, Charles. *The Descent of Man* (1871; New York: Dover, 2010).

———. *On the Origin of Species By Means of Natural Selection* (1859; New York: Dover, 2006).

Davis, Mike. *Late Victorian Holocausts: El Niño Famines and the Making of the Third World* (London and New York: Verso, 2002).

De Nie, Michael. 'The Famine, Irish Identity, and the British Press,' *Irish Studies Review*, 6.1 (1998): 27–35.

Deegan, Mary Jo. 'Textbooks, the History of Sociology, and the Sociological Stock of Knowledge,' *Sociological Theory*, 21.3 (2003): 298–305.

Delanty, Gerard. 'Cosmopolitanism and Violence: The Limits of Global Civil Society,' *European Journal of Social Theory*, 4 (2001): 41–52.

Dentith, Simon. *Nineteenth-Century British Literature Then and Now: Reading with Hindsight* (Aldershot: Ashgate, 2014).

———. 'Political Economy, Fiction and the Language of Practical Ideology in Nineteenth-Century England,' *Social History*, 8.2 (1983): 183–99.

Dickens, Charles. *A Christmas Carol* (1843; London: Bradbury and Evans, 1858).

———. *A Tale of Two Cities* (1859; London: Penguin, 2003).

———. *Barnaby Rudge: A Tale of the Riots of 'Eighty* (1841; London: Penguin, 2003).

———. *David Copperfield* (1850; London: Penguin, 1966).

———. *Hard Times* (1854; Oxford: Oxford University Press, 1989).

———. *Oliver Twist* (1837–38; London: Penguin, 2002).

[Dickens, Charles], 'A Crisis in the Affairs of Mr. John Bull,' *Household Words*, 2.35 (23 November 1850): 193–96.

———. 'On Duty with Inspector Field,' *Household Words*, 3 (14 June 1851): 265–70.

Eagleton, Terry. *Myths of Power: A Marxist Study of the Brontës*, rev. edn (New York: Palgrave, 2005).

Eastwood, David. 'The Age of Uncertainty: Britain in the Early-Nineteenth Century,' *Transactions of the Royal Historical Society*, 8 (1998): 91–115.

Eliot, George. *Felix Holt, The Radical* (1866; London: Penguin, 1995).

———. *The Mill on the Floss* (1860; London: Penguin, 2003).

———. *Romola* (1862–63; London: Penguin, 1996).

———. *Silas Marner: The Weaver of Raveloe* (1861; London: Penguin, 1996).

Ellmann, Maud. *The Hunger Artists: Starving, Writing & Imprisonment* (London: Virago, 1993).

Emami, Ehsan. 'Capitalism the Inhumane Form: A Lukacsian Comparative Reading of Capitalism in *The Mill on the Floss* and *Ulysses*,' *Theory and Practice in Language Studies*, 2.4 (2012): 759–66.

Fine, Robert. 'Cosmopolitanism and Violence: Difficulties of Judgement,' *The British Journal of Sociology*, 57.1 (2006): 49–67.

Finn, Margot C. *After Chartism: Class and Nation in English Radical Politics, 1848–1874* (Cambridge: Cambridge University Press, 1993).

'The Five Senses,' *The Leisure Hour: A Family Journal of Instruction and Recreation* (7 April 1866): 213–16.

Fourcade-Gourinchas, Marion. 'Politics, Institutional Structures, and the Rise of Economics: A Comparative Study,' *Theory and Society*, 30.3 (2001): 397–447.

Freeburgh Kees, Lara. '"Sympathy" in *Jane Eyre*,' *Studies in English Literature, 1500–1900*, 45.4 (2005): 873–97.

Freedgood, Elaine. *Victorian Writing about Risk: Imagining a Safe England in a Dangerous World* (Cambridge: Cambridge University Press, 2004).

Freeland, Natalka. 'The Politics of Dirt in *Mary Barton* and *Ruth*,' *SEL: Studies in English Literature, 1500–1900*, 42.4 (2002): 799–818.

Freitag, Sabine, ed. *Exiles from European Revolutions: Refugees in Mid-Victorian England* (New York and Oxford: Berghahn Books, 2003).

Fumerton, Patricia. *Unsettled: The Culture of Mobility and the Working Poor in Early Modern England* (Chicago and London: University of Chicago Press, 2006).

Funnell, Warwick. 'Accounting for Justice: Entitlement, Want and the Irish Famine of 1845–7,' *The Accounting Historians Journal*, 28.2 (2001): 187–206.

Gagnier, Regenia. *Individualism, Decadence and Globalization: On the Relationship of Part to Whole, 1859–1920* (Basingstoke: Palgrave Macmillan, 2010).

———. *The Insatiability of Human Wants: Economics and Aesthetics in Market Society* (Chicago and London: University of Chicago Press, 2000).

———. 'The Law of Progress and the Ironies of Individualism in the Nineteenth Century,' *New Literary History*, 31.2 (2000): 315–36.

———. 'On the Insatiability of Human Wants: Economic and Aesthetic Man,' *Victorian Studies*, 36.2 (1993): 125–53.

Gallagher, Catherine. *The Body Economy: Life, Death, and Sensation in Political Economy and the Victorian Novel* (Princeton: Princeton University Press, 2006).

———. 'The Body versus the Social Body in the Works of Thomas Malthus and Henry Mayhew,' *Representations*, 14 (1986): 83–106.

———. *The Industrial Reformation of English Fiction: Social Discourse and Narrative Form 1832–1867* (Chicago and London: University of Chicago Press, 1985).

Garson, Marjorie. *Moral Taste: Aesthetics, Subjectivities, and Social Power in the Nineteenth-Century Novel* (Toronto: University of Toronto Press, 2007).

Gaskell, Elizabeth. *Mary Barton* (1848; Oxford: Oxford University Press, 1987).

———. *North and South* (1854–55; London: Penguin, 1995).

Gauthier, David. *Morals by Agreement* (Oxford: Oxford University Press, 1986).

Gilmartin, Kevin. *Writing against Revolution: Literary Conservatism in Britain, 1790–1832* (Cambridge: Cambridge University Press, 2007).

Gilmour, Ian. *Riot, Risings and Revolution: Governance and Violence in Eighteenth-Century England* (London: Pimlico, 1993).

Gordon, Avery. *Ghostly Matters: Haunting and the Sociological Imagination* (Minneapolis: University of Minnesota Press, 1997).

Gordon, John. *Sensation and Sublimation in Charles Dickens* (Basingstoke: Palgrave Macmillan, 2011).

Gould, J.D. 'European Inter-Continental Emigration 1815–1914: Patterns and Causes,' *Journal of European Economic History*, 8.3 (1979): 593–679.

Gray, Peter. 'Famine and Land in Ireland and India, 1845–1880: James Caird and the Political Economy of Hunger,' *The Historical Journal*, 49.1 (2006): 193–215.

Green, Bryan S. 'Learning from Mayhew: The Role of the Impartial Spectator in Mayhew's *London Labour and the London Poor*,' *Journal of Contemporary Ethnography*, 31 (2002): 99–134.

Guinnane, Timothy W. 'Interdisciplinary Perspectives on Irish Economic and Demographic History,' *Historical Methods: A Journal of Quantitative and Interdisciplinary History*, 30.4 (1997): 173–81.

Guy, Josephine M. *The Victorian Social-Problem Novel: The Market, the Individual and Communal Life* (Basingstoke: Macmillan, 1995).

Hall, Robert G. 'Chartism Remembered: William Aitken, Liberalism, and the Politics of Memory,' *Journal of British Studies*, 38.4 (1999): 445–70.

Halperin, Sandra. *War and Social Change in Modern Europe: The Great Transformation Revisited* (Cambridge: Cambridge University Press, 2004).

Harrison, Brian. 'The Sunday Trading Riots of 1855,' *Historical Journal*, 8 (1965): 219–45.

Haywood, Ian. *The Revolution in Popular Literature: Print, Politics and the People, 1790–1860* (Cambridge: Cambridge University Press, 2004).

Herbert, Christopher. 'Filthy Lucre: Victorian Ideas of Money,' *Victorian Studies*, 44 (2002): 185–213.

Heywood, Leslie. *Dedication to Hunger: The Anorexic Aesthetic in Modern Culture* (Berkeley: University of California Press, 1996).

Hilton, Boyd. *A Mad, Bad, & Dangerous People? England 1783–1846* (Oxford: Oxford University Press, 2006).

Hobart, Ann. 'Harriet Martineau's Political Economy of Everyday Life,' *Victorian Studies*, 37.2 (1994): 223–51.

Holtzman, Jon D. 'Food and Memory,' *Annual Review of Anthropology*, 35 (2006): 361–78.

Honeyman, Susan. 'Gingerbread Wishes and Candy(land) Dreams: The Lure of Food in Cautionary Tales of Consumption,' *Marvels & Tales*, 21.2 (2007): 195–215.

Hopkins, A.B. 'Liberalism in the Social Teachings of Mrs. Gaskell,' *The Social Service Review*, 5.1 (1931): 57–73.

[Horne, Richard and Charles Dickens]. 'The Great Exhibition and the Little One,' *Household Words*, 3.67 (5 July 1851): 356–60.

Horton, Richard C. 'Mr. Thornton's Experiments: Transformations in Culture and Health,' *Literature and Medicine*, 25.2 (2006): 194–215.

Howes, David and Marc Lalonde. 'The History of Sensibilities: Of the Standard of Taste in Mid-Eighteenth Century England and the Circulation of Smells in Post-Revolutionary France,' *Dialectical Anthropology*, 16 (1991): 125–35.

Hume, David. 'Of the Standard of Taste,' in *Four Dissertations* (London: A. Millar, 1757), 201–40.

Humphries, Simon. 'The Uncertainty of *Goblin Market*,' *Victorian Poetry*, 45.4 (2007): 391–413.

Hunter, Leeann. 'Communities Built from Ruins: Social Economics in Victorian Novels of Bankruptcy,' *Women's Studies Quarterly*, 39.3 (2001): 137–52.

Hutchings, Peter J. *The Criminal Spectre in Law, Literature and Aesthetics: Incriminating Subjects* (London: Routledge, 2001).

Huzel, James P. *The Popularization of Malthus in Early Nineteenth-Century England: Martineau, Cobbett and the Pauper Press* (Aldershot: Ashgate, 2006).

Hyman, Gwen. *Making A Man: Gentlemanly Appetites in the Nineteenth-Century British Novel* (Athens: Ohio University Press, 2009).

Ingelow, Jean. 'Taste,' *Good Words*, 29 (December 1888): 413–14.

Itzkowitz, David C. 'Fair Enterprise or Extravagant Speculation: Investment, Speculation, and Gambling in Victorian England,' *Victorian Studies*, 45.1 (2002): 121–47.

Jones, Colin, Josephine McDonagh and Jon Mee, eds. *Charles Dickens, A Tale of Two Cities and the French Revolution* (Basingstoke: Palgrave Macmillan, 2009).

Jones, Jason. *Lost Causes: Historical Consciousness in Victorian Literature* (Columbus: Ohio State University Press, 2006).

Jones, Peter. 'Swing, Speenhamland and Rural Social Relations,' *Social History*, 32.3 (2007): 271–90.

Kabachnik, Peter. 'The Culture of Crime: Examining Representations of Irish Travelers in *Traveller* and *The Riches*,' *Romani Studies*, 19.1 (2009): 49–63.

Kant, Immanuel. *Anthropology from a Pragmatic Point of View* (1798; Cambridge: Cambridge University Press, 2006).

Kaplow, Jeffry. *The Names of Kings: The Parisian Laboring Poor in the Eighteenth Century* (New York: Basic Books, 1972).

Kelleher, Margaret. 'Hunger in History: Monuments to the Great Irish Famine,' *Textual Practice*, 16.2 (2002): 249–76.

Kineally, Christine. *This Great Calamity: The Irish Famine 1845–52* (Dublin: Gill & Macmillan Ltd., 1994).

Kingstone, Helen. 'The Two Felixes: Narratorial Irony and the Question of Radicalism in *Felix Holt* and "Address to Working Men, By Felix Holt,"' *The George Eliot Review*, 44 (2013): 42–49.

Kitson Clark, G. 'Hunger and Politics in 1842,' *The Journal of Modern History*, 25.4 (1953): 355–74.

Klein, Ira. 'When the Rains Failed: Famine, Relief, and Mortality in British India,' *Indian Economic Social History Review*, 21 (1984): 185–214.

Korsmeyer, Carolyn. *Making Sense of Taste: Food and Philosophy* (Ithaca and London: Cornell University Press, 1999).

———, ed. *The Taste Culture Reader: Experiencing Food and Drink* (2005; Oxford and New York: Berg, 2007).

Koven, Seth. *Slumming: Sexual and Social Politics in Victorian London* (Princeton and Oxford: Princeton University Press, 2004).

Kreisel, Deanna. 'Superfluity and Suction: The Problem with Saving in *The Mill on the Floss*,' *NOVEL: A Forum on Fiction*, 35.1 (2001): 69–103.

Krishnamurthy, Aruna, ed. *The Working-Class Intellectual in Eighteenth- and Nineteenth-Century Britain* (Farnham: Ashgate, 2009).

Kucich, John. *Excess and Restraint in the Novels of Charles Dickens* (Athens: University of Georgia Press, 1981).

———. *Imperial Masochism: British Fiction, Fantasy, and Social Class* (Princeton and Oxford: Princeton University Press, 2007).

———. 'Repression and Representation: Dickens's General Economy,' *Nineteenth-Century Fiction*, 38.1 (1983): 62–77.

———. *Repression in Victorian Fiction: Charlotte Brontë, George Eliot, and Charles Dickens* (Berkeley, Los Angeles and London: University of California Press, 1987).

Lamonaca, Maria. 'Jane's Crown of Thorns: Feminism and Christianity in *Jane Eyre*,' *Studies in the Novel*, 34.3 (2002): 245–63.

Leavey, Gerard, Linda Rozmovits, Louise Ryan and Michael King. 'Explanations of Depression among Irish Migrants in Britain,' *Social Science & Medicine*, 65 (2007): 231–44.

Ledger, Sally. 'Chartist Aesthetics in the Mid Nineteenth Century: Ernest Jones, a Novelist of the People,' *Nineteenth-Century Literature*, 57.1 (2002): 31–63.

Ledru-Rollin, Alexandre. *The Decline of England* (London: E. Churton, 1850).

Lee, Julia Sun-Joo. 'The Return of the "Unnative": The Transnational Politics of Elizabeth Gaskell's *North and South*,' *Nineteenth-Century Literature*, 61.4 (2007): 449–78.

Lees, Lynn Hollen. *Exiles of Erin: Irish Migrants in Victorian London* (Manchester: Manchester University Press, 1979).

Lengel, Edward G. *The Irish through British Eyes: Perceptions of Ireland in the Famine Era* (Westport: Praeger, 2002).

Lewes, George Henry. *Comte's Philosophy of the Sciences: Being an Exposition of the Principles of the* Cours de Philosophie Positive *of Auguste Comte* (London: Henry G. Bohn, 1853).

———. *The Physiology of Common Life* (Edinburgh and London: William Blackwood and Sons, 1859).

Lewis, Gwynne. *The French Revolution: Rethinking the Debate* (New York and London: Routledge, 2004).

Litvack, Leon. 'Dickens, Ireland and the Irish, Part 1,' *The Dickensian*, 99.459 (2003): 34–59.

Lloyd, David. 'The Indigent Sublime: Specters of Irish Hunger,' *Representations*, 92.1 (2005): 152–85.

Long, Leonard J. 'Law's Character in Eliot's *Felix Holt, the Radical*,' *Law and Literature* 16.2 (2004): 237–82.

Longmuir, Anne. 'Consuming Subjects: Women and the Market in Elizabeth Gaskell's *North and South*,' *Nineteenth-Century Contexts: An Interdisciplinary Journal*, 34.3 (2012): 237–52.

Lorwin, Val R. 'Working-Class Politics and Economic Development in Western Europe,' *The American Historical Review*, 63.2 (1958): 338–51.

Lysack, Krista. 'Goblin Markets: Victorian Women Shoppers at Liberty's Oriental Bazaar,' *Nineteenth-Century Contexts: An Interdisciplinary Journal*, 27.2 (2006): 139–65.

MacCulloch, Robert. 'Income Equality and the Taste for Revolution,' *Journal of Law and Economics*, 48.1 (2005): 93–123.

MacKenzie, Clayton G. 'Thomas Carlyle's 'The Negro Question': Black Ireland and the Rhetoric of Famine,' *Neohelicon*, 24.2 (1996): 219–36.

MacLaughlin, Jim. 'The Evolution of Anti-Traveller Racism in Ireland,' *Race & Class*, 37.3 (1996): 47–63.

Magnum, Theresa. 'Dickens and the Female Terrorist: The Long Shadow of Madame Defarge,' *Nineteenth-Century Contexts: An Interdisciplinary Journal*, 31.2 (2009): 143–60.

Malthus, Thomas R. *An Essay on the Principle of Population* (1798; New York: Dover, 2007).

———. *Principles of Political Economy*, ed. John Pullen (1820; Cambridge: Cambridge University Press, 1989).

Mandler, Peter, ed. *Liberty and Authority in Victorian Britain* (Oxford: Oxford University Press, 2006).

Markovits, Stefanie. 'North and South, East and West: Elizabeth Gaskell, the Crimean War, and the Condition of England,' *Nineteenth-Century Literature*, 59.4 (2005): 463–93.

Martineau, Harriet. 'The Anglo-French Alliance,' *Westminster Review* 63 (1855): 1–25.

———. *Autobiography*, ed. Linda Peterson (1877; Toronto: Broadview, 2007).

———. 'Conditions and Prospects of Ireland,' *Westminster Review*, 59 (1853): 35–62.

———. *Illustrations of Political Economy* (25 vols, London: Charles Fox, 1832–34).

———. *Illustrations of Political Economy: Selected Tales*, ed. Deborah Logan (Toronto: Broadview Press, 2004).

Marx, Karl. *Capital: A Critique of Political Economy, Volume 1* (1867; trans. Ben Fowkes, London: Penguin, 1976).

Matus, Jill, ed. *The Cambridge Companion to Elizabeth Gaskell* (Cambridge: Cambridge University Press, 2007).

———. *Shock, Memory and the Unconscious in Victorian Fiction* (Cambridge: Cambridge University Press, 2009).

May, Leila S. '"Foul Things of the Night": Dread in the Victorian Body,' *The Modern Language Review*, 93.1 (1998): 16–22.

Mayhew, Henry. *London Labour and the London Poor* (1851–52; 4 vols, London: Griffin, Bohn, & Co., 1861–62).

McAlman, Ian. 'Prophesying Revolution: "Mad Lord George", Edmund Burke and Madame La Motte,' in *Living and Learning: Essays in Honour of J.F.C. Harrison*, ed. Malcolm Chase and Ian Dyck (Aldershot: Scolar, 1996), 52–65.

McAlpine, Heather. '"Would Not Open Lip from Lip": Sacred Orality and the Christian Grotesque in Christina Rossetti's "Goblin Market",' *Victorian Review*, 36.1 (2010): 114–28.

McWilliam, Rohan. *Popular Politics in Nineteenth-Century England* (London and New York: Routledge, 1998).

Mendoza, Victor Roman. '"Come Buy": The Crossing of Sexual and Consumer Desire in Christina Rossetti's *Goblin Market*,' *ELH*, 73.4 (2006): 913–47.

Menke, Richard. 'The Political Economy of Fruit,' in *The Culture of Christina Rossetti: Female Poetics and Victorian Contexts*, ed. Mary Arseneau, Antony H. Harrison, and Lorraine Janzen Kooistra (Athens: Ohio University Press, 1999), pp. 105–36.

Mesnard y Méndez, Pierre. 'Capitalism Means/Needs War,' *Socialism and Democracy*, 16.2 (2002): 65–92.

Michie, Helena. *The Flesh Made Word: Female Figures and Women's Bodies* (Oxford: Oxford University Press, 1987).

Miles, William Augustus. *Poverty, Mendicity, and Crime, Or, The Facts, Examinations, &c. Upon which the Report Was Founded*, ed. H. Brandon. Presented to the House of Lords (London: Shaw and Sons, 1839).

Mill, John Stuart. *On Liberty and Other Essays*, ed. John Gray (Oxford: Oxford University Press, 1991).

———. *Principles of Political Economy with Some of their Applications to Social Philosophy* (1848; 7th edn, 1871; Oxford: Oxford University Press, 1994).

Miller, Andrew H. *The Burdens of Perfection: On Ethics and Reading in Nineteenth-Century British Literature* (Ithaca and London: Cornell University Press, 2008).

———. 'Lives Unled in Realist Fiction', *Representations*, 98.1 (2007): 118–34.

Mokyr, Joel and Cormac Ó Gráda. 'Emigration and Poverty in Prefamine Ireland,' *Explorations in Economic History*, 19 (1982): 360–84.

Moore, Grace. *Dickens and Empire: Discourses of Class, Race and Colonialism in the Works of Charles Dickens* (Aldershot: Ashgate, 2004).

Moore, Tara. 'Starvation in Victorian Christmas Fiction,' *Victorian Literature and Culture*, 36.2 (2008): 489–505.

Morash, Christopher. *Writing the Irish Famine* (Oxford: Clarendon Press, 1995).

Mukherjee, Upamanyu Pablo. *Crime and Empire: The Colony in Nineteenth-Century Fictions of Crime* (Oxford: Oxford University Press, 2003).

———. *Natural Disasters and Victorian Empire: Famines, Fevers and the Literary Cultures of South Asia* (Basingstoke: Palgrave, 2013).

Murphy, James H. 'The Literature and Culture of Nineteenth-Century Ireland,' *Victorian Literature and Culture*, 32.1 (2004): 209–19.

Nally, David. '"Eternity's commissioner": Thomas Carlyle, the Great Irish Famine and the Geopolitics of Travel,' *Journal of Historical Geography*, 32 (2006): 313–35.

———. *Human Encumbrances: Political Violence and the Great Irish Famine* (Notre Dame: University of Notre Dame Press, 2011).

———. '"That Coming Storm": The Irish Poor Law, Colonial Biopolitics, and the Great Famine,' *Annals of the Association of American Geographers*, 98.3 (2008): 714–41.

Neocleous, Mark. 'The Political Economy of the Dead: Marx's Vampires,' *History of Political Thought*, 24.4 (2003): 668–84.

Newman, Lucile F., ed. *Hunger in History: Food Shortage, Poverty, and Deprivation* (Oxford: Blackwell, 1990).

Nicholas, Stephen and Peter R. Shergold. 'Human Capital and the Pre-Famine Irish Emigration to England,' *Explorations in Economic History*, 24 (1987): 158–77.

Norton, Desmond. 'Lord Palmerston and the Irish Famine Emigration: A Rejoinder,' *The Historical Journal*, 46.1 (2003): 155–65.

Nunokawa, Jeff. *The Afterlife of Property: Domestic Security and the Victorian Novel* (Princeton: Princeton University Press, 1994).

O'Donnell, Ian. 'Lethal Violence in Ireland, 1841–2003: Famine, Celibacy and Parental Pacification,' *British Journal of Criminology*, 45 (2005): 671–95.

O'Farrell, Patrick. 'Whose Reality?: The Irish Famine in History and Literature,' *Historical Studies*, 20.78 (1982): 1–13.

Ó Gráda, Cormac. 'Famines Past, Famine's Future,' *Development and Change*, 42.1 (2011): 49–69.

Ó Gráda, Cormac and Kevin H. O'Rourke. 'Migration as Disaster Relief: Lessons from the Great Irish Famine,' *European Review of Economic History*, 1 (1997): 3–25.

Ong, Walter J. *The Presence of the Word: Some Prolegomena for Cultural and Religious History* (1967; New York: State University of New York Press, 2000).

O'Reilly, Shelley. 'Absinthe Makes the Tart Grow Fonder: A Note on "wormwood" in Christina Rossetti's *Goblin Market*,' *Victorian Poetry*, 34.1 (1996): 108–14.

Paley, Ruth. '"An Imperfect, Inadequate and Wretched System"? Policing London before Peel,' *Criminal Justice History*, 10 (1989): 95–130.

Parker, Bernard. *The Refugee Question in Mid-Victorian Politics* (1979; Cambridge: Cambridge University Press, 2008).

Parkins, Wendy. 'Women, Mobility and Modernity in Elizabeth Gaskell's *North and South*,' *Women's Studies International Forum*, 27 (2004): 507–19.

Perls, Friedrich Salomon. *Ego, Hunger and Aggression: The Gestalt Therapy of Sensory Awakening through Spontaneous Personal Encounter, Fantasy and Contemplation* (New York: Vintage Books, 1947).

Perry, Ruth. *Novel Relations: The Transformation of Kinship in English Literature and Culture, 1748–1818* (Cambridge: Cambridge University Press, 2004).

Peterson, Linda H. 'From French Revolution to English Reform: Hannah More, Harriet Martineau, and the "Little Book",' *Nineteenth-Century Literature*, 60.4 (2006): 409–50.

Pionke, Albert D. 'The Spiritual Economy of *Goblin Market*,' *SEL: Studies in English Literature, 1500–1900*, 52.4 (2012): 897–915.

Plotz, John. *Portable Property: Victorian Culture on the Move* (Princeton and Oxford: Princeton University Press, 2008).

'The Political Economy of Ragged Schools,' *Ragged School Union Magazine*, 9 (June 1857): 101–04.

Poovey, Mary. *Genres of the Credit Economy: Mediating Value in Eighteenth- and Nineteenth-Century Britain* (Chicago: University of Chicago Press, 2008).

———. *Making a Social Body: British Cultural Formation, 1830–1864* (Chicago and London: University of Chicago Press, 1995).

Porter, Bernard. *The Refugee Question in Mid-Victorian Politics* (1979; Cambridge: Cambridge University Press, 2008).

Potolsky, Matthew. 'Hardy, Shaftesbury, and Aesthetic Education,' *SEL: Studies in English Literature, 1500–1900*, 46.4 (2006): 863–78.

Prasch, Thomas. 'Eating the World: London in 1851,' *Victorian Literature and Culture*, 36 (2008): 587–602.

Price, Leah. 'George Eliot and the Production of Consumers,' *NOVEL: A Forum on Fiction*, 30.2 (1997): 145–69.

Prickett, Stephen. *England and the French Revolution* (Basingstoke: Macmillan Education, 1989).

Quinn, Eileen Moore. 'Entextualizing Famine, Reconstituting Self: Testimonial Narratives from Ireland,' *Anthropological Quarterly*, 74.2 (2001): 72–88.

Rappoport, Jill. 'The Price of Redemption in *Goblin Market*,' *SEL: Studies in English Literature, 1500–1900*, 50.1 (2010): 853–75.

Reuter, Thomas. 'The Fragmented Self: Cross-Cultural Difference, Conflict and the Lessons of Ethnographic Experience,' *Paideuma*, 52 (2006): 251–66.

Ricardo, David. *On the Principles of Political Economy and Taxation* (London: John Murray, 1817).

[Rigby, Elizabeth]. Review of *Vanity Fair* and *Jane Eyre*, in *The Quarterly Review*, 84 (1848): 153–85.

Rosenfeld, Sophia. 'On Being Heard: A Case for Paying Attention to the Historical Ear,' *American History Review*, 116.2 (2011): 316–34.

Royle, Edward and James Walvin. *English Radicals and Reformers 1760–1848* (Brighton: Harvester, 1982).

Rudé, George. *The Crowd in History: A Study of Popular Disturbances in France and England 1730–1848* (New York: John Wiley, 1964).

Ruggiero, Vincenzo. 'War, Crime, Empire and Cosmopolitanism,' *Critical Criminology*, 15 (2007): 211–21.

Saine, Thomas P. *Black Bread—White Bread: German Intellectuals and the French Revolution* (Columbia: Camden House, 1988).

Salmon, Edward G. 'What the Working Classes Read,' *Nineteenth Century*, 20 (1886): 108–17.

Savage, Mike and Andrew Miles. *The Remaking of the British Working Class: 1840–1940* (New York and London: Routledge, 1994).

Scanlan, John. 'In Deadly Time: The Lasting on of Waste in Mayhew's London,' *Time Society*, 16 (2007): 189–206.

Schlossberg, Linda. '"The Low, Vague Hum of Numbers": The Malthusian Economies of *Jane Eyre*,' *Victorian Literature and Culture*, 29.2 (2001): 489–506.

Scholl, Lesa. *Translation, Authorship and the Victorian Professional Woman* (Farnham: Ashgate, 2011).

Schorn, Susan. 'Punish Her Body to Save Her Soul: Echoes of the Irish Famine in *Jane Eyre*,' *The Journal of Narrative Technique*, 28.3 (1998): 350–65.

Seed, John. 'Unitarianism, Political Economy and the Antinomies of Liberal Culture in Manchester, 1830–50,' *Social History*, 7.1 (1982): 1–25.

Sen, Amartya. *Poverty and Famines: An Essay on Entitlement and Deprivation* (1983; Oxford: Oxford Scholarship Online, 2003).

'The Senses. I-Taste,' *Harper's New Monthly Magazine*, 12 (December 1855): 73–81.

Shakinovsky, Lynn. 'Business and Terror in Charles Dickens's *A Tale of Two Cities*,' *Australasian Journal of Victorian Studies*, 18.2 (2013): 1–16.

Shore, Heather. *Artful Dodgers: Youth and Crime in Early 19th-Century London* (Woodbridge and New York: The Boydell Press, 1999).

Shuttleworth, Sally. *Charlotte Brontë and Victorian Psychology* (Cambridge: Cambridge University Press, 1996).

Sicher, Efraim. *Rereading the City Rereading Dickens: Representation, the Novel, and Urban Realism* (New York: AMS Press, Inc., 2003).

Silver, Anna Krugovoy. *Victorian Literature and the Anorexic Body*, Cambridge Studies in Nineteenth-Century Literature and Culture, ed. Gillian Beer (Cambridge: Cambridge University Press, 2002).

Smith, Adam. *The Theory of Moral Sentiments* (1759; London: George Bell, 1907).

———. *Wealth of Nations* (1776; Oxford: Oxford University Press, 1993).

Smith, Mark M. *Sensory History* (Oxford and New York: Berg, 2007).

———. *The Smell of Battle, the Taste of Siege: A Sensory History of the Civil War* (Oxford and New York: Oxford University Press, 2015).

Sperber, Jonathan. *The European Revolutions, 1848–1851* (1994; Cambridge: Cambridge University Press, 2005).

Stallybrass, Peter and Allon White. *The Politics and Poetics of Transgression* (London: Methuen, 1986).

Stark, W. 'Liberty and Equality or: Jeremy Bentham as an Economist,' *The Economic Journal*, 51.201 (1941): 56–79.

Stern, Rebecca F. '"Adulterations Detected": Food and Fraud in Christina Rossetti's "Goblin Market",' *Nineteenth-Century Literature*, 57.4 (2003): 477–511.

Stevenson, John. 'Social Control and the Prevention of Riots in England, 1789–1829,' in *Social Control in Nineteenth Century Britain*, ed. A.P. Donajgrodzki (London: Croom Helm, 1977), 27–50.

Struve, Laura. 'Expert Witnesses: Women and Publicity in *Mary Barton* and *Felix Holt*,' *Victorian Review*, 28.1 (2002): 1–24.

Swift, Roger. 'Heroes or Villains? The Irish, Crime, and Disorder in Victorian England,' *Albion*, 29 (1997): 399–421.

———. 'Thomas Carlyle, "Chartism," and the Irish in Early Victorian England,' *Victorian Literature and Culture*, 29.1 (2001): 67–83.

Taylor, Miles. 'Rethinking the Chartists: Searching for Synthesis in the Historiography of Chartism,' *The Historical Journal*, 39.2 (1996): 479–95.

Thomas, Sue. *Imperialism, Reform, and the Making of Englishness in* Jane Eyre (Basingstoke: Palgrave Macmillan, 2008).

Thompson, E.P. 'The Moral Economy of the English Crowd in the Eighteenth Century,' *Past and Present*, 50 (1971): 76–136.

Tolson, Andrew. 'Social Surveillance and Subjectification: The Emergence of "Subculture" in the Work of Henry Mayhew,' *Cultural Studies*, 4 (1990): 113–27.

Tucker, Herbert F. 'Rossetti's Goblin Marketing: Sweet to Tongue and Sound to Eye,' *Representations*, 82.1 (2003): 117–33.

Twain, Mark. *The Prince and the Pauper* (1881; London: Penguin, 1997).

Uglow, Jenny. *Elizabeth Gaskell: A Habit of Stories* (London and Boston: Faber and Faber, 1993).

Vander Weele, Michael. '*Jane Eyre* and the Tradition of Self-Assertion; Or, Brontë's Socialization of Schiller's "Play Aesthetic",' *Renascence*, 57.1 (Fall, 2004): 5–28.

Vernon, James. *Hunger: A Modern History* (Cambridge, Mass.: Harvard University Press, 2007).

Visser, Margaret. *Much Depends on Dinner* (Toronto: McClelland and Steward, 1986).

Wagner, Corinna. *Pathological Bodies: Medicine and Political Culture* (Berkeley: University of California Press, 2013).

Wagner, Tamara, ed. *Domestic Fiction in Colonial Australia and New Zealand* (London: Pickering & Chatto, 2014).

Ward, Megan. '"A Charm in those Fingers": Patterns, Taste, and the Englishwoman's Domestic Magazine,' *Victorian Periodicals Review*, 41.3 (2008): 248–69.

Waters, Catherine. *Commodity Culture in Dickens's* Household Words (Aldershot: Ashgate, 2008).

Watts, Michael J. *Silent Violence: Food, Famine and Peasantry in Northern Nigeria* (Berkeley: University of California Press, 2013).

Wetzell, Richard F. *Inventing the Criminal: A History of German Criminology, 1880–1945* (Chapel Hill and London: University of North Carolina Press, 2000).

Wiener, Martin J. *Reconstructing the Criminal: Culture, Law, and Policy in England, 1830–1914* (Cambridge: Cambridge University Press, 1990).

Willams Renk, Kathleen. 'Jane Eyre as Hunger Artist,' *Women's Writing*, 15.1 (2008): 1–12.

Wilt, Judith. 'Felix Holt, the Killer: A Reconstruction,' *Victorian Studies*, 35.1 (1991): 51–69.

Winter, Sarah. 'Mental Culture: Liberal Pedagogy and the Emergence of Ethnographic Knowledge,' *Victorian Studies*, 41.3 (1998): 427–54.

Wisney Horowitz, Lenore. 'George Eliot's Vision of Society in *Felix Holt, the Radical*,' *Texas Studies in Literature and Language*, 17.1 (1975): 175–91.

Wood, Michael. *Literature and the Taste of Knowledge* (Cambridge: Cambridge University Press, 2005).

Wright, D.G. *Popular Radicalism: The Working-Class Experience 1780–1880* (London and New York: Longman, 1988).

Wright, Sam. *Crowds and Riots: A Study in Social Organization* (Beverly Hills and London: Sage Publications, 1978).

Zemka, Sue. 'Brief Encounters: Street Scenes in Gaskell's Manchester,' *ELH*, 76.3 (2009): 793–819.

Index

For Product Safety Concerns and Information please contact our EU
representative GPSR@taylorandfrancis.com
Taylor & Francis Verlag GmbH, Kaufingerstraße 24, 80331 München, Germany

www.ingramcontent.com/pod-product-compliance
Ingram Content Group UK Ltd.
Pitfield, Milton Keynes, MK11 3LW, UK
UKHW020954180425
457613UK00019B/674

9 780367 030636